"*First, Last, Only*... Is that look into the love, pain, and decisions that all relationships present us with. A great story that makes you yearn to know what happens."

-Liam C. Johnson, Actor

"What's interesting about this book is its exploration into all kinds of addictive loves: platonic, maternal, romantic. But it also shows us the difference between a love we desperately want and a love we don't necessarily need. She's our own Pandora's box that we are always tempted to open, but always leaves us broken. Through the voice of Chase, we all can identify with that one love in our life. And what we do to overcome it."

-Alex Bartley, Actress

First, Last, Only...

by

James Craigmiles

Cover art by Kendall R. Hart.

Interior layout and design by Kendall R. Hart.

Foreword by Wes Laurie.

Editing services provided by Edward Gehlert.

ReelPeople Entertainment

Genre: Romance / Slice of Life

ISBN-13 978-1-49937-947-1

ISBN-10 1499379471

Second Edition.

Printed in the United States of America.

This book is for my mom. She is, and always has been, the driving force behind me following my passions. Even now as I sit here in L.A. and write this, hoping for my next audition, she believes in me. She is proud of me. She is the reason that I am the man that I am.

Thank you, Momma.

Foreword

To love is one of the greatest joys in life. It can also be a curse...

Even when the heart is broken there can still be love found within the pieces. James Craigmiles has opened up for us and released a story that shows the tricky balance it can be to walk across those pieces. You're always in danger of being cut by a jagged edge, but the pain one feels is capable of turning weakness into strength. We hurt so that we may love again, love better, and love ourselves within the cycles of human emotion. Whether you are the smasher of hearts or the protector, this story shows you the mental and physical results of people daring to trust one another to the fullest extent. It is said that one can never truly know another person, but perhaps that is the driving force behind the power of romance, the great leap: faith.

The journey into another person's darkness can sometimes help shine a light into your own. *First, Last, Only...* is such a journey. It is a story that feels all too real and all the more powerful for it. It is a reminder that not all tears are cold, embrace every moment for what it is worth, and grow your love for better or for worse.

-Wes Laurie, Director

Acknowledgements

I would like to thank Brad Carter for sticking with me through these years. You were my first real friend in Tinsel Town. You have been a good one and I am grateful for your support and always staying true to your country roots. Congrats on your successes.

Mr. Leslie Jordan. It was random how we met and became friends. I am so grateful for your words of encouragement and your selfless acts of kindness in helping with my film. I look forward to future projects with you, sir.

My rock, Nina Henderson. Mom, you have always been my biggest fan but more so my biggest well of strength to draw from. Thank you for never being the kind of parent who said "Get a real job." Thank you for raising me the way you did to become the man that I am.

Thank you to all of my family. Thank you for always sending me kind words of encouragement and support. Thank you for always believing in me, even when the chips seem down. Especially Steve, Sheena, Casey and your families.

Mr. Troy Donehue. You were like a father to me growing up. I will always appreciate your support and you believing in chasing ones dream. So many children get to learn from you every day. I can only hope they see just how great of a teacher they have. Thank you for pushing me to follow my dreams.

Peter Wied. You have grown to become one of my best friends over these years. Your help and support in my times of need will never be forgotten. If it wasn't for you, lending a hand and always an ear I don't know if I would have lasted in this crazy town.

My good friend, Rose Nguyen. Our friendship was more recent than the others, but you saw to the core of me and the dreams I had inside. You held my hand and pushed me toward those dreams. I will be forever in your debt. I can only hope to repay you by one day aiding in your dreams as well.

To all of my Missouri, Austin, and Cali friends. I feel

blessed every day to know that I am surrounded by so many great people. You all make me a better man. Thank you.

Many have asked me if this is an autobiography. The answer to that question is no. Yet, this book *is* me. It is my life. I changed things, added things, removed things. But it is a chunk of me. I suppose the easiest way to describe it is this: until I'm ready to fully bare my soul and write a memoir, this will serve to do the job. The best thing to do, for now, is to think of my life and this book as two separate entities. Chase is not me, but a character through which I have lived as I wrote the book.

-James Craigmiles, Feb 2014

Kendall,

Man you are amazing. Honestly! Thank you so much for taking the time & energy to make my book & my film so beautiful. You are appreciated!!

1

Stark white walls. That's one of those things that always got my attention here. White, like nothingness. Not happy or sad, just apparent.

I notice the dust particles glistening, lazily dancing in the swath of the afternoon sunlight flowing through the dual-paned window. Is it possible that those tiny particles could feel? Could they ever know how beautiful and carefree their "lives" are? To be able to float around, dancing in sunlight, waiting until the next dust rag rolls along to take them on their next adventure.

A gentle squeeze of my left hand brings me back to reality. I'm not startled. I was aware of the frail hand lightly wrapped within my own. But a squeeze was a sign that my attention was needed back on Earth. As I turn my head toward her, my gaze glances over numerous machines and high-tech equipment. Lights blinking and sounds beeping out the song of their work. I know not what those numbers or readouts mean, but I need not understand the apparatuses to understand what is happening.

She was dying.

Her squeeze had begun growing slowly fainter with each breath. I wanted to look her in the eyes, to reassure her that it would be okay to move on, but I was scared. I was scared of how things would continue for me and for her.

What lies next? Is there a Heaven? A Hell? If there is, had she done the correct amount of good to allow her entrance into the better of the two? Or maybe there is reincarnation. Maybe I'll be picking my children up from school one day and they will have made friends with a little girl that has her eyes. Would I recognize them? Would she recognize me? Would I be able to handle it if either of us did?

She needs me now. Be strong. Be caring. Show her love.

My eyes start the ascent to hers. I see her chest rising and falling. The chest that was once so beautiful and full. Now it was barren, scarred, and broken; hidden beneath cheap cotton sheets. The thought of the pain she had endured pangs at my heart so hard that I nearly lose my breath and the welling of tears blur my vision. I bring my right hand up, never taking my left from her grasp. I put my hand over that chest, as if trying to send positive, calming energy through her to ease the pain. I don't know that I believe in such things, but I believe there is a great deal that I don't know and could never fully understand. Therefore, I send my energy into her with every last bit of will I can muster. After a long, thoughtful moment, I bring it back down and engulf her hand between mine.

I look further on, towards her neck. I remember kissing that neck. Tens of thousands of little kisses I must have placed upon it. That dark, Asian skin. I always loved how the sunlight at the beach seemed to cause her to shine so majestically. Her chin. Her lips. Those beautiful, soft lips; now chapped and broken.

Then I meet her eyes. She is barely holding them open. Even now they are so incredibly beautiful. That almond shape, the light brown color, and their depth show me the window to her soul. I reach up with my right hand and brush the hair off of her forehead. She looks up at me, deep in my eyes. I can feel her hesitating.

"I'm here. Let go. Be free. It's okay to let go now."

She can hear me. I can tell that she understands and that she is close now. Her eyes seem less scared. Her body slowly becomes less rigid. I hurt so much sitting here witnessing. God, if you are up there, help me take her pain away. I feel like I'm losing my strength.

Don't quit on her now, Chase. You gave your word. And a Midwestern man never goes back on his word. You promised her...

2

"Where are you guys?" came the annoyed voice of Amanda, my neighbor, through the cell phone.

"We are still at the bar listening to my friend's band," I replied, caught off guard by the unusual harshness in her voice.

Her tone was short when she replied, "Chase, I set this up so that you two could meet. And you're almost an hour late. Which is interesting, since you claim to be the one person in L.A. who never flakes."

That was the motivation I needed. She was right. I hate flakes. I hate people that give their word to call or be somewhere, and then don't follow through. And how hypocritical was I being at that exact moment?

My name is Chase. I'm a 5'10" guy with an athletic build. I have ear length dirty blonde hair and hazel eyes. I'm no Brad Pitt, but I have never been self-conscious with the way I look. I'm cute enough, and I have the kind of personality that people tend to be drawn to. That personality came from being raised by a strong country woman. She taught me about treating others as you wished to be treated, the "Golden Rule."

She also happened to be an ex-hippie. From this I learned about loving everyone and judging no one. I never knew, as a child, how much these teachings would impact the man I would grow to become.

Another great thing about my mom was that she was the most supportive woman on the planet. I knew, at age four, that I wanted to be an actor in Hollywood. From the first moment I proudly announced my intentions to her through my toothless grin until I booked my first part, she has always been my biggest fan, and my biggest source of strength. I owe the man I became to my mom and the country upbringing.

Here I was now, pseudo-flaking on a friend I had made a promise to. If I hated flakey people, then I should not be acting like this. I had agreed to go. I was asked a favor, and I said yes. That was the end of the story.

Why had I agreed to this? I hate being set up with someone. Most of the time they are never your type. Then there is the rare occasion that they are your type, but you aren't theirs. Then there is the even more rare occasion where you're both each other's type, but the situation is so awkward that nothing ever comes from it. Needless to say, I wasn't looking forward to it.

What I was looking forward to, though, was my buddy's band playing. My friend, Kurt, was in a band called Fossil 10. The *Los Angeles Times* had recently given them the most up and coming band in L.A. award and they were celebrating by having a gig at Wasted Space on Sunset. They were currently bringing down the house. As far as I could tell, the band was maybe halfway through their set and I sure didn't want to leave. But, like Amanda said, I hate flaking so I rounded up the troops.

The troops consisted of my two roommates. One of which was my best friend in L.A., Luke James. Luke was only about 5'5" tall in height, but his stature in size was offset considerably because of his fashion business. I had met Luke when I first moved to the city from Missouri. He was just a little guy with a great smile. I attended a party with some friends from work one night that Luke was hosting. We bumped into each other midway through the night. Though we were both young, and there were many girls at the party, we hit it off so well that neither of us was interested in the girls for the rest of the night. We chatted about cars, actors, movies, the universe, everything.

We had so much in common that we quickly became great friends and moved in together. Interesting side note about Luke, his last name is actually Garcia. But he was afraid that negative connotations came with a Latin last name in the fashion biz, so he goes by his first and middle name, Luke James. We decided to get a three bedroom house, which allowed us more space. But, we needed a third roommate. That brings us to Kobe Smith.

Kobe Smith was a friend of Luke's, but Luke vouched for him, and that was good enough for me. Kobe was an African-American man that stood about 6'2" tall, with a very lean frame. He was one of the most well-spoken and mannered men I had ever met. He also happened to be a bit of a recluse. It seemed there would sometimes be days that would go by where Kobe wouldn't emerge from his room. If he did come out, it was slowly and cautiously. We later found out that this was caused by paranoia due to the weed that he would smoke when he listened to CD's with his headphones on. It was his little piece of relaxation. I've never touched the stuff, but far be it for me to judge someone doing something that makes them happy. Besides, when he did make an appearance, he was funny as hell.

So why had I agreed to meeting with someone through Amanda? Well, that is an interesting story with odd connections. Luke, Kobe, and I had moved into our place about six months before that night. As good Midwestern boys do, I went to each neighbor and introduced myself. At each place I offered our phone number in case we were ever causing too much noise and promised to be helpful if the need ever presented itself. At the house directly to our right, we met Amanda. She was a beautiful Filipino woman that was very, as Kobe would later put it, "curvy in all the right places." She was very accepting of and excited to meet us. We even told her about our poker nights we intended to have on Friday nights. She promised to join.

A few weeks later, true to her word, Amanda appeared for poker night. She showed up with a case of energy drinks. We found out that she worked for a distributing company and she promised to bring a case for our party every week. True to her word, every week she did. As the months went by, we all became very close. I began to see Amanda as a big sister. She was kind and supportive, but with knowledge and good advice. I also began to see that her and Kobe were starting to make eyes at each other. For weeks they would lightly flirt.

Everyone in the house knew that they wanted each other, except those two. Finally, one Friday night, I had seen enough. I placed my arms around them and whispered, "Kobe, Amanda said that her sink has been leaking. Could you go over to her house and check it out?"

Their cheeks flushed red as they stared at each other. I smiled and gently guided them to the door, "Go ahead."

I knew that Kobe was too shy to do so himself, so someone had to lay the foundation. We didn't see them again until the next day and they were locked together at the hips from then on. It was really cute. I have always been a hopeless romantic at heart. So seeing them acting like school kids warmed my insides.

"Why don't I ever see you with a girl, Chase?" Amanda had asked me one day.

"I date here and there, but I haven't found anyone that I click with the way you and Kobe do," I said somewhat wistfully.

She sat for a moment, then asked, "Well, what's your type?"

"I do tend to go out with petite Asian girls more than most others. Is that a type?" I joked.

She joined in my mirth and playfully poked me in the ribs, "I'm going to do some thinking on that!"

Two days later she asked if I was free Friday night. I mentioned that I had a buddy's band to go see, but afterwards I had no plans.

"I want to introduce you to my cousin. She lives in Orange County, is Asian and petite, and she is a lot of fun. Will you please trust me and meet her?"

"Sure," I replied without thinking it through. It was Amanda. Of course I would do her a favor. Famous last words.

"We will be there in about fifteen minutes," I told Amanda over the phone.

"You better hurry, she is getting bored," came her reply.

Oh great, now I'm walking into an awkward situation that's even more intense, I thought. They were at Gotham Nightclub in Santa Monica. I drove, Luke in the front seat, and Kobe in the back. We jammed out to some 90's R&B, singing the whole way. The 90's had the best music for R&B. They sang about two things: making love and being in love. Sometimes they got fancy and sang about both in the same song. That was about it and that's okay in my book. Shortly we pulled up to the club, dropped the car off at the valet, and headed in. Here goes nothing.

Luke, Kobe, and I ascended the steps just inside the door that led to the dance area of the club. We had already paid our entry fee, which Luke had complained loudly about, "$20 a person just to get into this club? Seriously? Are the drinks served by models?"

Kobe had finally started to be less agitated about leaving the good music and was getting excited to see his girl. He really loved her. It's rare to see real love nowadays. Always makes me smile to reminisce about it. We reached the top of the stairs and walked out onto the dance floor in a very well designed club. The music was being spun by some DJ whose name I didn't recognize. But I must admit, his beats were great. They had me bobbing my head and feeling the energy of what was going on around me. It was impressive.

I don't know if I can say enough about how a DJ can influence the energy of a crowd. A great DJ finds the correct music that represents each crowd on any night. Sometimes it takes a few songs to figure this out. Once they do, the next few hours of their spinning will keep bodies moving and the dance floor packed. It's an amazing thing to watch.

Directly to my right was a long bar that stretched the entire length of the wall. It looked as if it were made of ice and was lit from beneath. Of course it was just really nice glass, but regardless it was a great illusion. The wall behind the bar had four long glass shelves that held every liquor bottle imaginable. These too were lit, causing each bottle to give off an inviting glow. Special attention had been paid to make sure colored bottles broke up the monotony of clear ones. A profound decision to make the business look like art, but it worked magically.

Three bartenders were working hard behind the bar. Two guys that looked to be corn fed country boys like myself, each over six feet tall and very well built. The third was a very pretty Latino girl with a killer smile. I made a mental note to get all my drinks that night from her.

Turning to my left, about 15 feet away, were very chic red velvet couches with ultra-high backs. I refer to them as couches, though it was probably actually just one couch that stretched the whole length of the wall and then bent around the corner. It wasn't just straight. It was designed in a way that it curved in and out, creating sections of couch that seemed to be one. Upon closer inspection, you could see that it never broke. It just continued on. The style was quite lovely. Everything between the bar and the couches was dance floor. About 30 feet wide and at least double that long. The only ambient light came from the bar or from the tiny sconces overhanging the couch.

That left the dance floor in near darkness. The only light that touched most of it came from the colored disco lights that danced with the beat of the music. They flew all over, never staying on one spot for more than a brief second. I realized that I hadn't been searching for Amanda; I had been too caught up in the view of the club. So, I turned my gaze straight ahead toward the back of the dance floor, and tried to spy her.

After a quick check, and a little luck, I found her standing next to a very attractive woman. Amanda gestured toward her friend, smiled big, and mouthed, "This is her." They were still a good 20 feet away, but I could already tell this night had just taken a turn for the better. I turned my attention to Jennifer. Life seemed to slow down as my brain took the time to process what I was seeing. The lights that had been flying to and fro just a moment ago, now lazily took their time. They passed over her, slowly revealing her to me. I forgot about Kobe. I forgot about Luke. I forgot about Amanda. Hell, I forgot where I was. I'm not sure if it was the beat from the DJ, but my chest was pounding. Maybe it was just my biological responses, kicking things into overdrive. But I had never felt something like this before. Especially considering I hadn't even met her yet.

We began to make our way toward them, it felt like I was moving in slow motion. I couldn't take my eyes off of her. Partially because her beauty enamored me and partly because I was afraid if I'd look away she would disappear. The light flashed over her torso. She was wearing flattering, but classy dark fitted jeans. They must have been a designer brand because they hugged her perfectly, as if they had been sewn for her body alone. Her shirt was a mini-sleeved button up that looked to be lavender. The pearly white buttons were clasped at the perfect height. Not so high to seem buttoned up, but not low enough to show too much cleavage. A way of saying, "Yeah, I've got a great body, that doesn't mean you get to see it."

Her body was athletic and her chest filled that shirt to its limits. I looked away quickly when I realized I was staring. Not looking, admittedly, was very difficult. So, I looked on. The light flashed near her feet and I saw that she was wearing heels. They were black, accented with a single shiny white gem over the toes, and probably in the area of three inches high. Her toes, which were freshly French pedicured, had been thought of beforehand.

A blue light caught my attention as it began to climb up her body. It was obvious that she took care of herself. The light lingered for a moment on her long, tan, toned neck. Then finally reached her face. That face. I will never forget the moment that I first saw her face for as long as I live. Juicy lips. Cute wide nose. Soft eyebrows. Shiny dark Filipino hair that was accented with a few highlights. And her eyes. Those almond shaped eyes that made me melt.

I stopped when I saw them. She looked right at me. Maybe it was through me, and she smiled. That smile would have made any dentist proud. It lit the room up and caused her eyes to sparkle. I swear to God they sparkled. We were maybe five feet away now.

Luke grabbed my shoulder and whispered in my ear,

"Chase, man, if you get her number, you're going to be my hero. My freaking hero, man."

I took the final two steps toward her, dropped down on one knee and said, "Hi, I'm Chase. Umm, will you marry me?" I was joking. I think I was joking. I may actually have been dead serious. Either way, it made her smile again. And that was enough for me.

"Chase, I'm Jennifer, I gladly accept your proposal of marriage," she replied while showing off her perfect teeth.

Her response proved instantly to me that she had a personality too! She had just accepted my nonsense, and played on it right back with me. My heart was pounding even harder now. Without another word, I led her to the dance floor, and we danced. We tore that floor up, only stopping to grab quick drinks and waters from the bar. For obvious reasons I now chose to use the corn fed boys instead of the Latino girl.

I don't think I learned a single thing about her that night. There was none of that awkward, "How many sisters do you have and what's your favorite food?" questions. It was just pure and simple fun. At 2:15 a.m. they turned the lights on and told us to leave. She was even more beautiful in the light. I had hit the jackpot on this one. Truly it would be a night that would be burned in my happy memories forever. I was grateful for it. Now, would it be possible to see her again? The five of us headed down the stairs and back out to the front of the club, where the valet had our cars waiting for us.

Mine was my first adult car. She was a brand new 2005 Infiniti G35. Silver with black interior. I had been in love with that car since they first debuted the G in 2002. I knew I wanted one, and I was finally able to get her. Beauty and sex appeal. The exhaust alone said hello without me ever having to open my mouth.

Kobe had decided to go home with his girl. So he got in Amanda's car first. I gave Amanda a big hug as she was about to get into her Lexus IS 350 and whispered to her, "You're amazing. She is perfect. For real, I'm in awe!"

She giggled and replied, "You are welcome. Now go get her number."

With that she ducked in her car.

I went around to the passenger side and grabbed the door for Jennifer. I wasn't coy when I declared, "I'm not going to try to act all cool and pretend I'm not interested. I know a good thing when I see it. I would love to take you out sometime soon."

She smiled at my overly excited words and slid a piece of paper in my hand. She had already written me something. Then she kissed me on the cheek, slid in her seat, and closed the door. With that they were gone.

Luke had been watching in anticipation. Sort of my silent cheerleader from the sidelines. I drunkenly (love drunk, not alcohol drunk) walked back to the car with a smile that felt like it was the size of the moon.

"What does it say?" he asked.

I hadn't even looked at the paper in my hand yet. I was still swooning. But his words brought me back to reality. Was it her number? Was it an apology that we can't see each other because she isn't interested? Was it the combination to a locker in Tahiti where I was to meet her? Well, a boy can dream.

The note read:

My first proposal. I am impressed. I hear you throw a pretty good poker party on Friday nights. Count me in on the next one.
Jennifer

A week. Seriously? She made me wait a week. I had no way to contact her. I just had to hope she would show up. If she and Amanda had been talking about me, Amanda was giving me no indication.

"I know you know something, darn you! Tell me at least if she's coming," I pleaded.

"I have no idea. I guess we will see if she shows up for the party tonight," was her response, giggling all the while as she spoke.

Our poker party occurred every Friday night and they always turned into an event. Luke and I really enjoyed having people over to the house. So every Friday night we threw our poker party. The obvious part is that we played poker. Texas Hold'em to be exact. We would always have 10 to 15 people show up to play. It was a $20 buy-in, tournament style game, with winner taking all and most games lasting until two or three a.m. We would also have another 10 to 15 people come over for the fun that wasn't poker.

Luke and I were basically big kids. We set our house up to be a play land for ourselves, which was perfect to entertain others. In the living room we had our 65″ plasma TV with my 500 movies that our friends could choose from. In the office we had karaoke set up on the computer for those that wanted to get their singing on. It was connected to the internet and had pretty much any song you would want to sing. In Luke's room we had the PlayStation 3 set up and Madden ready to go. In my room I had my modified Xbox, which I had paid a hacker $500 to turn it into an old school gaming system. So every single Nintendo, Super Nintendo, Atari, ColecoVision, Game Boy, Sega and XBox game ever made were hidden inside of it. It was pretty amazing. Sometimes all of us men crave to play *Contra*, *Mike Tyson's Punch Out*, or *Mario 3*. It's in our blood.

The best part of the party was the hot tub we had in the back yard. Eventually everyone would make their way out to the tub and finish off the night there. We kept it PG because we had neighbors, and we didn't like to be disrespectful. That didn't mean it wasn't still a great time.

Our usual guests for the party would show up around 7 p.m. or so and the game would start an hour later. Of course we had food and drinks for people to dig into, not to mention the games and fun all over the house to enjoy. So, as per usual, we all stood around, chatting and catching up on the events of the past week. At 7:45 p.m. I began divvying up the poker chips among the 13 players that had shown up. By 8:00 p.m. I was ready to start the game. I became aware that Jennifer had not come yet. I also noticed that Amanda hadn't either. I decided to run next door and tell her we were starting and ask where her cousin was.

I knocked on her door and waited, shaking my head again

at the awful brown color of the thing. The door opened, and there stood Jennifer, looking even more incredible than the first time I had met her, holding a glass of wine and smiling at me like I was the court jester. I suppose it had something to do with the look of surprise and excitement on my face.

"It's about time you came to get me. I was beginning to wonder if I would need to go to the party alone," she quipped.

Amanda looked at me after a moment and said, "Well, are you gonna' stand there and gawk, or are you going to escort this young lady and myself to your shindig."

She was poking fun at me. I'm glad. It cut the tension and brought me back around.

I held out my arm to her and playfully bowed while saying, "Your chariot, My Lady." She took my arm and walked with me the 25 steps to my house.

By this point we had a total of about 25 people at the party. All were good friends of Kobe, Luke and I, and all had been warned that I was head over heels for some girl. We walked in the front door, arm in arm, and the cat calling soon followed. My friends (girls and guys alike) were giving me thumbs up, whistling their approval, and some even vocalizing how they felt.

"Holy shit, Chase, well done!"

"When you're done, can I have a turn?"

"Mail-order bride?"

They were definitely enjoying themselves. "Okay, okay. Everyone, this is Jennifer. She is new to our group and may not be ready for the full amount of our nonsense," I announced.

She looked at me, looked back at them, then replied, "Herrrooooo. It 'bery nice to met' you," a small dramatic pause, "me love you long time."

That was it, that was the straw that broke the camel's back. She had just told a racist joke, about herself, to a room full of the least PC people you will ever meet, and laughed about it. She was officially one of the group.

We played poker 'til about 1 a.m. and she ended up taking all of my money. She did eventually go out in third place, not bad for her first time. We made our rounds saying hello to those watching *Gladiator* in the living room. We popped in and sang a couple of karaoke songs. My go to karaoke song is "This is How We Do It" by Montel Jordan. Hers was Mariah Carey's "Fantasy", which nearly caused me to faint when she was singing it, pouting her lips at me and acting all sexy. Sheesh. Women know just how to mess with men.

Then we went in and duked it out on *Mike Tyson's Punch Out*. I want it to be known, I never lose on purpose to a girl. So, I didn't feel bad when I destroyed her. Admittedly, she had no idea what the buttons did on the controller, but that is no excuse, darn it. I won. Finally. After a few more games we decided to join those that were in the hot tub.

She hadn't brought a bathing suit and, as I mentioned, we keep it PG in the hot tub. So I grabbed her some of my plaid boxers and a darker colored T-shirt before we hopped in. The water was just the right temperature. Warm enough to relax you, but not so hot that you have to keep getting out and sitting on the edge to cool off. We sat there in that water, surrounded by my silly friends, and finally talked. I got to know her.

She lived in Orange County in a house she rented that was only a few blocks from her parent's house. The parents were both in the healthcare industry and owned a beautiful house that sat on a hill overlooking the ocean. She had just finished school to be an X-Ray Tech and had been hired by a good hospital to work the night shift. She drove a cute little Honda Civic, though secretly wished it were a 5 series BMW.

All night long it went like that, talking. Not just asking the same old drab questions you ask on dates. But talking. Really talking. Laughing and telling stories and asking questions with genuine interest in what the other had to say. 3 a.m. came and went. 4 a.m. Soon everyone was gone or passed out in various places around the house. I decided I should make my way to bed too.

"At the risk of sounding like some creepy guy who would say anything to get you in bed with him; would you like to curl up in my bed and cuddle with me? I pinky promise not to try to get frisky," I said with a smile.

She cocked her head to the side and smiled up at me. Her smile curled up at the corner of her mouth and she licked her lips. I found myself being pulled toward her as we gazed into each other's eyes. Our lips gently caressed in a long soft kiss and again it seemed as if time stood still.

She slowly pushed me away and said, "If you really promise that you will keep your word, and that you will try nothing tonight, I will cuddle with you."

I nodded, only half realizing what she was saying through the intoxication I was feeling from the moment. I led her into the house and to my bedroom, numbly turning off lights and locking doors along the way. I gave her some dry boxers and a larger T-shirt to sleep in. Then we curled up together on my light blue satin sheets.

At first we were just laying side by side. The she grabbed my hand and rolled over. Slowly rolling me along with her until we were spooning with my body engulfing hers. I prayed right there to the big man upstairs, *"Please, God, please don't let me mess this up. Please keep me from getting overly excited right now and freaking her out."*

The warmth of her body flowed into me while her skin, so soft and smooth, pressed against mine. Her hair was right in my face and the aroma of honey and coconut wafted through my nostrils. Things awoke in the lower area of my body. I fervently began pleading again to God, *"Don't let her notice. Make it stop and PLEASE don't let her notice!"*

"I don't mind your body parts shifting back there, so long as you don't intend to use them," she giggled. Apparently my prayers had gone unanswered. I smiled to myself, hugged her close, then closed my eyes. We lay there until we fell asleep, spooning like newlyweds.

Thus became our Friday night routine. During the week we would flirt via text all day while we were at our respective jobs. Then, every Friday night, she would make the trek from Orange County to Los Angeles, have a glass of wine with Amanda at her house, then wait for me to come escort her to mine. It gave us something to look forward to the whole week. Every Friday night held the same excitement for me as Christmas morning.

These Fridays followed the same pattern. Poker, karaoke, video games, hot tub then curling up in my bed. And every Friday the urge to touch her grew stronger and stronger. We talked about sex. Sometimes we would kiss each other and the passion from the kisses alone would cause sweat to erupt from my body. Occasionally, she would lightly moan. At first I thought she was teasing me, but later I found out the moan was a sign that she was on the verge of losing control. I have been with women before. Not that I'm the most experienced man on the planet or anything. But I know when something feels different. And this was different. I had never felt passion like this. An extreme case of lust that was coupled with caring. Dare I call it love? No, it couldn't be. Not so soon. But what else could it be? What had changed within me? How was I feeling so strongly for someone that I saw only once per week? I decided that just wasn't enough.

"Okay, we have been hanging out for over two months now. I have yet to take you on a proper date. So, this is me, Chase, asking you, Jennifer, will you please allow me to escort you on the town for a night of fun?" I asked her.

She took her time in answering. I'm not sure if she just wanted to make me sweat or if she was considering the correct answer. Her tone became serious, "Yes. But, on two conditions. One, you must plan the entire night and it must be something different than just a normal date. Two, if you're hoping this leads to the next step in bed, you damn well better plan that one right too."

Holy Hell, my brain scream. I hadn't even thought about that. Had she just said what I think she did? Was she giving me the heads up that she was ready? Okay, okay, I had to slow myself down. I didn't want to assume or expect anything from that. If it happened though, I wanted it to be perfect. Not just for her, but for me as well. I wanted this one to be different. To mean something. I had much to plan.

"You drive a hard bargain, My Lady, but I accept your terms. May I offer that we plan for Saturday night? You will already be up here for poker on Friday. So I can plan our date starting from Saturday morning."

She laughed, "Your mind works fast. I like the sound of

that. Saturday morning our date starts. Friday night will go as usual then."

3

The blaring of the alarm at 8 a.m. woke me up that following Saturday. I quickly turned it off and I carefully removed myself from Jennifer's sleeping grasp so that I could sneak out. I paused a moment and watched her sleep. She seemed so peaceful. Yet, there was a light smile on her face. She was happy. That made me even happier. I had much to do though; so back at it I went. I headed to my local grocery store, Pavilions, and got the items I needed. Eggs, Texas toast, milk, powdered sugar, Dole Strawberry Pineapple Banana OJ, some honey dew, and some sausage were all tossed into my cart. I also added sodas, sandwich stuff, and snacks for later on.

I ran home and started to set up our date. Of course it had to begin with the right breakfast. I turned on the stove and got the flat pan warming up. Heated up the oven and tossed the sausages on a baking rack. I threw eggs in a bowl and beat them, adding milk and salt. In a separate square bowl I put in milk, vanilla extract, egg, and topped it with cinnamon. I took out a couple of slices of the Texas toast, dipped them in the cinnamon mixture, and tossed them onto the flat pan to make my French toast. I poured the egg mixture into a skillet and whipped up some really fluffy scrambled eggs. Grabbed the sausages out of the oven. Took out the two pieces of toast that were done, tossed in two more so that we would each have two, then started to set the plates up.

I put one piece of French toast down on one of the nicer plates I had in the cupboard. Then laid the other diagonally on top. It's important to sift some powdered sugar over it, making it look like a light snow. To the right of that I put a healthy helping of the fluffy scrambled eggs. A little pepper for flavor and looks. Below the eggs went the sausages. And for a little sweetness and color to the plate, I added some honeydew. I feel the light green, sweet flavor of honeydew really rounds out a great breakfast. I grabbed the serving tray out of the cupboard, placed the plate on it, added the juice, and of course salt, pepper, syrup, and ketchup then headed to wake her up. This was to set up what I hoped to be the best first date ever.

The door opened without a sound and I snuck inside. She was still lying in almost the same place that I had left her. I almost didn't want to wake her. Words can probably not do justice to how beautiful she really was. There was elegance to her. The way the sheet conformed to her body showing how insatiable she was, without giving too much away. The sun was now coming in through the crack in the curtains. It caused a triangle swath of sunlight to fall over the bed. The light was now touching her hair and the soft highlights were glinting, as if they were waking even before she did. I could have stood there just enjoying what I was watching. Luckily a car honked its horn outside and woke up my trance. Though I was enjoying watching her sleep, I also wanted to get this day going.

"Hey there, hot stuff," I said just loud enough to cause her to stir. She looked at me and took a second to process what was going on.

"What is all of this?" she asked as a smile crept onto her sleepy face. She sat up and I laid the tray over her, making sure to unfold the legs of it on either side of her so as to keep from causing a mess.

"Wait one second and I'll join you," I said and hurried back into the kitchen to make up my tray. Once finished I rushed back into the room to join her.

She was inspecting her bounty and exclaimed, "Chase, this is too much!" I had done a good job. We sat there and chatted as we enjoyed the food. She seemed very pleased and grateful for it all. And cleaned her plate to prove so. I must admit I enjoyed it as well. A man from the Midwest is always pleased when he has syrup coating his first meal of the day. It's like coffee for New Yorkers.

"What is next on the agenda?" she asked.

I looked at her and smiled. "I'm not telling you any of it. You just have to wait and see as it unfolds."

"You, sir, are earning major brownie points today. I very much like this side of you. Don't get me wrong; the poker playing, karaoke singing, goofball side is great as well. But this is nice and unexpected," she whispered.

What she didn't know is that my mom raised me. And Mom had always taught me to put a woman on a pedestal. My mom. She is an amazing woman. I suppose I get my drive and work ethic from her. Growing up she always tried to help mold me into a man. Encouraging me to play sports, learn about cars, build things, etc. But, she was a woman. She, unknowingly also taught me to be in touch with my sensitive side. She caused me to understand and love romance. To learn how to talk to and treat a woman with respect and kindness rather than being aggressive and indifferent as men can be. I became the embodiment of a "lover not a fighter."

I still grew into a man. I love to get under the hood of my car and tinker with my engine. And you would be hard pressed to beat me at a game of one-on-one basketball. But, at night, you can find me curled up watching a sappy movie as often as an action flick. And I'll cry right along with you at the end of *The Notebook*. What can I say? I'm a combination of sweaty man and sweet boy. Take it or leave it.

"How about you go hop in the shower? Afterward, throw on something light and comfortable, like shorts and a T-shirt," I suggested.

I grabbed a towel and started the shower for her. I had a speaker system set up in my bathroom so that you could plug in your iPod (iPhones were not available yet) and listen to your music. I plugged in my iPod and put on the mix I had made the day before. The mix was simply titled 'Jennifer Shower' and was filled with fun, up-beat songs that would make the time she spent getting ready more enjoyable. I put it on shuffle and the very first song to start was "Pony" by Genuine.

That set both she and I into a set of giggles. I grabbed her and kissed her gently on those soft lips, then let myself out of the bathroom and told her to take her time. There was a vanity in the bathroom and everything she would need to go along with it such as a blow dryer and flat iron. She wouldn't need to re-emerge until she was finished. This was perfect because I had much to do while she showered.

I cleared away the dishes and straightened up the kitchen. Then I moved to the bedroom, made the bed, and cleaned things up. I took my time to set up a few things that would be necessary for later, if the date went well. I went into Luke and Kobe's bathroom and took my shower. The hot water was invigorating. I took a few minutes to just stand there. Enjoying the way it felt as my muscles relaxed from the long week of work. I want it to be known that a hot shower is one of the greatest treasures we have on this planet.

Once I felt clean, relaxed, and ready to go I got dressed. I decided to wear comfy plaid shorts that show off my butt and a tight fitting V-neck T-shirt. I don't work out six days a week to wear oversized clothes. I styled my hair up using a little bit of Murray's pomade. It's perfect for the Jeep as it keeps my hair from going too crazy. Then I packed the cooler with ice, sodas, stuff for sandwiches, and some snacks. I loaded it into the Jeep then headed back inside.

Oh, the Jeep. How I love the Jeep. Her name is Jeepy. She is a 1991 Jeep Wrangler Renegade with a 4.0 inline six, one of the best engines Jeep ever made. It isn't fast, but I could tie it up to a house and pull it down the road. She is faded cherry red and has no top or doors, but has a 6-inch lift with 35-inch tires. Seriously, I love this Jeep. I had never asked Jennifer if she would like it. The wind can sometimes be hard on a girl's hair. I was taking a chance that she would appreciate it. I still had a backup car just in case. She was on standby should I get the idea Jennifer wasn't ready for the Jeep. Jennifer did have the tendency to be prissy once in a while.

I heard the blow dryer running in the bathroom and knew that meant she was almost done getting ready. I finished up the last bit of cleaning around the place, double checked my appearance in the mirror, then plopped down on the couch with my favorite magazine, *Popular Science*, and waited as if I had been sitting there all along.

She came out of the bedroom ready for the date. She had chosen to wear light brown comfy sandals, classy white shorts that accented her legs, and a yellow short sleeved button down shirt. I loved how she was able to float the line of classy and sexy. She had buttoned the shirt up enough to cover her beautiful breasts but still leave enough showing to keep your attention. She looked fantastic. She made me feel like I had dressed like a louse.

"Really, you're just going to sit there, all relaxed and wait for me," she said with a giggle. She knew better and was teasing.

"You know me, I'm super lazy," I playfully responded back.

"Well come on old man, let's get this date going," she said and walked toward the door.

I laughed and followed after her. She walked straight to my car. I stood back a bit and waited. She tried the door twice. She turned back to look at me and said, "Umm, you planning on letting me in?"

"Sure," I said, "but we aren't going in that."

I smiled and walked toward Jeepy. She saw what I was meaning, took in the sight of the Jeep being full with the cooler, and the biggest smile crept across her face.

"Hell yes. You always talked about taking this thing out, I didn't actually believe it existed!" She was excited. That made me smile. Considering the height of the tires and the lift, I had to help her up rather than get her door. Again we both burst out in giggles. I love when a woman laughs as much as I do.

"You're lucky I have a hair tie," she said, then tossed her perfectly highlighted hair up into a ponytail.

We slid the seat belts on, threw the Jeep in reverse, and off we went. We drove from our house in Burbank out to Will Rogers State Beach just north of Santa Monica. The Jeep isn't fast, but even at 65 mph the wind was whipping our hair around. Jennifer was loving the ride. I had plugged my iPod into the CD player and we were rocking out to some 90's

Hip Hop, singing along to old songs we remembered from our high school days. To start us off right I had started with Usher's "My Way" and it just grew from there.

In no time we were at Will Rogers Beach. I had chosen Will Rogers because it's a pretty beach that has lots of sand volleyball courts. Due to my planning, one of those volleyball courts was filled with about 15 of our friends. Some were poker friends and some were just friends we both knew. All were already engaged in playing some v-ball.

I knew that Jennifer loved playing sand volleyball. I had a feeling this would be a good place to start our post breakfast date. She was smiling from ear to ear as we walked up to the v-ball courts. She grabbed me and whispered in my ear, "Thank you."

I knew what she meant. I knew that the idea of being stuck inside all day was not her favorite thing. Though I wanted the day to be romantic, I also wanted it to be fun. We had plenty of time for romance later.

We played volleyball for two hours. Both of us jumping in and enjoying the physical activity. She was very agile while I was strong. Together we made a formidable team, even though I had only played a few times before.

Her movements were so cat-like. Her body, barely perspiring in the California sun, was tan and toned and often distracted me from watching for the set. Every time the ball would hit her arms I would see her whole body tense up, sending shock waves of carnal emotion through me. She would often yell at me to focus, laughing at me, trying to get me back in the game. We eventually won all three of our games, and then it was time to say goodbye. We gave hugs to our friends, who all knew that today was our first date. They made silly comments and we all laughed together. None of it bothered Jennifer. She took it in stride and gave it right back.

I rounded her and our stuff up, packed everything back in the Jeep, then coasted the few miles down to the Santa Monica pier.

We arrived at the pier just after 1:30 in the afternoon. I decided to take the road that led up and onto the pier so that we would have the best parking place, but driving over the planks of the pier caused Jennifer to jump a bit. Her nervousness was cute. I smiled. We walked into the amusement park area of the pier, bought a few ride tickets, and then hopped on the Ferris wheel. She didn't know, but I had paid extra to the attendant as we boarded, asking him to make it a good ride for a first date. He did. He loaded the other carts as normal, sent us on a few loops, then waited till we were at the very top of the circle, and stopped the ride.

We had the most incredible view of the ocean, Santa Monica, Venice, even our friends playing volleyball. It was perfect. She was staring out, soaking it all in. I was staring at her, heart beating triple speed, breathless. Here I was, sitting fifty feet up in the air, in a rickety craft only two feet from a woman that took my breath away. I was truly blessed. I reached for her hand, pulled her close, and then we locked in the most passionate kiss I had ever experienced in my life. It was deeper than the depths of the ocean, hotter than the sun, more electric than a Tesla coil. Indescribable were the feelings that ran through me. Here we were, surrounded by thousands of people, yet we were in our own world. Nothing else mattered. No one else was there. We were in a bubble all by ourselves. A void from the normal confines of this life.

I felt the ocean air against my cheek; felt it whipping her hair around us, still we didn't separate. I smelt the salt from the water mix with the scent of her perfume, still we did not break. I heard the waves breaking against the shore, sea gulls crying to each other, families yelling in happiness; still we did not disengage. It wasn't until I heard the "Uh Hem" clearing of the throat from the young guy who was running the Ferris wheel did we come apart. We had already spun a few more times and been the last to unload, and yet had no idea that we were no longer still sitting at the top. I slid the young man another twenty and mouthed, "Thank you."

He was pleased. Not only with the money, but, if I'm correct, I think he may have been a romantic and the idea that he helped out a young happy couple possibly find love made his day. I know he made mine.

We walked back toward the Jeep, stopping to grab some frozen yogurt along the way. She grabbed a raspberry sorbet and topped it with fresh pineapple and strawberries. I, on the other hand, opted for a peanut butter and chocolate yogurt mix topped with three types of chocolate chips, caramel syrup, Reese's peanut butter cups and a dash of Fruity Pebbles.

We got back to the Jeep, enjoying our yogurt and chatted away. By now we had grown so comfortable with each other that conversation came easy. There were never awkward moments, silent pauses, or dead air. Instead each moment was filled with laughter, smiles, and talking about life. I loved the way she talked about life. Like me, she too was a child of love. A lover of all things. Someone who enjoyed the sun on her face as much as the rain. We could talk politics, religion, sports, love, sex; it didn't matter. Even when our opinions differed, and they differed often, we respected each other's opinions and never argued. Just accepted each other's thoughts, then shared our own.

Back at the Jeep, I popped open the cooler and made us sandwiches and drinks. We walked over to the side of the pier and watched the tourists playing in the ocean for a bit. She began tossing pieces of her crust from her sandwich out for the sea gulls. At first it was cute and we laughed at their movements. Then they became crazed with the taste and started coming after us for more food. Jennifer yelled, laughed and ran toward the Jeep for safety. I batted at the birds and chased after her.

We reached the Jeep out of breath and in hysterics. An unexpected bit of fun to add for the date. Most assuredly a part we wouldn't forget. I looked at her, panting and sweating from the excitement. Watched as she brushed the brown and blonde highlighted hair out of her eyes. She stood and stretched, beads of sweat running down her neck and between her breasts. She was enticing. I liken it to watching flames dance.

As a flame dances it moves, rhythmically, to its own beat. It's beautiful. It calls for you to touch it. Yet you do not dare. For you know the flame is too hot. To touch it would be bad. No touching yet. Damn, what did she do to me? I was a little schoolboy hiding on the jungle gym staring at my crush from across the yard. Dare I sneak a peck on the cheek from her later? Risk the consequence? No, I must stay here on my jungle gym and keep an eye on everything. Seriously, this girl had me in knots.

The temperature was about 80 degrees and a nice breeze was blowing off of the ocean as we left Santa Monica. I was very happy with the way the day was going so far. We were sweaty and covered in sand, so showers must be had before any more of the date could commence. I pointed the Jeep east and headed back home. As we pulled off the freeway and down the ramp toward the main streets I stole a glance at her. Her hair was blowing around her face, the sun was gleaming off of her tan skin, and her smile, that incredible smile, was grinning from ear to ear. I felt a sense of pride well up inside me.

I thought to myself, *What do I wish to gain from this date?* I hadn't considered it until now. I knew I liked her. I knew she liked me. So what was the point of the date? It hit me. I loved her. I had fallen in love with her. This date was as much for me as it was for her. Tears welled up in my eyes and I turned my head so she couldn't see. I was overcome with emotion. I felt scared, hopeful, joy, elation, and love. So much love. My heart felt as though it could burst.

Had I truly met my wife? The mother of my children? Two months of Fridays and this date was all the time we had spent together and yet I knew her. I felt as though we had been friends since birth. I felt connected to her. I stole another glance, and noticed she was watching me. How long had she been watching. She grinned at me and laid her hand on my hand that was resting on the shifter. I could feel the energy coming from her. This was right. To whoever it is that could be listening up there. Thank you.

4

I looked back in her eyes. I squeezed her hand a little tighter. I could see how much in pain she was. Would my words be able to soften that pain? Was there anything I could do to release this poor broken woman from her prison of misery?

"I love the man that I am. I am that man, in large part, because of you. You showed me a love that I thought only existed in movies. I will love you until the day I see you in Heaven. I will think of you fondly, and often, until then. The love you gave me is something few on Earth will ever get to feel. Now, take a deep breath, let it out, and leave this failing body behind you. Leave this world with its failures and faults. Be free, my love."

Those last words caught me off guard. I knew it was going to be hard, but I was pretty sure I could handle this. However, I wasn't fully prepared to feel the finality of it as those words left my mouth. I felt a frog in my throat. That burning sensation deep down that is a pain you can't explain. Of course I wanted her pain to end. But, knowing she would be gone forever, that was going to hurt. It was a pain I feared would never go away.

I have lived through great times, sad times, pain and heart-ache. My story isn't a perfect story and Lord only knows if there will be a happy ending. I have loved. I have felt love so deep as to move mountains. Love that could build or crush nations with its might. I'd have taken a bullet, built an empire, and flown to outer space in the name of love. No matter what else I may endure, this included, my life can be measured as a good life. A life lived. A life that was worth living.

I need a moment to catch my breath, so I move to the window. I must admit, though cold and sterile, they have done a good job making these rooms more accommodating. She isn't sharing with anyone, so we are able to deal with this in private. Her room is on the 12th floor, so she has a view. I look out the window to the beautiful day outside. I see people driving, stoplight-to-stoplight, always in a hurry to get to their next location. I wish I could speak to them, to tell them to slow down and enjoy this life. They have no idea that just a few hundred yards away from them lays a woman, so young, dying. How many times had I been that motorist? In a hurry, rushing from place to place, completely oblivious to life around me. I am sure I have had my moments. I have also taken time to enjoy this life. I have lived. I have seen so much. Still, I should see more. I should slow down more.

I lean my back against the window, letting the sun warm me, and turn my head to watch her. She's lying there, painfully, fighting to stay though she knows it's time to go. Her spirit is so strong though her body is so weak. I wonder what is going on in her mind. Is she thinking about me? Remembering those times, long ago, which we shared. If so, do they help put her mind at ease? Or do they make her angry that this is happening to her? So young. I have to look away again to recompose myself. Times like these are when people blame God. They blame Him, asking why He would do such a thing to such a good person.

These days I'm not fully sure where I stand on theology. I tend to be a child of science, but there are so many things that science just can't explain. Let's leave it at I believe in something bigger than myself, though I'm not sure what that is. Regardless, I don't blame Him. If there is some omnipresent being watching over us I don't think that He/She/They would purposely cause someone harm like this. Plus, the child of science in me understands that the human body is so fragile. Though a woman her age dealing with this is rare, it is possible. Once it has progressed this far, there really is nothing to do but pray. Pray to God. Pray to Karma. Pray to who, or whatever, it is you pray to that they are able to help her pass to the next place peacefully.

Peace. No fighting. That her pain, her fears, her worries, her doubts are washed away. That she closes her eyes in this place and opens them in the next. Maybe she would open them and look down, realizing she standing on a ground made of puffy white clouds. Maybe she would be clothed in comfy white PJ's and be greeted by so many others, welcoming her to her new home. A home filled with smiles, laughter, acceptance and love. Sarcasm, racism, prejudice, and negativity are all gone. Ideas that get confused in this place we call Earth. Maybe she will find love. Always love. So much love. There can never be enough love.

5

I pulled the Jeep up to the house late that afternoon. I grabbed the cooler and went in, holding the door open for Jennifer. She went to the bedroom and began to clean off the day's activities. As there was light coming in the window, she hadn't turned on the bedroom light, only the one in the bathroom. It created a more dim and sensual atmosphere. I paused for a moment, letting the activities of the day settle in upon me. A great breakfast, volleyball with friends, time spent at the ocean, and laughter. Lots of laughter. Oh, and the itsy-bitsy realization that I was in love.

I had no idea if she felt the same way, if she felt emotion at all toward me. She hadn't given me any indication. I guess, from her point of view, neither had I. It was merely just what I was feeling inside. Thinking about all of this caused me to get goose bumps. The moment grabbed hold of me. I knew one thing and one thing only. I needed her in my arms that very second.

She wasn't facing me, so I snuck up behind her. I grabbed her around the hips and pulled her close to me. She was startled at first, but succumbed to my touch. She was wearing only square cut panties and one of my T-shirts since she was about to enter the shower. Like two puzzle pieces destined to fit together, our bodies perfectly matched. The feeling of her athletic rear pressed firmly against my body was elating. Her back arched and she sighed. An urge to take her right there entered my mind. Should I do it? I could feel from her body that she would allow it. She was craving me too.

With my left hand I swept all of her hair to the side, revealing her long tan neck. She leaned her head slightly, as if her body was whispering that she was ready. I wrapped my arms fully around her. I could feel her full breasts under my touch. I leaned down and kissed her neck. A long, soft kiss that lingered, taking time to make its presence known. She shuddered. Her whole body reacted as if touched by ice. I kissed her neck again, this time with less reaction; she became less tense. Her body was ready and craving it. I began to drag my lips up and down her skin, alternating spots to kiss. I wanted her. I was craving her.

I kissed her earlobe gently and held her still to halt her body's movements. I whispered in her ear, "You do something to me that no one ever has. I want you so badly right now, but I will respect you and won't try anything."

She slowly turned around, looked me in the eye, and said, "Thank you. I'm not sure if I'm ready for that yet. Just so you know, I want you too. Your touch on my skin lights a fire deep inside that I can't control".

With that, she slammed me against the wall, drew my face to hers, and kissed me with so much passion I thought I might explode. We stood there for what felt like hours, kissing and moaning, both wanting to finish what was started, neither sure if we should. Finally, she pulled away and smiled, "I definitely need a shower now." With a flash, she was gone and into the shower she went.

It took a moment to recover. I was sweating, panting, and yearning for more. Once I had calmed down, I hopped into Luke and Kobe's shower. I threw on some nicer clothes, and got ready for the fancier part of the date. She emerged from my bedroom wearing black heels and a form fitting dress that showed off every curve of her body. She looked elegant, yet enticing. I had opted for my dark grey suit with light pinstripes, a blue button up shirt, and a red tie. I felt like I looked good, but she put me to shame. We hopped in the Infiniti and headed toward Grant's in downtown Los Angeles.

Our reservations were at 7 p.m. and we were making great time. Grant's was known for its view almost as much as its steak, sitting on the 20th floor of a building in downtown. It was considered an Asian Fusion restaurant. The menu seemed to cater to those who loved beasts of both sea and land. I had chosen this place because I wanted to eat delicious food, but enjoy the beauty of Los Angeles from up high. Plus, she looked so elegant, I knew we needed to go somewhere she would shine.

Very dimly lit candles and antique wall sconces set the mood for romance. Smells of steak and seafood wafted through the air causing our mouths to water. Our eyes searched to find where the smells were coming from and we spied the kitchen. Adjoined to the kitchen was a meat locker, which had one wall made of glass allowing you to peruse the cuts of meat. We stopped for a moment and surveyed the raw slabs that would soon be sizzling and hot, coated in sauce, and being served.

We were seated at a table about midway down on a glass wall overlooking the city. The wall must have been 40 feet long, giving each table a view was breathtaking. The sun had just begun to set, so the City of Angels was now barely lit by a swath of oranges and purples. We were facing northwest. Our vantage allowed us to see from Hollywood to the ocean and everything in between. The sky, lit by so many colors, was inundated by planes heading to and from Los Angeles International Airport. Little white arrows cutting their path through the clouds, blinking red and green each in their own tune. And Jennifer, sitting in the dim light from the sconce above, the glow from the candle bouncing playfully off her skin. The talk came easily with her. Never was there a moment of silence. We laughed, told stories, and even had serious moments where we each opened up and shared something about us that made each seem more human.

For her it was her ex -boyfriend Hayden. She had been in love with him. She had thought he would be the man she married, but they had each only been 22 years old when they met. He had cheated on her with another girl from college, which had broken her heart causing her to not date for a year after.

As she told her story, I could see emotion build behind her eyes. I could see damage was done and, though it was now a few years later, there was still much healing to be done. I felt something myself. Was it empathy? No, it was something else. Something darker. Could I be feeling jealousy? Jealous some guy that was no longer in the picture, that wasn't here, but only in a story? Could that really be it? I put it out of my mind. Whatever the feeling was, I didn't like it.

For my story, I told her of my childhood. How my parents met and had kids too young (at 19). How they were both in the Navy and drank too much. That their drinking led to nights of fighting, anger, broken possessions, broken hearts, and police. Of losing my father at an early age because of his drinking. I don't share that story much, so talking about it brought back tough memories. She could see I was hurting and lay her hand on mine. Her soft touch was comforting. She made me feel validated in telling her my secrets and who I was inside. As we talked our food came and went.

For appetizers they brought out raw Kobe beef strips and a large hot stone that sat on a bed of jade. We used chopsticks to dip the strips in different sauces and then sear them on the hot stone. Each time they would hit the stone there would be a short sizzle, a hiss of steam, and an alluring smell. The flavor, though different each time depending on the combination of sauces, was succulent.

A large cut of Filet Mignon is what I opted for as my main course. The kitchen had prepared it perfectly to my taste. Medium, juicy, covered in A-1 sauce, side of mashed potatoes and sweet corn. There is something about Japanese corn-fed Kobe beef that just can't be beat. Delicious. She had decided on Lobster. It might have been the largest lobster I had ever seen. This must have been brought in from Maine, because I know it didn't come from anywhere close. It was served with steamed vegetables. She loved both the lobster and the asparagus equally, which I found cute.

Our dessert was a shared piece of chocolate suicide. Chocolate chip cake covered in chocolate cream icing with chocolate sauce poured all over it. I don't even know how we were able to stand after all of that. Though I was mindful of the time, we never felt rushed. Admittedly, I had probably planned too many things for one date. I just felt that I had so much to show her. She came from a financially better family.

The other side of the tracks, so to speak. I felt a need to impress her. I had been excited when I planned everything out, but had been equally as anxious. Part of me wanted to just grab her and head home. However, I still had more I wanted to show her.

The combination of the meal, the ambience, and her company could not have been any better. Arm in arm we walked back to the elevator, down to the valet, and out to the waiting car. I stole the valet's job and opened her door holding her hand as she stepped in. Just before I closed the door she turned to look at me, our eyes met, and I saw it. She flashed a hint of something. For just a moment I saw a glint in her eye, an unmistakable twinkle. I believe it was the same twinkle that I was sending right back to her. That second stretched on as our hearts searched each other out. I knew and she knew. Things were different after that moment. I don't know if there is an exact word that could describe it. The bottom line, we both knew that the other felt love. For the first time neither thought we were alone in our emotions. I will never forget that instant. For the first time, I knew someone loved me and I loved her back.

I joined her in the car. She leaned over, cupped my face in her hands, and kissed me softly on the lips. "Thank you so very much for today."

I let the moment settle in and took my time to respond. "You're welcome. I'm appreciative of your time. Don't get too relaxed, though, we still have a bit more to go."

Her eyes seemed to light up and she squealed, "More!? Oh my gosh, Chase. I don't know what to say."

"Shall we skip the rest?" I asked, wondering if I was right, maybe I had planned too much.

"No!" She exclaimed. "I never want this date to end. If you have more, please show me." She paused for a moment, and then continued, "I didn't mean to seem unexcited. I just can't believe how much you planned today. You, sir, have put me in awe. That's saying something considering how I already felt about you."

How she already felt about me? Had she felt strongly before tonight? Had we been heading on the same course, at the same speed, never knowing we were on the same track? I felt as though my heart may burst from my chest. This woman was amazing me at every turn. I started the car and put it into drive. She laid her hand on mine and there it stayed.

We drove from downtown L.A. to Newport Beach for the next part of our date. Newport Beach is a really quaint little beach town. A relatively high-end area nestled between other more popular beaches. What makes Newport so special is that much of its beach coastline has canals, similar to Venice, Italy. These canals snake through residential areas of some of the most expensive and elegant homes I have ever seen. Many of the owners of these homes, knowing their location and that people may see them, have hired professionals to decorate and light the outside of each home. So, at night, it's both beautiful and romantic. There just happens to be a company that does gondola rides, like Venice, through the canals at night. I had booked the last ride of the night, a 10 p.m. departure, and we were going to make it with about 5 minutes to spare.

We parked and I opened the trunk of the car, removing the oversized basket that I had packed and placed in there before leaving the house. We walked over to the dock, gave our reservation name, and met our gondolier, Mateo. Dressed in the traditional garb of black and white stripes, Mateo was a slightly overweight man that looked to be in his early 40's with a cheerful smile and a gleam in his eye. The kind of guy that seems to delight in the happiness of others. I took that as a great sign. He escorted us to our gondola. I helped Jennifer in first, and then she offered her hand to me. I sat down beside her and put the basket on the floor. Mateo joined us with a smile, pushed off from the dock, and out into the water we went.

The night air had a slight chill to it. I realized this even more noticeably when I saw the goose bumps begin to form on Jennifer's arm. I opened the basket, removed the blanket I had packed, and draped it around the both of us. She nodded a grateful smile, then hugged me and pulled me in close. Once we were firmly into the canals, Mateo reached down and turned on a little radio that I hadn't noticed. An Italian song softly started playing through the speakers. Not loud enough to disturb those already nestled down for the night in their homes. Rather, just loud enough to set a mood of romance for Jennifer and I. We turned a corner down one of the canals and realized we were facing a perfectly white full moon. Jennifer in my arms, music playing, I was entranced by the image of the moon swaying in and out of focus on the dark shimmer of the water. Jennifer too was watching the reflection. I wondered what she was thinking. Whatever it was, I now knew it included happy thoughts about me.

We had been floating through the canals for about thirty minutes when I decided it was time for a snack. I opened the basket and brought out some glasses, cider, cheese, grapes, and crackers. She poured the cider into the two glasses while I set up the cheese tray. We offered some to Mateo, but he never looked back at us. He was a romantic and felt he shouldn't break the wall for us. As far as he was concerned, he didn't exist in the boat with us. I thought that was a great quality. We enjoyed our nibbles and whispered sweet nothings into each other's ears. Though we were very much enjoying everything, I could tell we were nearing the end of our ride. There was one last surprise that even I was unaware of.

About a quarter mile before the dock there was a bridge. We began to slow as we approached the bridge and, as we went under, finally stopped. We were sitting dead still, held in place by the oar of our strong gondolier, Mateo. Without warning he began to sing a beautiful Italian tune. I realized that this was a moment for lovers; moment to embrace the passion of the night. I turned to Jennifer and engulfed her body with my arms, pulled her close to me, and kissed her. We kissed deep and sensually, our hands searching out each other's skin. Our tongues reaching for the farthest depths while playing unabashedly with the others. I felt my temperature rise as we kissed deeper. And then I felt the gondola begin to move as Mateo's song slowly faded then stopped. We were offered a moment of passion and had seized it. Admittedly, we both wanted more, but it was an excellent tease.

"Shall we head home?" I asked.

She smiled at me and nodded. She gave me the biggest

hug, then hopped in the car and reached across to open my door. Such a thoughtful gesture. I walked around and got in myself. We drove the rest of the way home in silence, hand in hand, soft music playing in the background. We arrived home around 1 a.m. I told her I needed to do something first, so I let her grab a quick bite in the kitchen as I went in the bedroom. A few minutes later I re-emerged and took her by the hand. I led her to the bedroom door, and slowly opened it. She gasped.

As her eyes adjusted to the dim light, she saw that, leading from the door to the bed, was a path of rose petals. Red, pink, white, yellow petals all intermixed and lined with the stems. The bed too was covered with the petals, as well as a huge bouquet of pink roses and an oversized stuffed teddy bear holding a card. Throughout the room were candles of various sizes and scents. The room smelled like a mixture of strawberry, apple, and spices. She went to the bed, picked up the bouquet and smelled them. She smiled and laid them on the nightstand. Then she grabbed the teddy bear and giggled.

She opened the card and read it aloud, "Jennifer, I have no idea how today will go. All I know is that I wanted to show you things I love while enjoying things you love. You make me feel a way that is new to me. Unexplored. I'm sometimes unsure of myself around you. I'm sure of one thing; I want to be with you. In every way. Emotionally, physically, intellectually, sexually. I don't expect that we will make love tonight. If we do, know that it means more to me than just a physical act. May today be the first of hundreds of dates to come. Chase."

She sat the card down on the nightstand and...

...She kissed me! Deeper and with more passion than she ever had before. Her left hand on my face her right hand grabbing my hair and pulling it slightly. She ran her hands down to my chest, started unbuttoning my shirt, never letting our lips break the solid bond they had made. After the last button was removed she slid my shirt off my shoulders and let it fall to the floor.

She ran her hands over my pecs and across my stomach. She smiled as she counted each one of my abs. I reached down to her knees, right where her form fitting dress ended, and grabbed the end. I slowly pulled it up and over her head. Our lips broke only for the millisecond it took to bring the dress past her face. Never looking down she undid my belt and unbuttoned my pants. I reached my hand around and undid the clasp on her bra. It fell to the floor. She pulled away from my kiss, knelt down, and slid my pants down as well. Then she started at my belly and kissed my abs, then my chest, up my neck and back to my lips.

I moved to her side, put my left arm behind her shoulders and my right arm under her knees. In one swift motion I picked her up and laid her on the bed of roses. Both of us now only in our underwear. The candlelight bouncing off of her barely covered breasts showing me more than I had ever seen of her. Her body was incredible. I climbed in bed with her, and rolled her over onto her stomach. Then I began to gently massage her. I kissed her neck, down to her shoulder blades, down the center of her back. Taking my time with each kiss. Letting them feel intense and linger.

We explored each other in that hour. Each of us searching with our bodies what our souls were craving. Finally, after my body eventually gave out, I collapsed on top of her. I couldn't speak because I was breathing so hard. I hurt, but I loved it. Then, the most magical thing happened. She whispered in my ear, "I love you".

I mustered enough strength to lift myself up and look her in the eyes, "I love you, too."

A tear rolled out of her right eye. I kissed it away and wiped her face slowly with my hand. I fell to the bed, pulled her onto my shoulder, and we passed out. Covered in rose petals, sweat, and battle scars. The perfect date was the perfect day. It had ended with us making love. Things would never be the same for her. For me. Or for us.

6

The next few months were a whirlwind. We went from seeing each other every Friday night to almost every night. This was a feat considering she lived 45 minutes away. We didn't care. All we knew was that every second apart didn't make sense. We were so in love. Exploding with passion. I craved her touch, her scent, and her soft wet lips against mine. Time stood still when we were together and zoomed by when we were apart.

During the day when she was at work, we texted each other. Sending cute little messages and pictures of ourselves to say hello. At night we texted while I was at work. Sometimes we would be cute, sometimes playful, and always sexual. We had a sexual connection that was like none I'd ever encountered. I asked my friends that had girlfriends if they felt the same passion for their significant other, none did. What Jennifer and I had was rare. We both knew it. And we held on to it for dear life.

On the days that we were both off of work, we explored life together. What made it more interesting was that we decided we had to explain why we chose to take each other on the dates we did, even if it was a silly reason. I went first and took her to Universal Studios, where I was working as Spiderman at the time. We spent the day riding the rides, watching shows, and playing games. A fun filled day.

When she asked me why I chose Universal Studios I answered, "I have known I wanted to be an actor since I was four years old. In kindergarten I was the Big Bad Wolf in the play *The Three Little Pigs*. I fell in love with acting even at such a young age. I worked hard, studied acting, and did every play/musical that I could get into until I decided to take the plunge and move to Los Angeles to chase film and television."

"There is a passion deep inside my heart that drives me. I can't even explain the emotion of being on set. My heart feels like it may burst. When I get to see myself on the screen, I feel complete. Much like I do when I'm with you," I finished.

"That is why I brought you here today. Though this is a theme park, we also went through the studio tour and you got to see where movies are made. A small sneak peak at what I do. I hope it brings a little more light to who I am," I said with a smile.

She grabbed me and held me so tight, "I love this side of you. I never thought that the acting was just fun for you. I know you, Chase. I can see in your eyes what it means to you. Much the same way I can tell what I mean to you. I don't come from a very artistic family; we are almost all in the healthcare industry. So it is tough for me to fully understand the passion. If you love it, it must be important."

One week she took me to Newport Beach. We spent the day walking and shopping at all the cute little beach stores. Some of the day we just laid out on the beach, enjoying the sunshine. Newport seems to be a more wealthy area. This tends to bring a higher class of people and fewer tourists. The beach is very well kept and is surrounded by many nice shops, restaurants, and art galleries. We perused the galleries, commenting our opinions on our favorites and the ones we didn't understand. We laughed heartily at the ones that we believed calling 'art' was a stretch.

She took me to a quaint restaurant on the beach and there we had dinner and watched the sunset. After dinner I asked her why she chose Newport for our date and she said, "The sun, the ocean, the sand all make me feel alive. I don't think I could ever live far from the beach. I love the smell of the salt water in the air, the sound of the waves crashing ashore and the beauty of it all. Newport seems to be the best place at bringing these things together, without being inundated with tourists and crazy Hollywood people. I love it here, Chase. Let's build a home here one day. On top of the hill with all of this as our front yard view."

"I will baby. I will do whatever it takes to make this dream come true for you." I was honest when I said that. I would have worked six jobs to make it happen.

In the beginning we were friends. After we had the first date, we became lovers. As time went on, we became more. I don't believe in love at first sight. At least, not true love. True love, in my humble opinion, comes from two people that truly know each other. The love that comes from the respect, understanding, caring, and absolute need to be around the other person at all times is rare and comes with time. I believe she and I had lust at first sight. An intense passion for each other. An organic chemistry that is rare. And, from that, we built true love. What we had was real. Tangible. You could reach out and touch it.

Our lives, though connected and similar in so many ways, differed greatly in profession. Her career at the hospital was growing. She quickly became the head of all techs and was being talked to about a possible management position. She was on a path. A direct path that her parents had planned out for her long ago. I, on the other hand, was on a much less direct path.

My path twisted and turned and the destination was unsure. During the day I was Spiderman in a stunt show at Universal Studios. A few nights a week I also bartended at a local dive bar. My jobs were merely a way to pay my bills as I was working toward my acting goal. I would go to auditions and occasionally call backs throughout the week. On the happiest of occasions, I would book the gig. Granted, they were all small gigs as I was just starting. I loved what I was doing, so I didn't mind the process or the time it took to get to where I was going; even if I didn't know where that was.

We decided to take a trip to Missouri. Missouri is where I grew up and where most of my family still resides. My mom picked us up at the airport and drove us the two hours to our Midwest home, where I grew up. Jennifer was so surprised by the country feel of everything. We rounded the last corner to our property and I pointed out where what we owned started. Many acres of land. Most of which we just used for hunting or renting to local farmers who needed a place to hold cattle for short periods of time. We finally reached our driveway to the house. It was a gravel road that stretched for about 1/4 of a mile. As we drove it toward the house I pointed out our front yard, which was the seven acres on our left. She stared in awe.

We pulled up to my childhood home with a slow crunch of the gravel. An adorable farmhouse sat before us that had five bedrooms, three full bathrooms, and 20 years of my mom's love to make it special. There were flowers wonderfully landscaped to add life to the front of the house. A wrap-around porch went from the front door to the back of the house. Out in the back there was a small one-acre garden where my mother grew her favorite vegetables and fruits. Six dogs, my brother Dean, my sister Letha, and my youngest sister Katy greeted us. Dean grabbed Jennifer's and my bags from the car while the girls said their hellos and started the chitchat. Women never seem to have a hard time getting to know one another.

During that trip Jennifer fell in love with my family, and they fell in love with her. We spent time out on the back porch at night, drinking Momma's sweet tea and everyone (but me of course) telling stories about me as a child. They told of my refusal to wear clothes for most of my early years. They told of how often I had to go to the hospital, resulting in various broken bones, stitch scars, etc.

"I always wanted to ask why he had so many scars!" she had exclaimed through her laughter. I have never been one that is shy about who I am or what I have done, so I laughed right along with them. Including when mom brought out the old photos. Except, of course, when she tried to show the naked ones. I finally had to put my foot down.

The time came and Mom took us back to the airport. As we were saying our goodbyes she pulled me in close and said to me, "Chase, there is something about this girl. She loves you very much. I can see it in her eyes when she looks at you. Don't mess this up. Oh, and I love you."

"Wow thanks!" I responded laughing, "I see who's important now." I knew what she meant. She wanted me to be happy more than anything. She believed that Jennifer could do that for me. I kissed her goodbye, then back to Los Angeles we flew.

On the flight I could see something was on Jennifer's mind. She was lost in thought. "Baby, are you okay?" I asked. She looked at me, started to say something, and then stopped.

She leaned in, kissed me, and whispered, "Thank you."

"You're welcome. I want you to be in my life, every part of it. That includes my family. It was important to me that you meet them. They loved you, which I knew they would. They are just like me; full of joy, eager to find happiness in any situation, and never judging."

She kissed my cheek and leaned back in her seat. I'm not sure, but I could swear I saw a tear fall down her cheek. She sat there, in silence, looking out the window for the rest of the flight. We landed, grabbed our bags at claims check, and loaded up. She seemed sad the entire time. Finally, I was so worried I could contain it no longer. "Baby, what is wrong!"

She started crying. She grabbed me and pulled me in close, holding me hard. I didn't understand what was happening, "Do I need to take you to a hospital? Are you hurting? Baby, please tell me!"

Finally she got control of herself enough to say, through her sobs, "No one has ever treated me like that. I love my family so much, but they aren't like that. They are constantly judging and pushing. They expect things. They aren't like your mom. Your family; they trust you. They support you and believe in you. They want you to live your own life. They took me in and accepted me. They were so kind to me and didn't care what I did or who I was so long as I loved you."

"Baby, it's okay. They adored you so be happy. You don't need to be sad that we have different backgrounds. There is nothing wrong with that." I said, hoping to calm her. But it didn't. She seemed even more frustrated.

"They aren't why I'm sad. They brought me so much joy. It's my family I'm worried about. Don't get me wrong. They are kind and great people and I had such a wonderful upbringing because of them. But, and it hurts me to say this,

I don't know that they will accept you the way your family has accepted me." That was the first time I realized how our different pasts could shape our future.

After that night at the airport I was dreading meeting her parents. Though I always put on a happy face and never let her know how I felt, I was worried. Would they accept me for who I am? I wasn't sure. Never in my life had acceptance ever been a problem before. Parents, coaches, bosses; it didn't matter whom, people generally always seemed to like and accept me. Most could see that I was a hardworking man of my word who treated people well. I only hoped I could show her parents the same thing.

Jennifer set a date for us to meet them. They had decided to have a big Filipino family dinner at their lovely house. When people from the Philippines get together it is a big to do. Lots of family comes and there is always enough food to feed a small continent. They cooked a lot of traditional food such as lumpia (little rolls filled with cabbage and meat), ponset (I have no idea), and even ballut (it's like a half hatched egg cooked). They also made sure to have some steak and potatoes for me, just in case. I drove down and picked Jennifer up from her place and we made our way over. She was visibly uncomfortable and her nervousness was making me more nervous. We pulled up after a short drive, I took a few deep breaths to calm the nerves, and headed in.

The house, which was enormous, had been impeccably decorated. A mixture of modern art and classic style went perfectly with the contemporary architecture. The common rooms were all open and spacious. This house was meant for a large family. And it had found just that.

There were children of various ages and sizes running around the house. The parents and other onlookers took time to shake hands hug their hellos, commenting on how much they had heard about me. The men stopped me for quick bouts of sports talk, "What do you think of Paquiou?" they posed to me.

I quickly remarked, "I think he is, pound for pound, the smartest and fastest boxer right now."

The women asked how Jennifer and I met and when I answered they replied, "So Amanda set you up did she? She is trouble, that cousin!" I just smiled and nodded.

We reached the upstairs living room where Jennifer's father, Mike, and some of the other family members were watching sports. Mike stood up and greeted me with a firm handshake and a welcoming smile. I thanked him for inviting me to dinner. He accepted, engaged me in a quick bit of conversation, then went back to sports. The exchange was comfortable. He was very nice and I felt a little more at ease after that. I walked into the kitchen to meet Jennifer's mother, Violet. She was a shorter and rounder woman with a great big smile. Her face, though older, bared a great resemblance to Jennifer's. I thought of how beautiful she must have been at one time. She saw me and gave me a great big bear hug.

In her thick Filipina accent she said, "Hello, Chase! My daughter speaks so highly of you. Thank you for taking care of my baby." I was taken aback. Jennifer had been so worried that they may not like me, but everyone was being so sweet.

Dinner came and went. The conversation came easily and we all talked of many things. With such a large group at the table, the topics changed quickly and opinions varied greatly. After dinner we moved to the family room where a large poker table had been set up and a group of 11 of us sat and played poker for hours. I felt very much at ease with her parents and didn't understand why Jennifer had been so concerned. I thought my country boy charm had won them over and everything would be fine.

After the game Jennifer and I headed out. We were all smiles as we drove back to her house. "Did I do okay?" I mused.

"Oh, Chase, you did wonderful. I was never worried about that. I knew they would love you as a person. It's the other stuff I'm worried about."

"What other stuff?" I asked, off-put by the notion.

"It is very important, in my culture, that the man have a career that allows him to take care of his family. I know how hard you work and what your career means to you. I'm worried that they won't see what I do," she said.

Confused I asked, "Should I not have told them that I'm an actor? That I bartend?"

"No, baby," she answered back, "I'm glad you were honest with them. I love that you're proud of who you are and who you want to become. I'm just worrying. That's all." I started to worry too.

The next morning we were lying in bed talking. Me lying flat on my back, her on my shoulder. We were just talking about random things, nothing of any importance, when her phone rang. It was her mother, who didn't know I was there.

"Hi, Momma", she said as she answered the phone. She was quiet for a long time after that. Minutes passed where she only said "yeah", "uh huh", or "I know". After about half an hour she finally said goodbye and hung up. She sat in silence for a moment, gathering her thoughts.

Then she turned to me, "Chase, they like you so very much. They think you're a good man and a joy to have around. However, they don't feel that you're the kind of man that could provide for, and take care of, his family. They are worried that we won't have a good life if I continue with this."

She went on to tell me that her mother had explained to her that we were from two different worlds. Her world was one where the idea that money does buy happiness. Indirectly, but most assuredly. That those who didn't see the world that way were from the other world. She told her that people like me went through life pretending to not care about money mostly because we were either ignorant of its importance or too lazy to care.

The seeds of doubt had been planted.

I was stunned. I had never been looked at like that before. I got my first job when I was 14 years old. I remember working at a gas station/convenience store stocking shelves back in Belle, Missouri. Since then I have steadily held one or multiple jobs. I have always worked hard and kept up my responsibilities. I had even tried school. Though, realizing after only one year, theater majors go on to teach theater. I had no interest in teaching, only acting, so I didn't go back. I didn't know what to say. I could see on her face that her mother's words had affected her.

"Jennifer, you know me. You know I will do whatever it takes to support our family. I'll work my fingers to the bone if I have to. You can't let the opinions of others hinder the love that is only understood between you and I."

She let that sink in and replied, "Chase, you're right. What they said is also right. I'm very confused right now. I know I love you with all of my heart, but I'm worried about the future."

I couldn't believe this was happening. "Baby, I'm your future. As you are mine. Nothing else matters. Not money, nor possessions, nor people who don't believe in us. Let's prove them wrong, let's make it work."

We went on like that for hours. The seed of doubt had been planted in her mind. I worked tirelessly to get her to see that our love was strong enough to overcome any obstacle. I reminded her that I grew up very lower-middle class. I had come from nothing. That my mom, who raised my siblings and I on her own since I was five, worked so hard to take care of our family. Though we weren't wealthy, we had a nice home, clothes, and were well fed. The rest aren't necessities. Now I owned two vehicles, lived in a nice house with my best friends, and had nice things. Finally, she seemed to calm down and I left to go to work that night feeling better.

The problem with the seed of doubt is that it rarely goes away. Even if it could, it takes a lot of time and effort to get through it. It's called a seed for a reason. Once a seed is planted it begins to grow. It begins to fester and spread. A disease of the mind. Some seeds, as this one seemed to be, could be stronger than others.

7

Weeks went by and everything seemed pretty much okay. I could tell she was a little distant, but I figured that was to be expected. I knew her family was still giving her their opinions and I would occasionally have to defend myself. I loved her, I didn't care. As long as she kept looking at me with eyes that said she felt the same way, I was willing to fight the world around us. My heart was filled with joy because of her. The rest didn't matter. Not money, negative people, or anything else life could throw at us. At least, that's what I thought.

I began to notice oddities. Little things that didn't add up or make sense. One night she got a call late in the evening, around 9, then erased the number that called. I thought this strange so I asked who it was. She nervously responded, "Monsterjobs.com calling me again trying to recruit me."

I took her word for it, but it did seem unlikely. Multiple times she disappeared for hours and I wouldn't hear from her, even though we had set the time to text each other. I had never been an overly jealous man, but these things began making me suspicious. I didn't like how I was feeling. When we were together, life was amazing, but when we were apart, I could feel distance building. I had to find out what was going on and put a stop to it.

One day I happened to be off work. So I drove down to the hospital around the time she got off. My plan was to wait outside and confront her. Catch her off guard and ask her to be straight with me. Tell me why things were changing. I parked across the parking lot with a good view of the doors she would exit. I saw her emerge from the sliding doors.

She was wearing lavender colored scrubs. They weren't flattering to her body, but she still looked beautiful. The wind caught her long highlighted hair and blew it around her face. I smiled. She seemed happy. That was the girl I had fallen in love with. I reached for the handle to exit the car and go to her. And then my world stopped.

A Caucasian man, about my height and build but with lighter spiked up hair, met her just outside the doors. He picked her up, twirled her, and kissed her. They stood there, kissing, for about a minute. Then they walked over to his black BMW 535i and drove off together. My heart stopped. I couldn't breathe. I didn't understand what was happening. Had I really just witnessed that? My knuckles were white from gripping my steering wheel. I realized I was drenched in sweat and there was a knot in my throat. I had to decide; follow her and possibly make this worse or just go home and figure it out later?

I had to know more; to understand what I just saw. I hated myself for doing so, but I followed them. They drove the familiar path to her house, and then he dropped her off. However, before he drove away there was a long exchange of laughter, kisses, and hugs. I thought about confronting her. I imagined myself, the broken man screaming and crying trying to make sense of her excuses. I couldn't do that. I was a better man than that. So I held it in. I swallowed my pride and went home. Once home I went straight to my room and I broke down. I had my moment of pity. I allowed myself a moment, only a moment, then I regained my composure. I loved this woman, so I would give her a chance to explain.

I texted her and asked if we were still on for watching our favorite show, *Nip/ Tuck* that night. She replied that we were. I sat down and waited the three hours till she arrived. She came in the door and bounced right up to me. I hugged her, so tight. My heart was beating a thousand miles a minute in my chest. She tried to kiss me, but I held back. I sat her down on the couch.

"We need to talk," I gruffly mumbled.

She looked at me. She could see the pain in my eyes and asked, "Chase, are you okay? What is it?"

My eyes flooded, but I held the tears back. I didn't want to be the victim. I was a man, but I was hurting.

"I have been feeling as though things are off between us. So, since I was off work today, I drove down to meet you when you left work. I saw you with him. Some blonde guy. I'm offering you a chance here. A chance to be honest and real with me. A chance to come clean and tell me what is going on."

She went completely pale. Beads of sweat broke out on her forehead. She cried. Quietly to herself tears streamed down her cheeks. She knew she had made a mistake. I waited patiently for her to answer. It took her ten minutes to compose herself enough to respond. She was still hysterical when she spoke and a lot of what she said was hard to understand.

" I'm so sorry you had to see that, Chase. I'm so sorry that I have hurt you. Ever since that night at my parents' house I have been dealing with a lot emotionally. My parents are telling me every day how my choices I'm making now are bad for my future. I'm confused and feel lost some days. I know how much I love you, but I don't know what to do. And then, the, the, the, the…" She was sobbing so hard she couldn't complete her thought.

"Tell me, baby," I said through clenched teeth. "Tell me who he is!"

She looked at me and screamed, "HAYDEN!" Then she collapsed in a sobbing pile on my couch.

Hayden. The ex-boyfriend who had cheated on her and broke her heart. The one she had told me about at dinner on our first date. I remembered that I had seen emotion in her eyes as she had told me the story about him. I also remembered feeling a sense of jealousy, even then. She was in pain. I hated seeing her laying there, crying. It broke my heart, but I was hurting too. What do you do in a moment like this? I had no idea. I was hurt and I was angry.

"Why, baby? Why have you done this? What all have you two done?" I asked her.

She looked at me as if in a daze. "My parents talked to him. They like him because he is a real estate broker and makes a lot of money. They told him about you and how in love we seemed. It made him jealous and he started calling and texting. I have love in my heart for him, Chase. I love you too. I love you more, but it is there. When he started coming around, plus what my parents were saying, it caused me to get confused. We never did anything more than kiss. I swear to you on everything that is special to me. I'm so sorry. I AM SORRY!" Again, she was sobbing.

"Can you tell me, right now, that it will end? That I'm the only one? That it can be just you and I? Will you tell him, in front of me, that it is over?" I asked her, believing in my heart that our love was the kind that could overcome this. She would choose me and this would become but a bad memory locked in the depths of our minds. I waited for an answer. Minutes went by. My mind was racing, my heart beating so hard I was afraid it might run out of energy. Why hadn't she immediately accepted? It didn't make sense. We were so in love.

"Jennifer, this is very important. I need you to look me in the eyes and tell me that it is over with him. Please, baby." She stood up, looked me in the eyes, and then turned away. She couldn't do it. The final dagger was placed in my heart. I was at a loss for words.

"You know where the door is", and I turned and walked to my bedroom. I locked the door and lay down on my bed. I was emotionally exhausted. A few minutes later I heard the front door open and close. She was gone. I was defeated. Emotionally, physically, mentally I was beat. I closed my eyes and slept right there in my clothes.

Two weeks came and went without us talking. I began to settle back into my routine of life without her. I was sad, but managing. I spent more time with the guys. We went out, played sports, watched movies, and enjoyed our guy time together. They could all see I wasn't as happy as normal and knew why, but they let me be myself and didn't push.

Amanda, Jennifer's cousin that introduced us, seemed especially hurt by the ordeal. I assured her that it wasn't her fault. That life sometimes changes and there is nothing you could do about it. I was appreciative of the time that Jennifer and I had spent together. I loved feeling that way toward someone. I was sad regardless.

Amanda told me one night after poker, "I see you like a little brother. I worry about and care for you. She may be my blood relative, but you're closer to me." I'll never forget that. Those words meant so much to me. I carry them in my heart even today.

The next Friday night I was working at the bar and it was especially busy. I was exhausted when I left work so I took my time as I walked to the lot where I always parked. I saw my Jeep come into view and headed toward it. I parked near a streetlight, hoping that would help keep it from being stolen. Out of the corner of my eye I caught something move from the shadows behind the Jeep. I immediately got on the defensive, just in case I needed to protect myself. As I got closer to the Jeep, I saw what had moved come into the light. It was Jennifer.

She was dressed in grey sweat pants, a light blue tank, and the matching grey sweat top. It seemed unusual that she would be in public in that attire. Of course, considering what had transpired recently, I suppose her being there at all was unusual. My heart began to race as she approached me.

"Please give me a moment to speak, before you say anything," she said to me in a very calm yet decided tone.

I motioned toward the Jeep, she nodded and we both got in. I gave her a look that said I was ready, and she began. " I'm an emotional wreck without you. What happened between us is my fault. I can accept that now. I let others influence my decisions rather than looking at things through unbiased eyes. You were kind to both my family and me. You respected me and cared for me. What I did was dishonest, wrong, and disrespectful. I understand that you may never take me back or that it will take time to win you back. However, if you'll allow it, I'm going to fight for it. I'm going to get you back. I'm going to prove to you every day that you are the only one for me. My days are empty, my nights are lonely, and my heart is lost without you. To show you how serious I am, I'll start tonight by calling Hayden and telling him exactly what I'm telling you. I love you baby. I love you so much. Please, don't make me go on without you."

I sat there in silence for a minute. I was stunned. I had yearned every second of every day to hear those words. My face went flush. I was shaking. I wanted her to worry, to stew in the pot of her own words. On the inside, though, I was rejoicing like an entire school of kids that was just given free ice cream. I was so happy, but I held my best poker face.

"Please say something, Chase. Yell at me, scream. Tell me anything. I just need to hear a response."

I looked at her, smiled my boyish country smile and responded, "Jennifer, I fell in love with you again the moment you stepped out of the shadows. In the immortal words of Jerry Maguire 'You Had Me At Hello.' I'm so glad you're here. I'm happy that you're ready to do this for real. It's you and I against the world from now on. I love you and I'm willing to do this with you, if you promise me that these things won't happen again."

She hadn't expected this response. She must have assumed that I would fight a little more. This surprise caused her to launch out of the passenger seat and onto my lap. We sat there, just she and I in the glow of the streetlight, and we held each other. Things were back to the way they should be. All the pain, the hurt, the anger just washed away. All that mattered was the love we felt right there in that Jeep.

We spent the next year building our love and setting up our future. The first order of business, of course, was the conversation with Hayden. I sat there, next to her, as she made the phone call. She was calm and matter of fact, but let him know that what happened with them could not happen again. She said that she loved me and that her future was with me. She kept the conversation short, but made sure to get out all of the important information. I watched her face. I was looking to see if it hurt her. There was worry in my heart. I wondered if she meant what she was saying. I didn't see pain. Instead, she seemed at ease. As if this was the easy and right choice for her. I don't know if she knew how much that meant to me, but I vowed to show her in time.

Next was her family. We knew that, for us to work, we were going to have to have a talk with them. We took them to dinner with the idea we would tell them that we understood their worries for their daughter, but that we were going to be together. I was very scared that night. Though they were sweet people, I knew how they felt about me in their hearts. I have never been a fan of confrontation, but I stood when I spoke to them.

"I want to first thank you all for coming. As you know, Jennifer and I have been through quite a lot in a short time. I know that you are all worried about her. But you need to understand I was brought up with country values that are similar to your those of your own culture. Though I can't promise you that I will get a job in an office where I have job security, I can promise that I will work hard and break my back to take care of my family.

I love your daughter and she loves me very much. What we have is rare and beautiful. We have the opportunity to build something that can last a lifetime, but we need your support. Your words and wisdom mean a lot to her, and to me as well. So we are asking that you love us as a couple. Care for us as a unit, both being your children. Allow me the opportunity to prove to you that I am the right man for your daughter. With my love, respect, honesty, and hard work I will make you proud that I am a part of the family."

We spoke back and forth for a bit. At the end, we all agreed and it turned out to be a good night. Though I never saw full trust in their eyes toward me, I didn't complain so long as they quit planting seeds in Jennifer's mind.

Jennifer, knowing she had damaged her bonds with my friends, made it a point to repair those relationships as well. She called each one individually and told them of her love for me. She promised them not to hurt me again and how much she would appreciate their blessing for us. My friends, though all worried for me, respected her effort and did so. We all began to hang out again. At first, of course, there was some resentment and hesitation, but over time, it faded. Soon we were all enjoying poker nights again.

As the months went by we began to settle in with each other. Not in the way where people settle in and lose the passion. Instead we got used to the driving. We grew accustomed to our different lifestyles. We even got comfortable with the neuroses' we both have. For her it was the future. She was constantly worried about the future. It was so much for her that sometimes she was daunted by it. I would calm her down each time and try to help her live more in the present. She was imperfect and I loved it.

Imperfections are what make us perfect. If we were all the same, we wouldn't be interesting. I'll be honest; I absolutely have my imperfections and neuroses'. I have a tendency to be a little ADD. I have the energy level of a 12 year old and can sometimes be a little too hyper. Most of the time I believe that to be an endearing trait. There were times, though, where she had to calm me down.

Laughing she would say, "For the love of God, can you be still for two minutes?" When she would mention something like that I knew it was time to chill out. We balanced each other. When she was sad, I would be happy for her and help. When I was too excited, she would be the calming sea to soothe me. A yen and yang. Earth and sky. Together we were a pair destined to be.

Things weren't always perfect. And that was okay. A relationship isn't about being perfect for the other person. It's about learning how to work with your significant others imperfections and minimize the impact of your own. People should fight in a relationship. They should argue. They should feel strong in their convictions. So long as they are willing to listen to the other persons' opinion, and grow within the relationship.

The important part isn't that you fight; it's how you treat each other during and after the fight. Can you forgive? Can you apologize? And can you respect the other's opinion, even if you disagree with it? These are important. I believe that you can have a lifelong relationship if you can master these things. Though we weren't the best at it, we worked hard and really respected each other when we disagreed. We almost always ended a fight in laughter or lovemaking. We both agreed that making love was our favorite way to end it. We continued building our love. Laying the groundwork for our future. One day she came to me and told me she had made a big decision.

"I have decided I want to buy a home," she stated.

"That's amazing, baby," I replied, unsure of how far along she was in her decision.

"My parents agree that paying rent makes no sense. I love Orange County so I have decided to buy a home here. I have a real estate agent looking and I want to buy soon. I hope that is okay with you?" She had obviously given this a lot of thought.

At first, admittedly, I was a little disappointed. I suppose I had always thought that we would eventually move in together. I figured it would be somewhere in Los Angeles. However, buying a home in Orange County was much smarter. The housing prices were still somewhat manageable, the schools were better, and the area was much cleaner.

I put on my best happy face and said, "Of course it's okay, baby!" I knew she would want to be near her family. I should have anticipated it. As long as I was with her and within driving distance to auditions, I was happy.

That got my mind to whirling. Why had she asked if that was okay? Had our relationship progressed to the next point? Was she expecting me to propose soon? We were just now at about the year mark, and I wasn't sure if that was enough time to wait before jumping into it. The thought made me excited, scared, nervous, and flustered all at the same time. I was overcome with confusion. Then I laughed. A year of craziness and she still got me all shook up. I loved that feeling. I knew I wanted to marry this girl. And now I felt like she was feeling the same way. So I put the thought in my mind that I should start considering the proposal.

8

"I've made up my mind. I'm going to do it. I'm scared as hell, Momma, but I'm gonna take a chance."

Proposing was a huge decision. And, as with any of my big decisions, I had to call mom to get her input. Though, to be fully honest, I already knew her thoughts. She was a supporter. So long as her kids followed their hearts, treated others well, and followed the Golden Rule, she would always give positive responses.

"Chase William!" she shrieked, nearly blowing my eardrum, " I'm so excited right now!" Anytime I heard my middle name I knew I was either in trouble, or that mom was excited. I was guessing she was excited this time.

" I'm so proud of you. I know you two have issues, Lord don't we all. She looks at you with so much love that I'm sure you two can overcome any. She calls me anytime she is worried about you. Sometimes she just calls to talk. Oh, My God, does that mean grand babies soon?"

"I'll let my siblings get you the grandchildren soon, Mom. For me, let's just focus on the task at hand. How should I do this?" I honestly wanted her opinion. She had always given me such good advice when it came to dealing with my relationships. This was definitely uncharted territory for me.

"It has to come from your heart. Make it special. Don't do something funny. Sit down and think about her. What does she love? Does she prefer big crowds, quiet moments, or fun? This will be a moment you two will remember forever, so don't take it for granted. I swear on all that is holy, if you just hand her the ring I will disown you son." I laughed to myself. She was silly, but she was right. No man should ever just propose lightly. A woman should feel that the man took the time to plan it, that she means so much to him that he put effort into the moment.

I didn't know if she would say yes. However I knew that I never wanted to spend a day without her. I did as mom suggested and I sat down to plan out proposing. I knew I wanted it to be special. I knew I wanted it to be memorable, and I didn't care if it was cliché or overdone. So long as it made her smile as I did it.

Like me, she really loved views from high places. So I decided to incorporate that. I knew that she loved orchids, so that would have to play a part. For two hours I sat there brainstorming. Imagining what each proposal might look like from her eyes. By a lake, on a building, at a sporting event, or on the beach. Daytime, nighttime, sunset, etc. Lots of people, no people, close friends, etc. I wrote so much my hand cramped. I suppose when I get excited I have a hard time slowing down. I was definitely excited.

Then I realized something. I needed a ring, and not just any ring. It had to be something she would be proud of. Something she would want to show off to her friends. Something that would make her think of me each and every time the sun glinted off the diamonds and caused that famous sparkle. Admittedly, she was a little more materialistic than most girls I had dated before. It was uncharted territory for me. I knew I had to impress her parents almost as much as I impressed her. I got anxiety just thinking about that, but she was worth it.

Off to the jewelry store I went. I spent six hours there that day. First I took their class on the three c's. Cut - Clarity - Color. Before that day I thought diamonds were all the same. Only the size was different. What can I say; I'm a country boy. I was very wrong.

I learned about the cuts. That there are many different shapes to diamonds. Square, round, oval, princess, etc. I took time examining each one. Some I liked, some I felt were awkward. Oval was my least favorite. It just seemed an odd shape to me.

Again, what do I know; I'm a country boy. I fell in love

with the princess cut. Maybe it was the name, or maybe it was the beveled shape and the long point. Something about it said it was meant for Jennifer. So princess it was.

I learned about clarity. Sure, all diamonds sparkle, but some sparkle and shine more than others. Some of that comes from its clarity. Is it perfect? Or does it have inclusions? Inclusions are tiny imperfections within the diamond. Depending on how easy they are to see, how many of them there are, and the severity of them; the beauty and price of the diamond are affected.

I learned about color. I assumed all diamonds were "diamond" color. Clear with sparkle. This, apparently, is not actually a color. Instead, there are many colors. Clear, black, pink, yellow, and cloudy. The more cloudy they are, the less rare. The more pink they are, the more expensive.

I sat there as they brought me hundreds of diamonds to look at. I saw some that were really large, but less expensive because they had inclusions and were cloudy. I saw some that were small, but very expensive because they were technically flawless. I took all of this into perspective. Keeping in mind that I'm not a rich man, but I wanted something to show my love that I care about her, I decided to go with a balance. I wanted a good-sized diamond that was very pretty. I would sacrifice a little bit of size for a more quality diamond, but still keeping it relatively big so she could be proud.

Magnifying glass in hand, I looked at each diamond under that bright light. Each time taking into account its size, quality, and price. Finally I picked one. A 2-carat princess cut that had only one tiny inclusion. That inclusion could only be seen with a microscope and it had nearly flawless color. I was so happy. I told the salesperson I had chosen and prepared to pay. Then she dropped a bomb on me.

"Have you already chosen your setting?"

I had totally forgot. I picked the diamond, but it had no ring. I laughed, "Well, here we go again."

We started the process all over. This time they taught me about the different types of gold, silver, and platinum metals. I looked at antique types, modern types, and outlandish types. I looked at some that would have only the diamond I chose and some that had more diamonds than I could count.

I found this process even harder than picking the diamond. There were so many types. What would she love? What would look good on her finger? I wanted it to be perfect. Slowly I began seeing a pattern with ones that I liked. I liked some diamonds, but not too many. I didn't like other stones, especially colored ones. I didn't like outlandish shapes, but did like the antique look. I narrowed the selection down to ten then held the diamond against each ring, trying to see which setting fit it best. It was the focal point, the ring was the accent. I wanted the ring to flow seamlessly into the diamond. On the seventh one, I fell in love.

The ring was platinum. Looking at it from the top you would notice that it beveled and had very minute beading along the seams of each bevel. On all three sides were single rows of tiny diamonds. The diamonds run in straight lines to the four prongs that held the large diamond. Each prong held two matching tiny diamonds. The ring was beautiful. It had an antique look with a modern feel. I took them over to the window and held both up in the swath of sunlight that was spilling in. Each sparkled and gleamed like stars intermittently casting their shine to the world. This caused heads to turn within the store.

One girl walked by me, smiled, and said, "She's a lucky girl."

We signed the paperwork and set my pick up date. The process had taken over six hours. I had looked at thousands of diamonds, hundreds of rings, and wracked my brain. I couldn't have been happier with my purchase, though. Granted, I would be making a payment as large as my car payment each month to pay for it, but I didn't care. She was worth it. And money is nothing without the people in our lives that make it worth spending.

I left the store on a high. I called Mom and told her about the ring.

"Chase, it sounds just wonderful. If she doesn't love it I'll gladly accept it as a Mother's Day gift, " she joked. Leave it to mom to make me smile even more than I already was.

Ring picked out, decisions made; now all that was left

was the scariest part. I set the date. New Years.

I suppose some women dream of the moment they are proposed to for their entire lives. They imagine how they want the guy to do it, where, the weather, everything. They don't relay those images to us men, unfortunately. We are left to try to figure it out for ourselves. We don't dream of that moment. We dream of the moment she says, "I do", wrapped in white, looking more beautiful than ever before. The proposal is more of a dreaded rite of passage. Leaving our fate in their hands. We are frightened of it, but we respect the process. Truth be told, I was somewhat enjoying setting it all up. I believe the reason was because I felt that if I did a great job she would say yes.

It was the beginning of December and I decided that New Year's would be the best time to propose. Sure, it is very cliché. But I ask this, 'what is wrong with cliché'? Things are only cliché because someone else realized how amazing something was and did it. Then others followed suit. Just because many have done something doesn't mean it can't be amazing if you do it as well. Sure, I could propose on a random Tuesday for no reason and it wouldn't be cliché, but it also wouldn't be as memorable. Just another day. New Years was special. A new beginning, a fresh start, even an end of one era as a new one is ushered in.

I decided that I would need a little bit of help to make it perfect. So I enlisted the help of Amanda, Jennifer's cousin. I knew she could keep it secret, but would also be great at helping me with the moment.

"I'm going to propose to her," I told Amanda one day while grabbing coffee at a local cafe.

"I had a feeling that was coming soon," she giggled, "You two are never apart. It makes sense."

"Well, I want you to be a part of the process, if you're willing." I asked.

"Oh Chase," she exclaimed, " I would be so honored to be a part. I have grown really fond of you as a friend, and the idea of you as family makes it even better. I consider you my little brother. " These words broke my heart. She had mentioned that to me before. For her to say it again really hit home. The fact that she saw me that way, coupled with how well she treated Kobe, one of my best friends, I couldn't have been happier.

Next I had to do something that was scarier than the proposal itself. I knew that it was important for me to ask her father before I asked her. It was both important to me as a country boy and it was important in her culture. However, I knew her parents still weren't extremely pleased that we were together. They were kind to me, but still hoped that she would meet someone more professional. Regardless, I made the drive down to their house. Her dad answered, looking very surprised that it was me.

I sat him down on the couch in the living room. My heart pounding in my chest, scared out of my mind, I told him of my love for his daughter. He sat patiently, listening to everything I had to say. I went on for a good half an hour. At the end I said, "Sir, I love Jennifer. I came here today to ask for her hand in marriage. Out of respect, I feel I should ask you first. I know you have your reservations about me, but allow me to show you the kind of man that I am."

He took his time to speak. Seemingly arranging his thoughts before he began, "Chase, we like you. You are good to our daughter. We see how much you love her and how much she means to you. We also know how much she loves you and what you mean to her. She is happy with you. Happier than she has ever been. Of course we worry about her and her future. What parents wouldn't?

However, we think that you will be true to your word and will make sure that she is taken care of and protected at all times. If you want to marry my daughter, I give you my blessing. That being said, I want you to do me a favor. I want you to sit down when you go home today. I want you to take a moment and imagine having children with her. Imagine building a home for those children. Imagine if you had a career that could support your family so that you had a home like this one. A big home with a yard, filled with nice things, and less stress on the bills. If you consider these things, and they interest you, Jennifer's mother and I are committed to helping you along the way. Just food for thought."

I left the house full of thoughts running through my head. Sure, he had definitely said his piece about my career, but he had given his blessing. He hadn't demanded that I change. Merely that I take some time to think about it. Maybe it was just more seeds being planted. Only this time they were planted in my own mind. Either way, I had his blessing.

December passed by quickly and soon the date was upon us. I awoke at 6:30 a.m. on the morning of the 31st. I felt waves of excitement course through my veins. I threw on some jeans and a T-shirt, slid on my baseball cap, and headed downtown.

Downtown L.A. has an area called the Flower Market, which is about six blocks with nothing but shop after shop of farmers selling their flowers. The farmers that grow the flowers all around L.A. bring all of their freshest items to the Market to sell really early in the morning. They arrive around 4 a.m. and open soon after. However, only florists are allowed to shop at first. They get there early and get the first pick of the bounty to fill their shops for the day. Then, at 8 a.m., the market opens to the public.

Though the florists do buy a lot, what is left is all still fresh, beautiful, and best of all, incredibly priced. Large bags of rose petals for $3. A dozen roses, every color imaginable, for only $10. Every flower and plant you could imagine. When you're in the need to buy a lot of flowers at one time, this place cannot be beat. I happened to be in the need to buy a lot of flowers, so I had planned ahead. I had borrowed Amanda's SUV. I was ready.

I took my time. I walked around, shop to shop, looking for what would fit for a night I would never forget. I was smiling and excited. *Am I really doing this?* I thought to myself, grinning. Yes, I was.

I bought five orchids. A white, a purple, a blue, a white with pink edges, and a lavender one. Next were roses. I bought ten dozen red, then also a dozen each of yellow, white, and pink. I found the bags of rose petals with multiple colors and bought ten of those. In a shop close by I stumbled upon cute tea lights, and bought a box of a hundred Soon, I had an SUV full of flowers. A florist on wheels.

I drove to Amanda's house. Together we unloaded the bounty and set to fixing them. The only downside to buying flowers so fresh is that they haven't been done up to look their best yet. The roses still have thorns, the orchids need cleaning, and everything is wrapped in newspaper. We spent two hours together working, laughing, and talking as we got the stuff ready for what lie ahead. She could sense my nervous energy and made fun of me for it.

"You look like a scared little schoolboy," she laughed.

I threw a rose at her and laughed as well. Once everything was set and looked perfect, we set it aside. She and Kobe would later pack it back into her SUV and deliver it for me.

I drove over to the jewelry store and picked up the ring. I spent a good amount of time examining it, making sure it looked perfect. The diamond fit the ring so well, a seamlessly perfect match. Back at the car I sat there, staring at it, watching it glisten in the sun. *Am I really going to do this?* I thought. *Have I really decided to make this jump?* Then, I thought about her eyes, and the answer was immediately yes. No doubt, no hesitation. Only yes. I only hoped she felt the same way.

Amanda and Mom were the only ones who knew of my plans. I didn't want anyone spilling the beans. It was going to be a long, anxious night. I awoke from a nap and began getting ready for the party. Knowing that I was going to a New Year's Party, coupled with the fact that I was going to propose in just a few short hours, I chose to dress very well. I put on my black Express suit that had really fine pinstripes. Very classy. Shined up my Aldos, threw on my Movado (the elegance of Movado seems to me to be unmatched by other watches) and looked in the mirror. It was the best I had looked in a long time. Every advantage I could get tonight was important.

Jennifer was already at the party when I arrived, wearing black dress pants and an elegantly colorful shirt that draped off of one shoulder. The only thing more beautiful than the way she was dressed was her smile. We would catch each other's eyes from across the room occasionally and both would smile playfully. It was as if our love was bouncing back and forth across a crowded room. We would always come back together for moments throughout the night. Giving soft kisses and whispers of love and thankfulness.

Amanda and I kept in contact via text as the night wore on. She was with Kobe at a New Year's Party herself. I didn't want my plans to interfere with their romantic moment at midnight, so she knew to set everything up after. She knew where to go and what to do. The excitement and tension began to grow with each text. On more than one occasion goose bumps would form on my skin, causing me to turn red in embarrassment.

As it got closer to the ball drop, I made my way over to Jennifer. She was talking and laughing with some of the younger family members. I approached her from behind and wrapped my arms tightly around her. She slid her head sideways so mine could snuggle up to hers, causing the kids to laugh and poke fun at us. We merely smiled at them. Then her mom yelled out that the ball was dropping. A minute to go.

We turned to the TV and watched with the family as the Big Ball dropped in the

Big Apple. Thirty seconds, twenty seconds, we counted down 10, 9, 8, 7, 6, 5, 4, 3, 2, and 1.

Everyone yelled "Happy New Year" and I spun Jennifer around and kissed her. Knowledge of events about to come, heart beating a million miles a minute, face flushing with excitement, I kissed her. The family, the noise, the party, everything faded away. All that mattered was the moment. Another moment that took my breath away.

We finally came back to reality and joined the rest of the family. After about half an hour of fun, Amanda texted to let me know they were on their way to set everything up. I waited for about ten minutes, and then grabbed Jennifer.

"Baby, Amanda and Kobe just left a New Year's Party in Hollywood, and their car broke down. We are going to need to go help them," I said to her.

She looked at me puzzled, "Chase, why would we drive 45 minutes to help them when they could just get a tow truck or AAA?" I hadn't thought of that. I figured she would just accept what I told her.

"Jennifer! It's your cousin! They are stuck up on Mulholland Drive in a dark place and they have asked for a favor. How do we say no to them?"

I had put her in an awkward spot. Saying no would make her feel bad, so she reluctantly agreed and we headed up to L.A. That was the first time I ever saw a quiver of negativity from her. I ignored it, thinking that she just didn't want to leave the party, which was understandable. Then again, it was her cousin.

On the drive up she fell asleep in the passenger seat. I drove along, occasionally stealing glances at her, wondering to myself if this was the start to our engagement. Would she say yes? Would she like the effort I put into it? A month of planning, worrying, stressing all came down to these next few moments. She lay there, peacefully, with no idea of what lie ahead.

I texted Amanda that our ETA was about ten minutes. She responded saying they were putting on the finishing touches. This was it. In roughly ten minutes I would be pro-posing to the woman I had fallen in love with. The butter-flies started going crazy in my stomach, felt flushed red with anxiousness, and my palms began to sweat. I even felt a little dizzy. One last curve on Mulholland and I pulled up to the spot I had picked out.

Mulholland Drive is a road that runs the ridge of the Hollywood Hills from the 405 freeway all the way into, and past, Hollywood. It snakes along the top of the hill, rarely in a straight line, for many miles. Along this road are a few little roadside parks. They are small, usually consisting of just a few benches and a parking spot or two, but the view is incredible. The spot I picked is about a mile west of where Crescent Heights Boulevard and Mulholland meet. It's a cute little park with two benches and parking along the road. From this spot you can see all of Hollywood, downtown

L.A., West Hollywood, Beverly Hills and Century City. On a clear day, you can even see the ocean.

We pulled up a little after 2 a.m. At this time of night, the ocean was not possible to see. What was possible to see, though, was the city, all lit up, providing the natural ambience for a romantic moment. We were in the middle of such a large city, yet it was peaceful and serene. Airplanes in the sky, blinking as they headed toward LAX. Lights of every color of the rainbow glowing with purpose. The lights, in patterns that went vertical, horizontal, up, down, curving, and every other possible angle, provided enough light for us to see our way.

I parked, pausing to steal a look at Jennifer. She was still sleeping, unaffected by the movements of the car. "I love you," I whispered before sneaking out and going to double check everything.

Amanda and Kobe were standing by Amanda's SUV about thirty feet ahead of my car. They were hugging and admiring their work. To my left was the park, smack dab on the edge of the mountain, overlooking the city that was stretching out for miles into the dark oblivion beyond. There, sitting in the middle of that incredible view, was what Amanda and Kobe were admiring.

They had stretched out an oversized blanket under a large tree right near the edge. From this spot was the perfect vantage point to see the beauty of the city laid out before us. Surrounding the blanket were more tea light candles than I could count. They were arranged in a sort of imperfect large circle around the blanket. In doing so, they had created a romantic safe space within the lights. On each corner of the blanket was one of the orchids. The fifth orchid stood at the opening to the circle, as if inviting us in to the safe space. In the middle of the blanket were a dozen red roses, waiting for their moment.

Intermittently placed inside and out of the circle were the rest of the red, yellow, pink and white roses. Save for one of each color, tied in a cute little bouquet lying near the vase with the dozen red roses. Amanda had even thought ahead and set up something for me to hand to Jennifer. She was good. Covering about half of the ground within the circle were the rose petals. As the candlelight flickered different petals would light up causing all of the colors to be shown at different times. It was perfect.

The beauty of the city beyond, candles providing light, flowers everywhere, and my heart so full of joy. This was it. I reached my hand down into my suit jacket pocket and felt the soft outer covering of the ring box. I went to my trunk and grabbed my video camera, taking it to Kobe. I asked that he film until the answer, then they could go home and enjoy the rest of their night. I grabbed Amanda and hugged her so tight. I felt tears well up in my eyes, but I held them back.

"Thank you a million times. This looks amazing. Thank you for helping, thank you for coming up here so late, and thank you for being here to support me in this. I love you, big sis." I had always considered her like a big sis, especially after she had told me of similar feelings, but it was the first time I had ever told her.

I saw tears form in her eyes too, gleaming in the glow of the candlelight as she answered, "You're so welcome. Now go get your soon to be wife."

I walked the thirty steps back to the car, which felt like five miles. My breathing became erratic and I felt more nervous than I ever had before. I slowly opened her door and knelt down to kiss her. She stirred, slowly opening her eyes and looking very confused. I gave her a moment to get her bearings.

"Are Amanda and Kobe okay?" she asked.

I smiled. "Yeah, they are okay, but they want you to come say hello. Do you mind coming with me for a second?" She nodded her head then took my hand as I helped her out of the car.

She stood and stretched, admiring the view of the city. "It's very pretty up here," she said, completely oblivious to the scene just to the right of her peripheral vision.

I grabbed her hand and began to lead her toward the circle. I watched her face, waiting for the moment when she would realize that something was happening. I saw her recognize Amanda and Kobe. I saw her look confused when she realized Kobe was filming. Then I saw her eyes as they caught sight of the circle, the wheels turning as her brain scrambled to process what she was seeing. She turned pale.

My worst fear began to unravel. She started pulling back from my hand and began repeating, "No, no, no, no, no."

My heart slumped. I had a pretty good assumption of what her answer would be. I knew this was a possibility, but I thought I had read all of the signs right. I thought she wanted this as much as I did. Though I knew at this moment it was highly unlikely for her to agree to marry me, I decided to proceed anyway. I was going to say how I felt. If she said no, if she wasn't ready, or if I wasn't the one; she could tell me no and I would respect it. I had to try. I couldn't come this far and not at least ask.

I pulled her into the circle of lights. Past the inviting orchid and over the rose petals. I lead her to the blanket and I got down on one knee. I had her standing so that the city was on her left, Amanda and Kobe were in shadows to the right, and I was right in front of her. In the flickering lights of the candles I could see the tears falling from her eyes. She was crying.

Seeing her like that broke my heart. I didn't understand why the thought of me asking for her hand in marriage was making her so sad. I began to cry as well. I now doubted myself. I doubted my decisions. I doubted myself as a man. Was I not good enough for her? Was she realizing that now and that's why she was upset? It didn't matter. I was going to say my piece and accept my fate. I reached down, grabbed the bouquet and handed to her. Then I took a deep breath, looked her in those eyes, and began.

"I have quoted the movie *Hitch* to you on numerous occasions. There is that quote that I will never forget; 'Life isn't made up of the number of breaths you take, rather it is measured by the number of moments that take your breath away.' You have given me so many of those moments Jennifer. The first night we met when I playfully proposed to you. The first time we kissed. The first time we made love. Seeing you walk out of the shadows the night we made up. You fill my soul with happiness. I believe in my heart that life is too short. To me, that means waking up happy, going to bed happy, and filling every moment in between with happiness.

I won't settle with anything in my life just to follow a pattern set forth for me by others. I know what fills my heart with joy and I know my life will be happier with you in it. I can't imagine a single day where we aren't together. I can't fathom a holiday, a birthday, hell even just a Friday where I can't hold you and hear you whisper that you love me in my ear. I know there are the types of people you date that you want to go to bed with, and then there are the types that you want to wake up with. I want to wake up with you, every day, for the rest of my life."

I got choked up. The frog in my throat had grown and I felt it difficult to breathe. I could see by the look on her face that what I was doing was futile, but I was going to finish what I started, regardless of the outcome.

"I know in my heart that on days when I need a hug, a long hug, a strong hug, a nose in the neck hug, I need it to be from you. On my bad days, I will need your shoulder. On your bad days, I want you to use mine. I have my imperfections. I certainly can't promise that they will all go away or change, but I can promise that I will be a good man for you. I will work my fingers to the bone to provide for our family."

I began wishing I had rehearsed this, that I had spent time writing it down instead of just saying it from the heart. I had thought that being in the moment and saying what came to mind was the most important. Rather than words on paper that were practiced. Now I was regretting my decision. I didn't know what to say to make her realize that I was the right man. That I would make sure she was treated well and cared for. I didn't know what else to say, so I choked back the last of the tears, reached my hand down, grabbed the ring, and finished.

"Baby, I love you. I have loved you for longer than I admitted to you or to myself. I will love you for the rest of this life and any other lifetimes to come. Two weeks ago I went to your father and asked for his blessing. Today, with the city that I love as our back drop, I ask you for your hand in marriage."

I opened the box and held it up to her. I had asked it. I had held my heart in the palm of my hands where the ring box now sat. There was nothing more I could say. This moment was hers and hers alone to decide. I prepared for the worst. My heart, scared and sad, awaited its answer.

She stood there for a few moments. She stared at the ring, but didn't take it. She glanced down at me, then to the city, then to the ring. She seemed lost in the world locked within her mind. I dared not rush her, though I was fairly sure of her answer. Knowing there was a possibility she could still say yes, I waited.

Slowly, a smile spread across her face. Two more tears dropped from her eyes. Without warning she tackled me. Literally, she tackled me as if I were a quarterback on an opposing football team! In one motion she had grabbed the ring, lunged at me, and took me to the ground. She kissed me. A hundred times we kissed. Some were small and fast, some were deep and passionate. Rolling around the blanket, causing rose petals to stick all over us. We laughed together. We cried together. We held each other so tight I was sure bruises would be found the next day.

"I'm sorry if I seemed like I didn't want this. You just caught me off guard. I wasn't prepared and this was too big of a decision to take lightly. Seeing you, kneeling there, spilling your heart to me, made me realize what I already knew." she said to me.

I responded, "I certainly appreciate that. But, for the rest of us that don't already know how you're feeling, could you give me an answer!"

She laughed, "Yes, Chase, a million times yes. I want to spend forever with you!"

She grabbed a tea light and began examining the ring. "Oh, my God! It's so beautiful. It's a princess cut and it has antique etching. How did you know those were my favorites? Never mind, I don't care. It's perfect."

She handed it to me to slide on her finger. I did so, laughing at her love for it. She stared at it with a smile that would have put the shine of the sun to shame. Amanda and Kobe quietly brought over the camera, laid it down by the circle, then left, congratulating us as they waved good-bye.

We spent the rest of the night and into the morning sitting there, wrapped in the blanket, talking of our past and of our life to come. We watched the sunrise and she commented on how the ring sparkled in the early morning light. We had done it. I took a chance and she had said yes. My best friend. My lover. My fiancé.

9

I walk over to the monitors. Few of them do I recognize and understand. The ones I do, however, tell me with numbers what I can see with my eyes. She is growing weaker. There isn't much time left. I'm torn. I want her to leave so her pain can end. Yet, I want her to stay because there is still so much love in my heart for her. I see a nurse walk by and poke her head in. She looks at her and then to me. I nod that things are about the same. She nods back and tries to give a polite smile, then off down the hallway she goes.

They have been very sweet to her since I've been here. They have tried to make her as comfortable as possible. I noticed that the female nurses have taken an especially sincere interest in her. Like a secret bond between those in the society of woman hood. Once a nurse even came in after a 12-hour shift and spent three hours working on her hair.

The whole time, whispering to her, "We may not be able to prevent you from being taken away, but by God we will make sure you look your best if you are." It touched my heart. A little bit of kindness in a place like this goes a long way. I make a note to my-self to do something special for that nurse and her family once all of this is over.

I think of her family, huddled together in the waiting room. They love her so very much, but they can't stand to be in here watching her pass slowly. They, along with her, decided, before I arrived, that I was to be the one to stay with her until she passed. They felt that too many people in the room would make it harder for her. All knew that I would be able to handle the task.

"You are a good man, Chase," her mother had said before I entered the room. "She will leave this world happy because you are with her to help send her off." That had broken my heart. I had

never known that her mother had cared for me or thought of me in high regards. So much had happened in these few years. I appreciated her kind words. Those words would be needed to make it through this.

The family would wait, then come in after she passed. They had all already said their goodbyes and were now holding each other, waiting for me to emerge. It has been 14 days now since I got to the hospital and this began. Each day watching her sink more into oblivion and each day a part of me dying with her. The family spends the nights at a nearby hotel, always at the ready should I call, but during the day they stay in the waiting room. Talking, praying, telling stories, celebrating her life rather than mourning it. I note this. I truly hope that when I go, my family can celebrate as well. It's a beautiful thing.

10

We realized, now that we were engaged, maybe living in two separate places wasn't conducive to what we wanted to accomplish. In the end, the choice was pretty clear.

She owned a house with a yard. Her place was larger and a closer step toward a real life together. I lived in a house, but I didn't own it and I had roommates. It made sense that I would move in with her. That meant a long drive for auditions, but it seemed worth the sacrifice.

As Jennifer's' house was already furnished, we didn't need a lot of my things. We put my foosball table, poker table, electronics, DVD collection, and a few other of my belongings in her garage, but the rest we sold. I no longer owned any furniture. I had no bed, no couch, no dressers, and no other home furnishings. I didn't need them, though, as Jennifer's house was full. Full and decorated tastefully.

Some of it I had even helped pick out as she was filling and decorating the home.

Together we painted walls and hung art. For her bedroom I decided to build her an amazing bed. I took the black platform bed that she currently had in use as a starter point. Then I built a box that connected to the back of it. The box was the same length and height of the headboard, which was only about three feet tall, but was a foot wide. Then I built sections into it. Five sections total. I added a board on top to serve as a base, but sunk it about two inches lower than the headboard. This would allow for the top finish. In the outer two sections and middle section I added an 8-foot tall and 7-inch diameter tan bamboo. This bamboo stood solid and straight from floor to ceiling.

Then, in the two sections between the big bamboo, I added 6-foot tall green bamboo that were only about an inch thick. Each section had seven pieces which were all set at different angles, entwining with each other. In the "lid" section that was sunk lower than the bed height I put in smooth black rock. I used it to fill in all the space around the bamboo and up to the headboard height.

I tucked candles intermittently throughout. When lit, the candlelight danced beautifully off the bamboo and gave an incredible romantic presence. I added a better mattress and satin sheets that matched the bamboo. It was the most intricate thing I had ever built. I was so proud of what I had done for her, and so proud to show her. We loved the home were building together, though it was really hers.

We also realized that me having a car, a Jeep, and my recently acquired motorcycle was a bit too much. So, we first sold the motorcycle. I had wrecked it once already, which had scared her. Let me say how atrocious it is that eighteen wheel trucks are allowed to re-tread their tires. A re-tread is just a two-inch piece of rubber added to a balding tire. Rather than replacing the balding tire they use these to save money, but these have a tendency to come off while they are driving. One did, hitting me at 70 miles an hour one night while riding my bike on the 710 Freeway. Not only did the tire hit me, destroy my bike and almost cause me to wreck completely; but I also had Luke on the back as I was giving him a ride. I almost killed my friend because of a cheap trucking company and the laws that allow it to happen. Yet I have to wear a seatbelt in a car. Sometimes I'm at a loss for governmental policies.

Needless to say, Jennifer and I decided that I should sell it. I was down to just the Jeep and the car. After a short while, she believed that was a bit much too. We began having conversations about not needing the Jeep. How the economy was bad and how bad it was on gas. How I only used it for fun, rather than as a useful vehicle. Soon it was sold. In just a few short months I had gone from having three vehicles, lots of furniture, and my own life to no furniture, one vehicle and a shared life. I didn't mind. These things made her happy, and she made me happy. They were merely possessions. It was a cycle that I was willing to be a part of.

Her family seemed more accepting of our relationship. They congratulated us and were very sweet. They even started helping with the planning of the wedding, though we had yet to set a date. They made mention often if I had given what her dad said any thought, which I had. I thought of giving up acting and getting a better career, but thinking those things made me sad. A sadness in my soul. Like I would be losing a part of who I was. Acting wasn't like my motorcycle. My motorcycle was a possession. A material thing that I paid money for. I was brought up to believe that an object doesn't make us who we are. Acting, however, was inside of me. I had known I wanted to be an actor since I was four years old. I still think back and remember how it felt the first time I saw a crowd react to something I did. To give up acting would be to give up a part of who I was. A piece of my soul lost to oblivion. Like asking Mozart to give up music, Jordan to give up basketball, or a lawyer to give up lying. It hurt to consider it.

As time went by, however, I saw it slipping away. I had to find a job closer to where I lived. That meant I started missing auditions for work. When I lived in L.A., even if I was at work I could just sneak away for half an hour and run to an audition, but living an hour away with traffic made that no longer an option.

My obligations around the house began to grow as well. The pool needed cleaning, shelves built, garage organized, and lawn mowed. I began spending more time at home when I wasn't working. I stopped going to acting classes to spend more time at night with Jennifer, as our conflicting schedules made seeing each other more difficult. Though I was only about 30 miles from Hollywood, my acting career began to seem further and further away.

Soon I began looking at schools. I would browse online about different programs and careers each school offered, but nothing really seemed to interest me. Jennifer and I started talking about things that would provide a better life for our family. So, I quit looking at things that interested me and instead looked at things that would eventually pay well. Since she was a good ultrasound technician she had made her way up the ranks and was doing quite well. She loved what she did and suggested that I start looking at other jobs in the medical field as well.

I realized that an MRI tech might be a good fit for me. They sit in a little room and watch a screen, taking the images from the giant MRI machine. Very little blood or other crazy stuff involved. However, one cannot simply become an MRI tech. First you must go to school and get an associate's degree as an X-ray technologist, work for a few years as an X-ray tech, then eventually cross train into MRI.

I never made the decision to give up acting. However, in order to go to school and work, that is basically what happened. I would get up early each morning and go to school. Then I would come home and handle my chores and necessities around the house, along with my homework and studying that needed to be done. Then I would go to work at night.

To get an associate's degree in X-ray, you must first go through the prerequisites. Once the pre-requisites were done then you could apply to be in the two-year program that would eventually make you an X-ray Technologist. I worked hard. I was a fast learner and became good enough that I held study sessions at our house. Jennifer would hide inside while the class and I would meet in the garage to study. I realized I was good at the human body. I never loved it, but I understood it.

Soon the end of my classes and the finals came. I studied hard and went in confident. I was the first to turn in my exams in each class that I had. I thanked my professors and felt that I did fairly well. Once my grades came back, I realized my hard work had paid off. I had earned a 3.97 GPA. The others from my class all texted telling me of their high grades and thanking me for helping them get through the semester. I had finished what was required of me so that I could now apply to be in the actual program. That's when I found out some bad news.

The healthcare field had become very popular as of late and had become saturated with students wanting to earn specialized degrees, i.e. X-ray. With only so many programs being offered, only so many students were allowed in each year, while the rest were put on a wait list, which I had been added to. Unfortunately, the average person was on the wait list for around two years. TWO years! Just to start the program. I will never understand why they allow so many students to believe they can begin the program. They should only allow so many to start the pre-requisites in the beginning. I was told, however, having such a high GPA would help me. Also, if I went to seminars and other events it could move me higher up the list. Otherwise, it was a solid two years. I was disappointed. I hadn't had an audition in over three months because I had started this path. Now it felt like I had done it for no reason.

Jennifer was encouraging and told me that I should just take other classes and learn more while I waited. Maybe get a second job working in a hospital, just to acclimate myself to the environment. We had been engaged now for nearly eight months. This new obstacle seemed to be adding a toll on our relationship. We were short with each other. We made love less and were quicker to fights. There was a lot more stress involved.

Jennifer had her own stresses as well. When she had bought her house she had bought it from a mortgage broker who was her friend's boyfriend. He told her little of the different types of loans and payments. More or less he just said, "You are approved, here is your home."

So the entire time she had been making the negative amortization payment on her mortgage (it's an option that allows you to pay half of the interest each month, instead of the full interest or more. The other half just gets added to the end of the loan, actually causing you to owe more on your house each month. This should not be allowed. I fully feel that it is criminal and is a huge reason that led to the eventual collapse). The bank realized that she had added over $20,000 in debt to her home, and they increased her payments to compensate for it.

At the same time she had maxed out a credit card with an $18,000 limit, using the money to furnish her home. She was only making the minimum payment on it, as the minimum payment was over $1,000 each month. These two financial stresses were taking their toll on her. I had no idea this was going on. Then one day she snapped at me for no reason, and we had our first really big fight since we had got engaged. We nearly ended the engagement, but, after a lot of yelling, we were able to pinpoint where her stress was coming from. I took a look at both of her statements and was confounded at how she could allow herself to do that with the credit card and how her friend's boyfriend had allowed her to make these payments. Had someone explained to her what doing these things would cause, she wouldn't have been in this position.

I started making calls. As I had no school at the moment, I spent my whole day researching and figuring out how to fix her mess. Finally, after days of digging, I figured it out. I called the mortgage broker and I told him what I thought of his practices. I then offered him the opportunity to make it right.

The government had just lowered the APR again. I figured out that Jennifer could refinance her home. Since the interest rate was so low, I got him to include $19,000 extra in the loan to pay off the credit card. Then I set it up so that she had a fixed rate that would not fluctuate and her payments, which would include full interest and payment, were just a little bit above what she was paying currently for the credit card and mortgage combined. By doing so, she no longer had the stress of the credit card and her mortgage would be paid off in 30 years, unless she started paying more, in which case it would end sooner.

I was very proud of myself. I was mentally exhausted and didn't want to see any more numbers for a while. When she came home that night I showed her what I had worked on and explained it to her. Once she understood what I had done, though she would still have to sign the paper work for it to be finalized, she began to cry. Like so much weight was taken off of her shoulders that she was able to breathe. For a moment we were free from our stresses and we saw each other as we had only months before. We made love that night. Deep, passionate, sweet, love. Candles were lit, music was playing, and we were good again.

We woke the next morning and things felt lighter. I made her breakfast before she went to work. We made love again, quickly as she couldn't be late, but there was still so much passion in it. Our kiss as she left lingered and felt strong and connected. I had helped relieve her stress, and in doing so she had helped relieve mine. As she pulled away to leave, she began to say something, but stopped herself, smiled an awkward smile, and left.

I wondered to myself what it could have been. Was she going to tell me she loved me and was grateful? Was she going to explain how much I had just changed her life? I felt good in my heart, that good things were coming because of my hard work. I was wrong.

She came home from work that night very jittery. The conversation felt awkward and, more than once, it seemed as though she needed to tell me something, but couldn't. I didn't want to force her. So I didn't prod her, rather just continued to try and be my normal happy self. We returned home after, then I suggested that we sit by the pool and chat. I knew she needed to get whatever was bothering her off her chest.

"Jennifer, you have seemed uncomfortable about something all day. I can't quite pinpoint it, but I know you're upset. If I have done something wrong, if you need something, if you just need to vent, please know you can do so with me," I offered to her. She looked at me for a long time. Her eyes began to fill with tears. She held them back, but resigned to the idea that she was going to tell me where they were coming from.

"Chase, what I'm about to say will be the hardest words to ever leave my lips. After what you have done for me, you deserve to hear them," she whispered.

My heart began to pound and my pulse quickened. I felt myself becoming short of breath. What did she need to tell me? What could I possibly deserve to hear? I didn't say a word, as I didn't want to cause her to stop telling me. I was curious, scared and worried, but I had to know.

"Oh, my God. Here goes. Chase, you're amazing. I know you're amazing. But, sometimes you are gone too much. When you were in school and working it was tough for us to find a moment to be together. You are content with a life full from the moment you wake up until the moment you literally pass out from exhaustion, but I'm a woman. I have emotional needs that must be fulfilled and taken care of. There was a moment, when you were in school, when I felt lonely…" She stopped suddenly. She looked at me, as pale as a ghost. There was something she had to say.

My mind was whirling a million miles a minute. What had she done? Was it a tiny mistake? Could it have been something reversible?

"Jennifer, I'm not trying to rush you, but you need to tell me what has happened," I said with a calm, yet firm tone. On the surface I must have seemed okay, but underneath I was a volcano with hot molten lava about to explode from my core.

She sniffled, and then went on, "I've been lonely. One night, while you were at work after being away at school all day, I felt all alone. Hayden called. He said that if I just needed to talk to someone, he would come pick me up and take me to get ice cream…" She paused, looking at me for comfort.

I could barely breathe. I felt that familiar pain light up within my heart. The frog in the throat. The pit in the stomach. My eyes pleading with her, "Please don't let this be what I think it is."

"At first I said no, but he was so persistent. He kept telling me that we could be just friends. So I agreed. I knew I shouldn't, but I did. We went to ice cream and we talked for a good hour. I even talked all about you and your sacrifices. It did feel as though we were just good friends catching up. Afterward he brought me back to the house and asked how the renovations were coming along. Then he asked if he could see them. I knew it was a bad idea, that I shouldn't let him come in, but I was so proud of the work that we had done. Before I knew it I was showing him the kitchen, then the living room..." Once again, a pause from her.

Thick, juicy, beads of sweat began to form on her upper lip. The beads seemed to quiver and move, rhythmically dancing for me, as those maroon coated lips continued to open and close. Those lips that had, many times before, whispered that they loved me when we made love. Though they moved, I heard no sound.

My nails dug deep into the wood of the patio chair. Pain erupted from my fingers,

begging me to stop, but there was no control. My mind was leading me through her sinful journey. Through clips and images that my subconscious displayed I was shown a moving picture of the kitchen, the living room, the bathroom, and finally our bedroom.

The last part of the movie was of them kissing. He picked her up, threw her down on the bed, then lay on top of her. Eyes full of water, I looked at her. Searing white hot pain erupted from me in one soft word, "No."

She saw my pain and finished, "It was meaningless. I didn't want to be with him, it just happened, and as soon as it was over I asked him to leave. I can't keep hiding it from you. I know that what I did will make being together difficult, but I can show you that I'm a good woman. I promise to give you the best from now on."

I sat there in silence. She waited just a short time, but needed me to speak.

"Say something." She said to me. Silence. "Say something damn it!"

I couldn't speak. I was broken. My heart was broken. My soul was broken. I was no longer a man in that moment. I was a child who had lost his mother. I was a desert that had had no rain. I was the moon without the rays from the sun. None can exist fully without the other. On their own they are lost, dark, alone.

I thought to myself, *Please, God, please let this be a dream!* This was supposed to be my wife, the mother of my children. My confidant and best friend. I was busy because I was doing the things she wanted me to do. I never wanted to be in the medical field. Now I was being punished for doing what was asked of me! How could she have done this? In our home? On our... OH MY GOD!

"Did you have sex on the bed?" I asked, very direct and pointed. Emotionless, needing to know the truth. "Was it on the bed?"

She looked at me, confused why I would ask that of all questions. Then I saw the realization on her face.

"It doesn't matter where it happened. Just that it happened. I'm trying to make it right. I know that you're upset and you're going to react to what you just learned, but let's just stick to what's important." she offered, trying to divert the emotion.

"DID IT HAPPEN ON THE BED!?" I shouted, becoming much less calm. I could hear my heart pounding in my ears. My anger was building.

"YES! Yes, I'm sorry, yes."

Those words rang in my brain. Bouncing like millions of tiny marbles clanging off of every fold. The bed that I had hand built for her. That I had spent my time, sweat, and money to make special for her. Our bed! The mattress that had been brand new and only used by she and I. The sheets that I had laid on countless times since. She had desecrated something that was holy between us. My anger reached a boiling point, and I forgot that my heart was broken. I forgot that I was sad. I saw only red. I lost control.

I grabbed drawers in the dresser and threw them out, emptying them on the bed; as if trying to hide the disgrace from my sight. She had allowed me to sleep in that bed, on those sheets, with his disgusting germs floating all over it. Letting me wallow in their combined juices from their night of unwarranted passion. Weeks had passed since school had ended. How long had she allowed me to sleep there? My ears began to ring. I saw her shouting at me, but I heard nothing.

I went to the closet and grabbed armloads of stuff. Into the shower they went, which I turned on full blast, hot, as if my brain thought steaming the clothes would help rid the sin in the room. I had no idea what I was doing. I had no plan. I was just destroyed and hurt. I went to the patio and grabbed all of the patio furniture. One by one I tossed them into the pool. One by one I watched them sink to the bottom. Like our love, sinking and lost. I glanced at her as she watched through the sliding glass door. She was crying. For the first time, though, my heart didn't hurt because she was crying. I felt nothing. Like someone who is drunk and falls down. They feel nothing, no pain, until the next day. For the moment, my pain was on hold. Only anger was allowed.

I went to the sliding door to go back in, unsure of my next act of business. She had locked it, had locked me out. I moved to the side door, locked. I went to the front door, also locked. She had shut me out. Then I saw her on the phone. She was calling someone. Maybe she was calling Hayden again. This sent fumes through my veins and I pounded on the glass, acting like a crazed loon. I didn't know what to do or what I was doing. I only knew anger. I wanted to break down the door and smash things. I would never put my hands on her, as I'm against that, but by God, I wanted to break things. Then, as if things couldn't get worse, her father and brother showed up. Out of nowhere they appeared, brandishing weapons.

Threats were thrown back and forth. Suggestions of police being called and bodily damage being inflicted by both sides. For an hour this went on. Jennifer stayed hidden inside. I stood there, a man against the world, absolutely dumbfounded at what had transpired. Hours ago I was happy, waiting for my fiancé to come home to me. Now, here I stood, everyone against me, and I had done nothing wrong. Finally, it set in. She had cheated on me. She had done it with her ex, Hayden. The one she had messed around with on me before. Only this time they had gone the distance. They had done the mortal sin. They had done it in our bed.

I lost the will to fight. My survival instincts fluttered out. My anger subsided and the red faded to the grey of the night. I fell to the ground and vomited. I composed myself, then looked at the carnage around me. The furniture sitting at the bottom of the pool, clothes strewn everywhere. What had I done? More importantly, what had she done? At that moment, I didn't see how we could come back from that. The damage was done.

I stood up to get away from the vomit. I was dizzy and confused. Her father and brother were watching me, waiting for the right moment to pounce. Though I could hold my own, the two of them with their weapons, baseball bat and a rake, would have eventually done enough damage to overtake me. I absent-mindedly walked to my car and drove away. I didn't know where to go, so I went to school, parked in the parking lot, and fell asleep.

At about 4 a.m. I awoke extremely uncomfortable. I drove back over to the house. Her father's car was gone and the lights were off. I let myself into the garage, made a pallet to sleep on, and feel asleep. I set my alarm for 8 a.m., as I had to go by school for a meeting with the counselor. I had set it up to talk to him about my career path. I got up at 8, threw on my clothes from the night before and went to the meeting. I have no idea what he talked to me about. That whole morning was a blur.

I went back over to the house, having no idea what I was going to do or what lay ahead. I saw Jennifer's dad's car in the driveway as I pulled in. I walked up and saw him changing the locks on the house. That answered a lot of questions that I had.

"I'm here to get some of my stuff. The rest you can move into the garage. Do not change the lock on the garage until after I have removed all of my belongings. If you agree to this I will cause no problem," I told him, matter of fact. He nodded his head in agreement. I could see that he wanted no more fight from me and he was just happy that his daughter was no longer with the loser. I went in, grabbed some clothes and more valuable items, and headed north to Hollywood.

I was unsure of my next move. I knew I needed to find a place to stay and I needed to figure out how to proceed with my life. Everything in the last couple of years had revolved around her. My routines, my choices, my life had all been set and dictated according to our unit. The unit was now broken and gone. I called a good friend of mine, Paul, and gave him a quick overview of what had happened. He had a spare room in his condo that he offered to me to use until I figured out what I needed to do. I drove straight there.

For two weeks I stayed with Paul. He was a gracious host and tried very hard to keep my mind off of Jennifer, but my emotions were a wreck. Each time I would start getting sad about what happened my mind would wander and fantasize about Hayden touching her, caressing her, kissing her and it would cause me to get enraged. Then I would get upset that I was angry and be sad again. Over and over I went through a multitude of feelings, diving deeper and deeper into what was beginning to feel like a depression. My work began to suffer. My relationships with my friends began to feel strained.

They all noticed. Everyone knew what had happened and all were trying to be supportive. I appreciated their offers of help and kindness, but I had no idea what I needed in order to feel better. I had no way of telling them how to help. I was only 30 miles in distance from her, but it felt like I was a world away. The distance, both in space and emotion, began to take its toll on me. Showers became the worst. As I would be standing there, lost in my thoughts and surrounded by steam, I would be overcome with the reality of what was happening. It would break me down. I would sometimes slump into a ball on the floor, huddled there for hours, letting the fall of water from the shower head wash away any tears until I was nothing but a naked, shivering, wrinkled mess.

After two weeks, I could no longer stand the way my life was headed. I needed a change. I needed my heart to heal, and it couldn't do so in my present environment. I called my best friend.

"Luke, I need your help brother. I'm making a drastic decision to try and put myself in a better place emotionally. Tomorrow I'm going to get all of my stuff, have a going away party, then the next morning I'm moving back to Missouri. I need to be around family. I need to be back where my roots are so I can find myself again. If you're willing, I need a Luke style going away party," I told him.

Luke spoke, and though I could hear the hesitation in his voice, he agreed, "Chase, you're a good guy, my best friend, my brother. What she did to you was wrong. If you need to get away for a while, I understand. We all do. I'll set your going away party up and I promise you that it will be amazing!" We hung up and I felt a little better. I had something to look forward to.

Next I called Tim. Tim was one of my other good friends and was one of the most reliable people I knew. Tim had made it to every poker night that we ever had at the house. He was always one of the first to arrive, last to leave, and always willing to help clean up. Tim was a great guy and I knew that, especially in my time of need right now, he was the perfect one to call for a favor.

"Tim, hey man, I need your help. Any chance you can go with me tomorrow and help get my stuff from Jennifer's house? I need an able bodied man for some manual labor."

He laughed. It was so nice to hear laughter right then and replied, "I got you, man. What time do you want me at your place?"

My plans were set.

11

I was 22 when I had made the drive from Missouri to Hollywood to chase the acting dream. I still remember the 30 people standing outside the house my friends and I had rented back in St. Louis, all of them waving goodbye, wishing good luck, and sending their prayers. Some were crying, some were cheering, but all had faith in me.

Now here I was, only six years later, giving up. Giving in. Leaving the town I had fallen in love with. So many people only know L.A. from what they see on TV. But, if you are an actor and you love this business, it is so much more. There is an energy to this city that is unmatched in most places. For a country boy with acting in his heart, there was no better place on the planet. The Hollywood Sign, something I had used as a beacon and a source for inspiration. The Walk of Fame with so many names I recognized and yearned to join. The beach where I would go to hear the ocean and collect my thoughts. The studios, littered all over the place, where movies were made and dreams came true. Here I was, packing up and saying goodbye. I caught myself and had to choke back tears. Not today, I thought. Today I had to be strong.

Tim showed up at 8 a.m. with another energy drink for me. I had just finished the first and was in dire need of another blast of caffeine. We drove to U-Haul together and decided to rent a medium sized truck as I had lost so much in the move to Jennifer's place just a short time ago. I had sent Jennifer's father a message letting him know of my intent to retrieve my belongings. They unlocked the garage for me, then all left the house as none of them wanted to be around when I got there. We pulled up around 9 a.m., after having stopped at a nearby 7-11 to grab a few more energy drinks. We opened up the back of the truck as well as the garage door, and set to our task at hand.

Though I no longer owned any normal furniture, I still had quite a lot of stuff to pick up. There was my foosball table. Not the plastic crap they make now days, but the old school kind that was made of heavy wood with elaborate players and heavy balls. My poker table, which was my pride and joy. The poker table was a circle table, made of heavy wood and stained a light maple color. When the top was on it was a beautiful dining table. Flip the top over to reveal a felt poker table replete with built in chip and drink holders.

My DVD collection had grown to over 600. They were housed in DVD towers that matched and linked up with each other. There was also a 55″ TV, three surround sound units with speakers, a full computer and quite a bit more. Load after load, we filled the truck until the only thing left was the basketball goal.

The basketball goal was something I was torn over. I loved that goal, but it was a Christmas gift from Jennifer. Keeping it meant keeping something that she had given me. That would be a constant reminder of her and of what she had done, so I didn't see how I could keep it, even though I was attached. I sat down on a little rock wall about ten feet from the goal and sipped on an energy drink. For twenty minutes I mulled over what to do. My heart torn. My mind torn.

Then an idea came to me. Her little cousin and I had played on it many times. His family didn't have much money and I had grown quite fond of him. I left a note on it, letting everyone know that it was his and his alone. I couldn't take it with me, but I could at least be happy with dictating where it went.

We closed the back of the truck, pulled out of the driveway, and said goodbye to a life that I had left behind. I realized as we were pulling away that I had not looked at the house once since we had gotten there. I was solely concentrated on the task at hand and ignored it. I sneaked a peak before it was out of sight, and I understood why I had not looked. It hurt. Seeing the house that I was supposed to raise my family in hurt. Knowing what she had done in that house, in our bed, hurt. For the second time that day, I fought back tears. I swallowed the frog in my throat, my pride, and continued on.

Tim drove the distance from Long Beach back up to the house where Luke and Kobe still lived. As we drove I sent out text after text, explaining what I was doing as I sipped on my fifth energy drink of the day. In the text I told of my intentions to leave and that I could only take what would fit in my car. Since not a lot would fit in a sports car, I was giving the rest of my stuff away. Rather than sell it on Craigslist and have people I didn't know haggle me over money, I would give it to friends who loved me and would cherish the things that I loved. Obviously, for his help, Tim got first pick.

"If I have first pick, and if I can have anything I want, would it be okay if I took the poker table? The Friday nights that we shared on this table were some of the best nights of my life. My best friends, hot girls, and silly fun. Times that couldn't be duplicated if I tried. If you would allow me, I would be honored to take it and care for it until your return," he said.

The words he spoke to me were like a confirmation that I needed to hear. They made me feel that giving the stuff to friends was better than selling it. No amount of money could have made me smile as much as he did just then.

Once we arrived at Luke and Kobe's place I filled my car with what I would take with me. My clothes were obvious. Important papers and documents. My DVD collection. Not the towers that held them of course, but all of the DVD's. I filled my trunk to the absolute brim with DVD's.

Soon my car was full and I could take nothing else. It was perfect timing because people began to show. Like Tim, one by one my friends arrived and picked through what I had, taking what they wanted. Some brought energy drinks. Each stopping to tell me what they were taking and why. Some told stories of what the item meant to them. Others just took what they thought was cool or fun. Each time I would sit there, enjoying the story. It allowed me to smile, to put the pain on hold. Like natural morphine for my heart.

After a couple of hours the picking was done and only about 1/5 of the truck was left. The rest of the items I took to Goodwill. Though neither my friends nor I could use the stuff, someone would be able to. Someone would be able to appreciate my clothes, the electronics, or the giant stuffed teddy bear. That made me feel good. I liked knowing that my negative situation could cause a positive reaction for someone. Another smile.

We dropped off the U-Haul and then I took Tim to dinner. We aren't the fanciest of people. One of our absolute favorite things to eat was greasy Tommy's chili cheeseburgers with fries. We loaded up on the chili and sat down to enjoy.

"You have no idea what your help meant to me today. I know I asked the favor, and to you it was just a simple 'sure I'll help'. I know it is just your nature to want to help, but to me, it was so much more. Having you there helping me, talking to me, keeping my mind off of what was going on, I can't even say thank you and it be enough. I'm forever in your debt, my friend," I told him. I knew I didn't need to say the words. I knew he needed no thanks. It was just the kind of thing a guy like him would do. We were so alike in that aspect.

He answered back, "I'll always be here for you as I know you will always be there for me. I have no doubt that you will be back here soon, once you have healed. I see you as a brother. I have two brothers already, but I see you just as strongly as I see them. I have heard others say this to you, Chase, and I agree with them: you are a good man."

Tim had decided to stay by my side the entire night. He knew I was hurting and said he didn't feel right going anywhere else. It was only 7 p.m. and we still had three hours until we were supposed to go over to the club Luke had set up for my going away party. I was getting anxious just waiting around. Miraculously, as if on cue, people began to arrive at the house. Like moths to flames they all came saying that they wanted to see me outside of the club before I left the next day. Within an hour there were 25 people in the house and it was like a Friday night poker party. We brought out the karaoke machine and all hell broke loose.

Amanda heard the commotion from next door and decided to join. She brought over her usual case of energy drinks as if to throw gasoline on the flames. I don't know if karaoke and energy drinks are meant to go together, but for us, there was never a better combination. About thirty minutes into it we invented a new game. This entailed about five of us guys grabbing energy drinks, counting down from three, then ripping them open and chugging. The first one done got to decide on the karaoke song and the others had to back him up with singing and dancing. This was both fun for those of us doing it and for the other 20 people who were just amazed at the ridiculous spectacle that was laid before them. We were all laughing. Sometimes in life it's the simple and silly moments that will really mean something. They will last a lifetime.

Over and over we had our races. Each time we chugged an energy drink. I knew that I was drinking a few too many of them. Today, I didn't care. With each sip came a boost of happiness. Like liquor, but without the lethargy that comes with it. I was getting drunk off of caffeine, surrounded by my best friends as my support group. In the middle of my saddest time, I was as happy as I could be.

10 p.m. rolled around and we filled into cars to drive over to the club. Luke had set us up at Cinespace. It's a well-known club in Hollywood that always had high-end clientele, great DJ's, hot girls, and some kind of fun show. Tonight Luke had made sure to get the silk performers. We arrived just a little after 10:30 and were all escorted to a roped off section in the back of the club where 4 tables were reserved for us.

Each table had bottle service and lots of energy drinks. I popped one and headed to the dance floor. Many of my friends followed and before long our group took up about half of the dance area. I did a quick count and realized we had more than 100 of our people there partying. I made my rounds hugging and saying hello to everyone. If friends were there by themselves, I searched them out a date. If someone was thirsty, I made them a drink. It was just pure and simple fun. At midnight we sat back at our tables as three ladies descended out of the ceiling on silk fabric. A sensual feeling took hold as each twisted and turned their taught bodies up and down the silk.

By this point I was so inundated with so much caffeine that I couldn't sit still. I stood up

and began dancing in rhythm with the silk performers. Everyone laughed and many gave cheers. Dark, disco lights, crazy music, hot ladies in silk, made everything surreal. Then I fell. I fell right through the velvet rope that surrounded our seating area and onto the dance floor. I was shaken and aware of what had happened.

I had pushed my heart to the limit. It was pumping so hard that it caused me to lose balance and almost consciousness. Between the stresses, heart break and energy drinks my heart was losing strength. Then a thought hit me. Was I really going to let myself be the headlines for the next day? Did I want some no name reporter doing a story aptly named *Heart Explodes From Bad Day*?

I realized I wasn't hurting. I was having too much fun to feel the pain. So, as any addict does, I grabbed another and continued on. Sixteen total energy drinks I had that day. Sixteen. The back of most cans tell you that three is the limit. Sometimes, just on that rare occasion, you have to say, "Fuck the world."

I awoke at around midmorning, grabbed some Advil to counteract my caffeine hangover, hopped in the shower, dressed, then quietly said goodbye to the home I'd had for two short weeks. It was just me, myself, and my thoughts. I left a note for Paul, along with a really nice bouquet of flowers, thanking him for all that he had done and headed out to my car.

The car was such a sight. had enough room to see out of all the windows and through the mirrors, but that was about it. I put it into drive with teary eyes and said goodbye to L.A. Goodbye to the city that I had dreamed of coming to since I was four years old. Goodbye to the home that I had made, friends I had acquired, and the life that I felt I was supposed to live. I knew leaving was wrong. It hurt, but the idea of being close enough to her to possibly run into her made my stomach knot, my palms sweaty, and pain to run rampant in my heart. The only thing I could think to do was to leave. Start fresh and begin again back where I grew up. That way family and friends could surround me as my heart began to heal.

One thing about Midwestern people is that we are some of the most inviting and comforting people on the planet. I began calling family and friends to tell them of my homecoming. We live by the Golden Rule of treating others as we wish to be treated. As each one of the people I called heard my story, they all wanted to help. Many offers of spare rooms and couches were sent my way. I needed and appreciated that love and support. Though I thanked them for their offers, I couldn't imagine going anywhere but home.

12

Mom got off work about four hours into my drive. She called me as soon as she did to make sure I was being safe and to help me figure out where I was going.

"I have every intention in coming home and staying with you, Momma," I told her. I felt like I was 16 again coming home from a weekend away at camp. I knew there was no safer place to be than mom's house. Surrounded by love and fried chicken. I knew I was going to gain weight by going home. The thought of that made me smile.

"Son, you know you are always welcome here. That being said, I don't want you to make a decision on that yet. You have a long drive ahead of you. Take your time, do some soul searching, and I think you will know where to go."

I was taken aback. Had she really hinted that she didn't want me there? My eyes welled up with tears. I couldn't believe she would be like that in my time of need. "If you don't want me there, I'm sure I can find a place more suitable," I said to her with obvious hurt in my voice. She sensed it, realized how I had taken her words, and began slowly.

"Chase William, you know damn well I love and want you in my home, but I am being realistic. The truth is, you won't be happy being stuck out here in the country. If you choose to come home I'll make you fried chicken, mashed potatoes and corn on the cob every single night just to put a smile on your face. All things considered, I think you should take time and think through where you're going to go. Your heart is hurting. If you run home you may feel stuck. You will know what to do when you're ready. When you make that final decision, I will happily and fully support you no matter what."

She was right. Of course she was right. I probably wouldn't be happy being stuck so far out in the country. Her house was over ten miles from the nearest town and at least a mile from the nearest neighbor. Though the serenity of it would be nice for a short time, I would eventually grow tired and restless. I had much to ponder as I drove.

On more than one occasion my sight would blur from the tears of too much emotion and I would need to pull over to compose myself. I was a man, but in these moments I was reduced to a child. Human emotion is the most powerful force in the universe. The strongest part of human emotion is love. I had felt love, true love, deep love. It had been taken from me. My heart felt as if ripped from my chest, leaving a gaping hole.

Yet it had not. I was alive. I was healthy, just very sad. I would remind myself that I was my mother's son. The son of someone who had raised her children on her own with nothing. If she could be strong, so could I. I would swallow my pride, take a steadying breath, grip the steering wheel, and burn rubber back onto the asphalt.

I was already on Interstate 40 and a good seven hours into my trip when my phone rang and startled me. It startled me because it was the song "Walked outta Heaven" by Jagged Edge, which I had recently made as Jennifer's ringtone. I was frozen. We hadn't spoken since the night of the fight. I didn't know what to do. I was craving the sound of her voice. I wanted to hear her whisper those three little words in my ear as I imagined how her face looked while she did so. I also wanted to scream at her. To call her names and cuss at her and ask why. Why had she allowed us to get to this point? Why had she forsaken the love that we had made? Why had she brought another man into our bed? OUR BED! I couldn't answer the phone. I was frozen solid, barely able to focus on the driving. It vibrated the usual six times; replaying the chorus to the song twice, and then went blank.

I stared at it in my hands. The screen said simply: Missed Call Jennifer My Love.

Then went black. I was overcome with too many emotions. The sound of the music from the radio, whistling from the wind through the windows, engine growling all disappeared. I only heard that buzzing sound in my ears that meant I was completely lost in thought. I was barely paying attention to the road. I felt the car slowing. Cars began passing me faster and faster.

Then it rang again, cutting the silence in my head with the loud ring. "Jennifer My Love" flashing across the screen with her smile. That picture that I had saved to her contact info so long ago beaming at me as I'm trying not to wreck. I threw the phone into the passenger side floorboard with so much force I was sure it had broken. I could still hear the ring, but at least I couldn't see it.

What had she wanted? Why was she calling me? I was trying to move on, to rebuild, to heal my wounds. Here she was, as if blocking the ambulance from entering the hospital. Why now? After weeks of silence, why when I'm driving, leaving her and that life behind?

It rang again. And again. Over and over I had to hear Jagged Edge serenade me from my passenger floorboard. I turned the volume up on the radio, but could still not drown it out completely. I lost count after 15 rings. I began to cry. Not soft tears coming down my face, but sobs. I had held my composure for so long, only letting the emotions slightly overcome me here and there, but this was too much. I couldn't drive anymore. I saw an exit with a gas station a mile ahead and decided it best to go there and try to calm down.

I pulled up to the gas station, a very large one that accommodated the 18 wheel trucks that use Interstate 40 as their connection from east to west and everything in-between. I left the phone where it lay and went into the shop. It was one of those that was gas station, food mart, and little diner in one. I needed something comforting. I went into the diner and ordered up a double bacon cheeseburger with chili fries. While that was cooking I went into the food mart and bought an energy drink. I sat down at a table and enjoyed all of the grease, washing it down with floods of caffeine. I suppose I was like a smoker, getting that first drag of a cigarette to calm my nerves. It worked. I settled down enough to go back to the car.

I walked to the passenger side, opened the door, and looked at the floor where the phone lay. It was upside down, pushed up into the corner where a person's foot would normally reside. I paused for a moment. There were many things that I thought, hoped, wished, imagined in that moment. The reality of the situation was that I was standing there, at a gas station in the middle of nowhere, heading home to repair a damaged heart. There was no taking back or forgetting what had happened. My life was forever changed. I was changed. I took a deep breath and reached for the phone. Just as I grabbed it, it rang again. Her face showed on the screen again. I swallowed my pride, I swallowed my pain, and I put on a strong face. I would never let her see how hurt I was. I assumed she was calling for some mundane reason, like I had forgotten to take a shirt or something. The last thing I wanted was her to know how deeply she had cut me.

"This is Chase," I answered in my business tone. Silence. "Hello, this is Chase," I repeated. I waited a few seconds and then started to hang up.

"Chase, can we talk?" came a soft voice from the other end.

I wasn't prepared for that voice. I had assumed she would be mean or strong, as she normally was. I was a sucker for that soft voice. The voice that had told me late at night that she loved me. The voice that had whispered "I want to make love to you" when we were in public. Soft, sincere, beautiful. It hurt to hear it. It was hard to take. I was caught off guard and my defenses dropped immediately. I was lost in the moment.

"Yes. Of course," I replied, soft as well.

"Don't leave me baby. Don't leave me please," She said, slightly less soft than before.

"I can't, Jennifer. The damage is beyond my repair. I feel lost and alone and I can't be there anymore," I said all I could say while still keeping some form of composure. I was standing in that parking lot, trucks zooming past, people walking by, but I felt as if I were standing in the middle of a field of tall grass. The sun beaming down on my face, only the sound of life around me coming from crickets chirping, the wind, and her voice in my ear.

"You aren't alone," came her reply, "I'm here, waiting for you."

I crumpled in the car. I was so in love with her. I had loved her so much I had already planned on growing old with her, having a family, building a life together. My heart yearned to hear those words. I was lost. I had no idea what to say, what to do. I was at least 20 hours from being home, but I was already eight hours from the life I had left.

"Why are you doing this? What do you want from me?" I asked her, frustration mixed with hurt coming from my voice.

"I love you, Chase William. I love you more than you will ever know. I love you from the bottom of my heart. A love that will never go away. I want you. I need you, baby. Come back to me."

I was becoming increasingly confused. I began to think that maybe I should go back. I loved her so much. I needed to see her. I needed to hold her in my arms. To feel her skin on my lips. To bury my head in her hair and breathe her in. I hated that I was so far. Then I was brought back to reality.

"Chase, come home."

She had made a fatal error. She had said "home." Home triggered me to think of her house. Which made me think of her bedroom. Which made me think of her bed. Which made me think of her in that bed, back arched, while sweat dripped from his chest as he took her. All of this flashed in an instant. I felt the rage and anger well up inside of me. I wanted to scream at her. To yell and curse and say mean things, but I wasn't going to this time. This time I was going to tell her that what she did was wrong.

"I have no home with you there, Jennifer" I said in my controlled, business like voice, "The home we had has been desecrated. I never want to set foot into that building again. Or see it for that matter. I felt like I was helping to build a home with you. You destroyed that. You chose a moment of passion over a life of love. You made your choice. I never wanted this. The fact that you blamed it partially on me being gone a lot because of school and work shows me the true type of person you are. I was gone a lot because I was doing what you wanted me to. I was living the life that you told me to. My reward for this? You had sex with your ex. So no, I won't come 'home' to you. I'm going home to where my heart is. Where I can be surrounded by people who mean what they say. I do, and will always, love you. I will just never be able to forgive you." With that I hung up.

I sat there on the edge of the passenger seat, half hanging out of the car, emotionally exhausted. It had been so close. I was so close to turning my car around. I would have been miserable had I of gone, but for a moment I couldn't see that. In that moment all I could imagine was us together. That would have been a huge mistake. I made a mental note not to answer any more of her calls. And call she did. She called a total of 64 times over the course of that drive. She left 17 voice mails and sent 137 text messages. They ranged from the sweetest I had ever read to the meanest. I realized that she was going through emotional turmoil as well. I had left her, and she was left to deal with the fallout of that.

I enjoyed the scenery of the drive. Often, our lives are moving too fast to notice things anymore. We live in the age of instant gratification. I'm as guilty of checking Facebook on my phone as anybody... Morbidly curious about what ridiculous posts my friends may have made. For that trip I slowed my mind down to enjoy what I was witnessing.

Plateaus. Have you ever seen a plateau? They are a wondrous piece of nature. I saw many of them as I crossed through Arizona and New Mexico. I know how a plateau is made, and yet, as I drove by them, I was amazed and confounded at them. In the middle of nowhere, no other mountains around, they rise up like giants out of the flat desert terrain. There is no peak. It's as though someone took a knife and chopped the top off, leaving a flat hill. The sides are steep, suggesting to the onlooker that the land literally just shot straight up. Fascinating.

Fireworks and casinos. Along the drive I noticed that firework stands and casinos are the common business along the freeway. I don't know if truck drivers just always get a hankering for a good old-fashioned bottle rocket or what, but they must be big business considering the number of stands I passed. The casinos were everywhere. Though, admittedly, calling most of them casinos was a stretch. Most seemed to be in a small converted house. Maybe it used to be a two-bedroom family home and now it was a casino. They were tiny. Dilapidated. Not what we think of when we imagine the casinos in Las Vegas or Reno.

My phone rang when I was about eight hours from mom's house. I was only about five hours from the Missouri state line and I could feel my excitement growing. I looked at the phone and saw that is was my buddy Brad Dozer from high school. We had played basketball together growing up and kept in contact over the years.

"Dozer! What the hell is up man?" I asked as I answered the phone, excited to hear his voice.

"Life is good my friend," he replied. "Life is really good. I'm in a great place, but I hear that you aren't having as much fun as I am right now."

I laughed, and he laughed. He had said it to test how my mood was. I was doing okay. My heart was heavy, but I was excited to restart and be fresh. I answered in a smart-ass tone, "True man, so true. Life is interesting right now. All things considered, though, I'm good." I laughed again. It felt good to laugh.

"That's why I'm calling you, Chase. I know you're going through some shit right now. I may have a way to take your mind off of it a little bit. I talked to your brother and he said you planned on moving back home. I totally respect that man. I probably would do the same thing if I were in your boat. What she did was pretty fucked up. However, if you aren't exploring any other options, I have a proposal for you."

And a proposal he had. He went on to tell me that, after college, he had moved to Lake of the Ozarks. The Lake of the Ozarks, we just call it the Lake, is a giant lake that sprawls for many miles in finger like projections in the heart of Missouri. If you took the coast of the Lake and stretched it straight it would be longer than the entire West Coast. He told me that he got a job for the cable station and was in charge of making all of their local business commercials.

Oh, and he had bought a house. The house, he told me, was where I needed to come stay. I would have the entire downstairs of his house as my bedroom. He had already spoken with two of the local bars and had jobs lined up for me. The best part was the backyard. He lived in a very sought after cove that had direct access to the main channel. His house sat right next to the water, only separated by a little yard.

His proposal, should I choose to accept, was simple. I could come stay at the house for as long as I needed. All I had to do was start doing repairs to the place in my spare time and keep up with general maintenance such as mowing. I didn't know what to say. In the middle of such a dark time I was being offered a hand up. Though I'm a prideful man, I needed that hand, and I accepted. I accepted with as much appreciation and gratitude as any man can muster. I took down his address and adjusted my trip to head there. Which actually made my drive two hours shorter, yet another bonus.

"Okay, I'm only going to say this once. So listen carefully and don't ask me to repeat it," I said playfully.

I was on the phone with mom now. I had entered Missouri and was looking at only about two hours left in my drive. She laughed and accepted my request.

"You. Were. Right. Ugh," I sighed at having to say it, but she had been right. She had known that coming home wasn't what I needed. It was just all I knew. Making the decision to go to Brad's instead was the best idea.

"Baby, I don't care that I'm right. I just want you to be happy. I mean, don't get me wrong, this conversation is being recorded and will be downloaded to a hard drive and stored in a temperature safe lock box for any future reference should the time come that it be needed as evidence," she said. She could be such a smart ass sometimes. I suppose that's where I got it from.

Total drive time was about 32 hours. The navigation had me go down a gravel road and let me know I had less than a mile left. I was so close. I pulled up to a cute lake home with about 12 cars parked out front. I assumed parking must be a problem causing the neighbors to have to park there. I was wrong.

Instead, as I was parking, about 20 people came filing out of the house. Led by my mom and my brother and sisters. Brad and his girlfriend, high school friends of mine that I had grown up with, Darnel (my childhood and still best friend to this day) and a few others also came out. Each shouting their excitement that I was home. It felt incredible. My heart had been in such a deep dark place, now it was exploding with rays of sunshine. Let it be known that I said the love of a friend or family member can be like morphine for the soul.

I was brought into the house where Mom had been in the kitchen for the past couple of hours. As soon as she had heard that I was coming to Brad's, she loaded up some groceries and headed there. Together they had put together my welcoming party and all, including myself, were salivating at the smells coming from the kitchen. Mom had made my favorite meal. Fried chicken with mashed potatoes, corn on the cob, and German chocolate cake for desert. The chicken was cooked well and remained crispy on the outside. The potatoes were done to perfection with just the right amount of butter to make them creamy, but not sloppy. The corn, on the other hand, was so sloppy with butter that it was dripping down my face as I ate it in the same fashion as an old school typewriter would move typing back and forth. I loved it. Don't even get me started on how good the cake was. Man, it was good to be home.

After we ate, Brad showed me to my room and I settled in with the light stuff, deciding that the bulk of the carrying could be done the next day. Everyone was excited for me to see the back area. I knew Brad lived on the lake, and that was pretty cool. I didn't understand why everyone was so excited though. I mean, it's a lake house right?

Wrong. Considering my state of mind at that time, it wasn't just a lake house. It might as well have been renamed the Recovery House. For that was its purpose. On the back wall of my room was a door that lead to the outside. I opened it and understood why they were excited. It was right at sunset and I was losing light, but there was still enough for me to get a good view of what was back there. Directly in front of me was a little sidewalk that went down toward the water. I took that for 20 steps and arrived at a large gazebo. The gazebo had a built in bar with DJ system, replete with lights and huge speakers. One merely had to plug in an iPod and they had a full on club, right next to the water. I could imagine the fun to be had already.

I walked through the gazebo, admiring that it had a great balance of party guy stuff, mixed with a little bit of class. It was a great combo. At the back of the gazebo was a little gate. I opened it and stepped down onto the dock. I was now standing above the lake. To my right the cove went for about a hundred yards, then ended. All surrounded by beautiful homes and their attached boats. To my left was the cove as it headed out to the main channel. Flagged on both sides by homes, some with floating trampolines and water toys. The oranges and yellows from the setting sun were moving with the surface of the water. I noticed that the water was so still it almost looked like glass. Brad later told me that it was so still because the main channel was far enough away to break up the waves before they got this far down. Meaning the only waves would come from the boats in the cove coming or going. Which wasn't often in this sleepy part of the lake. A lot of the homes weren't even used by their owners but maybe a couple of times a year. It was beautiful there, serene.

I looked in front of me. That is when I saw what I would refer to as the best distraction in history. His dock had a boat that looked fun enough, but next to it was the distraction. A super charged Jet Ski. Jessi I named her. Jessie was the Corvette of Jet skis. Built for one purpose and one purpose only, to go fast. I fell in love with her the moment I saw her. Jennifer was gone and a new lady had replaced her. Jessie. And Jessie wanted to play.

I turned around and stared toward the house. About ten of the welcoming party had left. The rest were now gathered in the gazebo. Someone had gotten the music started up and all were in high spirits. I felt the weight on my shoulders lift a bit. I knew I could be myself here. I didn't need to pretend to be someone else. I agreed to wait until the next day to worry about jobs, school, life, etc. For tonight, it was time to dance. The music was turned up, the disco lights came on, and I danced along with my friends and family. We played and had fun and I laughed until I passed out in my bed many hours later. I was home.

13

I awoke the next day full of life and vigor, or spit and vinegar as my grandmother would always say. Brad had left the keys to the jet ski in plain sight, right in the middle of the dining room table. He had already gone to work for the day, but knew I would want to ride it. I was so blessed to have such great friends in my life. I poured myself a bowl of Applejacks, man sized of course, and sat down at the table. I opened up my lap top and did my usual look at Facebook, commenting to myself how odd I thought it that so many people chose to post pictures of their food. I stared at my bowl of Applejacks and chuckled. What would the comments be if I posted a picture of that? I could only imagine.

My eyes kept glancing at what was sitting on the center of the table and I enjoyed the breakfast. Two simple keys connected to each other by a keychain that doubled as a floating device, Brad explained to me that was in case you dropped the keys in the water. Pretty ingenious. I was about 3/4 done with my cereal when I decided I could wait no more. I snatched up the keys, ran downstairs, threw on my board shorts, and dashed out into the sunlight.

It was a gorgeous day. I guessed it was around 85 degrees with a light wind and just a few clouds. The right amount to make the blue sky have a little character. I paused for a moment, standing there, sun on my face, sucking in a huge breath of clean country air. Then I laughed as I ran along and literally jumped onto the Jet Ski. I used the remote for the lift and lowered it down into the water. I started it up and let it sit for a moment, checking its gas and oil levels, as I didn't want to be stranded out in the lake. Soon I was ready to go.

I had ridden jet skis many times. They are fun little watercraft. Like a motorcycle for the liquid road. This one, however, was unlike any I had ever ridden. It was supercharged. For those of you that don't know what that means, here is a simple explanation. There is an extra piece added to the engine that makes it go fast. Real fast. And it craves speed. I eased out of the dock and into the cove. I respected the cove neighbors and kept the Jet Ski very slow and basically idled out to the main channel. I didn't want my wake to be causing any trouble my first day living there.

It took about ten minutes to hit open water, but when I did, all bets were off. I peered around, got a sense for where other boats were around me, and then I pushed my thumb all the way down on the throttle. The sheer abrupt power nearly threw me off. I held on tight and within seconds I was flying at incredible speeds; humming across the surface of the lake. I passed people in fishing boats, looking for that night's dinner. I passed young people on party boats where clothing was an option that some opted out of. I passed other jet skiers who all waved hello in an envious gesture, I assumed because Brad's jet ski was so fast. There must have been hundreds of boats containing thousands of people.

I spent hours out there that day. Drenched in fresh water beneath the Midwest sun. I had to refill on gas in the middle of the day because it had gotten to the point that I was running on fumes. It was invigorating. I was overwhelmed with the realization that something so simple could be so therapeutic. I made a promise to myself to make the Jet Ski ride my morning routine. Like a jogger who needs his morning run to start his day off right. I needed the water, sun, and speed. I had found my new addiction. It was making me forget what I had just gone through.

Finally I decided to head home for the day. I had a smile from ear to ear as I pulled into the dock and used the lift to pull the Jet Ski out of the water. I cleaned it off, taking great care in doing so. I respected the fact that it wasn't my property and that I had better take great care of it. Brad allowing me to stay in his home and have use of that machine was more than I could have dreamed of. I knew I owed him big. And I vowed to work hard on his home, as I had told him I would.

He arrived shortly after that and we cooked a hearty meal together. Breakfast at night. Pancakes, eggs, bacon, sausage, rice and raisins. A meal fit for a king. Well, probably an underage king, but a king none-the-less. We poured syrup over the entire plate and threw baseball on the TV. Then we sat there, two guys who hadn't seen each other in years, and caught up. He told me of his father's alcoholism and I told him of mine. We compared horror stories of ex's and lamented on what we had thought we would be doing by now.

Brad and I had been close in high school. but he had never known how close the way I did. Brad was my nearest neighbor growing up, though his house was a mile away. In middle school I used to walk that mile to go to his house and play video games, use his pool, and play basketball. Basketball was our life back then. If we hadn't have been two white guys that were under six feet tall, we would definitely have gone to the NBA. Well, maybe not, but that was what we believed.

We talked a lot that night. We made plans for the house, my job situation, the gazebo, parties, everything. We bounced ideas off of each other, laughed at each other's jokes, and argued over sports. It was as if the Big Man Upstairs knew that my heart needed something to distract it. Though Jessie had me covered during the day, at night it was Brad. He eventually got tired and went off to bed. I shut off all of the lights and headed downstairs, intending to go to bed too. Instead, I walked down to the gazebo, listening to the sounds of the crickets and the moving water. I grabbed a sleeping bag out of a cupboard, curled up on the swinging bench and closed my eyes. Though only the moon in near darkness illuminated me, I could perfectly see the world around me in my head. The stillness of it all was beautiful.

I awoke the next morning and was quickly reminded that I was no longer in California. See, in California, the air is not very humid. Dry air is not a great breeding ground for insects. However, Missouri has very humid air. Being next to a lake in very humid air is a GREAT breeding ground for insects. Especially mosquitoes, as evidenced by my poor arms, each covered in at least five bites. I was annoyed at myself for not remembering and even more annoyed when I saw the insect repelling candles sitting mere feet from where I lay. Okay, lesson one of being back home learned: light citronella candles when sleeping outside. Check. I laughed it off and began my day.

Again I started my day with a ride on Jessie the Jet Ski. I was even more comfortable with it this time. I pushed it harder, went faster, and tried a few tricks. Some were successful; others caused me to have to swim about 50 yards to catch back up to poor Jessie. Luckily, when you ride a jet ski if you fall off the engine shuts down, yet another ingenious idea. One that I greatly appreciated. My ride was shorter as I had interviews at the jobs Brad had set up for me.

I interviewed at both bars. The first bar was in a chain restaurant and I agreed to work there in the afternoons and early evenings. The second was a bar with an incredible deck that went five levels down to the lake. I agreed to work there at nights. Getting two jobs so quickly filled me with pride and helped built my self-esteem back up.

The weeks wore on. I began working a lot. I started to build a regular clientele at both bars. I even took over as lead bartender at the night bar, including overseeing all liquor services at the main bar. Every morning I would start with my ride and each night I would relax with a movie. During my days off I kept my word and worked on Brad's place. I mowed the yard, built landscaping, redid the plumbing in the downstairs bathroom, patched up the gazebo, painted, and so much more. The true country boy in me coming out each time I got to get my hands dirty. And each time Brad was extremely grateful. A great circle of life.

My life was feeling whole once again. Mom and the siblings visited often. I was enjoying every moment. Though there was still a dark, cold part in my heart. I felt happy. Had I not of come home and surrounded myself with family and friends, I don't know that I could have done it.

14

I notice a fly come into the room and head toward the window. Its flight pattern is erratic, not in a straight line but rather circles and zigzags. It flies high and low, searching. Finally, it spies what it needs, an opening. Sunlight calls its name. It flies at full speed toward the window. I watch it slam hard against the glass. I see that, even after the initial contact with the window it continues to bang against it, presumably hoping to find the one spot that may grant it's freedom.

Is that how we are? Do we continue to aimlessly bang our heads against unseen barriers in hopes of finding the week spot? Are we as oblivious as the fly, unknowing that we merely need to turn around and head in a different direction and we could be free of the barrier that blocks our way? Was she lying here, now banging her head? Could she see the light, but was blocked from getting to it from some unforeseen force? Could I be that force? Could the love that was still in her heart be keeping her from passing?

"I love you too, but this world has nothing more for you. It has failed you. This body has failed you. I have failed you. Go where life will be better and you can start fresh. Go where your pain will be gone," I tell her.

Sometimes I hate having to be the strong one. All I want to do is to curl up next to her in that bed and cry myself to sleep as I hold her.

At that moment the fly lands on her face. For all of its banging on the window, it survived, but to land its infested little legs on someone I love was its biggest mistake. I shoo it away and then squash it once it is clear of her. I sit back down next to her, kiss her forehead, feeling as though, at least in some small way, I'm still the one who gets to protect her. Then I start to reminisce about the day we had our first date. She and I had shared many good times together. I know that she enriched my life. And here she lies, ailing in a body that I can't fix. Knowing my hands, the hands that had promised to work to the bone for her, could do nothing but comfort her. I was helpless.

I lay my head on her chest. I could hear the air barely being brought into and out of her body. I could feel the frailness of her skin. I brought my head up and nestled in her neck. The familiar spot that my head had lain a thousand times. I turn my head and kiss. I didn't even have to think to do it. It was something I had done enough that it was merely muscle memory now. I close my eyes. I wish I could take some of her pain away. I wish I could make her well. That I was strong enough to fix her, but I am not. I am merely a man living in a body only slightly less fragile than she. Mine just hadn't broken down yet. If she only needed a body part, a kidney or lung, I would offer mine. Her body was in too much disarray. She will pass soon and be gone from this world. All I can do was watch.

No, damn it, that's not true. That is not all I can do. I can support her. I can comfort her. I can let her know that she is loved and will be remembered. That her life was a good life. So I do. I began to tell her of stories that we shared. I tell her of funny ones, of sad ones, and of ones that didn't involve me, but that she would remember.

Maybe her mind would overlook the pain if I took its focus off of what hurt and put it on memories. I grab her hand and talk. Telling stories. Sometimes I laugh as I tell them. Sometimes I get sad, but I refuse to stop. If this is all that I could do for her, then this is what I am going to do.

15

Two months went by with nothing. I had even begun to think of her less. I started thinking about my future and what path I may want to take. Life was still a struggle sometimes, but I was happy. Considering it had only been a few months, I felt pretty good about that.

Then, out of the blue, I got a message from Jennifer. One afternoon, after my ride on Jessie, I came back to the dock and checked my phone. A single message was displayed across the screen, "Check your email." That was all it said. She had messaged me to check my email. My heart began racing. I had been doing so well. I took a few deep breaths, calmed down, and assured myself that it was probably just another message whining about how I shouldn't have left, how her cheating was my fault, etc.

I got on my computer, pulled up my Yahoo account, and saw one new message. The subject line read "Itinerary." *What the hell could that mean?* I thought to myself. I opened the message and my jaw hit the floor. It was a confirmation for a flight itinerary from Southwest Airlines for Jennifer to come to Missouri.

The message attached read, "I can no longer sit here in our home and wonder if you are going to come home to me. I love you so much that I'm coming to you. I need to see you. I need to speak to you. Face to face. You always claim you are a good man, a good friend, one someone could count on. Well, I'm putting that to the test. Here is my flight itinerary. If you're at the airport to pick me up, I will know that what you say is true. If not, I will believe that you are nothing more than talk."

"Holy fucking shit! She's coming here!" I screamed aloud.

The flight was Saturday afternoon, only three days away. I was at a loss for words. There, against the backdrop of the beautiful lake, I screamed and stammered like a child. Multiple times I jumped into and out of the gazebo, running around like a crazed mad man. Had a bird of flown overhead he would have seen this young man in such a beautiful place, absolutely losing his mind. I went on like that for the better part of an hour.

I became calm and collected my thoughts. The facts were thus: she was coming, my core values had been called into question, I was in a better place emotionally than I had been in a while, and I was pseudo happy. Something was obviously still missing in my heart. I thought to myself, *What do I do with this knowledge? How do I proceed? If I go, I risk hurting myself again. If I stay, I risk a person being left in a place by themselves, alone. And that is not my nature.*

When Brad came home from work that night we sat and talked about the dilemma over fried chicken and mashed potatoes. Butter dripped from our corn on the cob as we went back and forth over what to do.

His opinion was simply, "Leave the bitch at the airport. She can find a flight home just as easily as she found one here."

It should be noted that Brad was built from the same threads as I and was a man of his word as well. He had also watched his buddy go through a traumatic experience, and therefore hated whatever it was that caused that pain.

I went to bed having not made any decisions. Too much weighed on my mind. Over the next two days it went like that. I went to work, rode Jessie, and worked on Brad's home to constantly keep myself busy. All the while having a raging battle on the inside as to what I should do. I hated that I was put in this position. I hated that I was healing and I was doing better, yet now, here I was, right back in the middle of the bullshit. In the back of my mind, I craved her.

I admit it. I craved her. I missed looking into those gorgeous almond eyes. I missed her smell. I missed her lips pressed against mine. I missed the way her skin felt while being held in my arms. My heart craved her. My body craved her. This understanding infuriated me. Why did I have to love her so much? Why was I allowed to feel this pain? It wasn't fair.

Saturday morning arrived at lightning speed. I awoke and took Jessie out. We didn't search for boats this time. We just went fast. Really fast. I wanted to feel my body going as fast as my mind was.

"What do I do? What do I do? Give me a sign please!" I asked the heavens.

Nothing came. No signs. No miraculous realizations. Just me, my thoughts, and a big decision to make. I stopped in the middle of the largest part of the main channel, turned off the engine, and lay down on the seat. I closed my eyes enjoying the sunshine. I didn't want to think anymore. I just wanted to exist. I just wanted to go about my daily activities and not have to engage, decide, communicate. That, of course, was not a possibility.

"Fuck it!" I yelled.

I had to know. I had to see what the hell she was thinking. It was worth the risk. Though I was aware it was probably not a great idea, I also couldn't imagine the thought of her standing alone at the airport wondering if I was going to show. I raced back to the house, docked Jessie, and ran in to shower. Though I was in a hurry, the drive to St. Louis airport was about two hours and I didn't have much time to spare, I did take the time to look good. Even then, in the midst of all of that, I still wanted her to like how I looked. Odd.

The drive to St. Louis was long, which forced me to think about everything. I worried if what I was doing was a mistake. Worst-case scenarios played through my mind like old war movies. Moments of hope. Visions of marriage, kids, and the white picket fence all crept in at times. I arrived and parked in short term parking at the Southwest Terminal. I headed into the baggage claim area.

I saw businessmen, dressed up for work, hurriedly heading down and straight out to the cabs or their waiting drivers. They obviously had this down to a science and didn't need a checked bag. There were families coming back from vacations. I saw sunburns and tropical themed clothing. Even though I knew they were coming home from a vacation, I could tell that they were exhausted. They all needed a vacation from their vacation.

A group of Asian businessmen got on the escalator and made their way down. It was quite the sight to see. There were about 35 of them and they pretty much took up the entire thing. Short Asian men, all well dressed in nice suits. I can't imagine having to fly like that. It made me smile seeing them. I watched them all the way down and as they exited the escalator. One person in the group, the presumed leader, stuck a flag up in the air that had no discerning marks on it, other than the color green, and off he went with 34 like-minded people in tow.

The second I put my eyes back to the top of the escalator I saw her. My mouth immediately became dry. I felt my heart stop beating. I couldn't breathe. She was actually here. I panicked; for an instant I wanted to run. To run and never look back. I wasn't the man that I used to be. She had changed me. Pain had changed me. I don't know if I could ever see her the way I used to. I was frozen solid. I hadn't been sure that she would actually come. Part of me hoped that she wouldn't have.

Yet, there she was. She was wearing a light blue sweatshirt with UCLA emblazoned across it in their signature yellow. Her hair was down and curled around her beautiful face in such a way as to give you the idea that she was a picture in a frame. How does one describe beauty? I suppose it's akin to describing wind, or love, or the idea of an unending universe. Our mouths could never describe exactly what we see through our eyes or feel in our hearts. It's one of the few systems that are inept within our bodies.

I saw her scanning the crowd. She was looking for me. I slinked over toward a corner where it would be more difficult for her to notice me. At this point I was much more content to watch from afar. For a moment I was allowed to be anonymous.

My plan was short-lived, for all at once our eyes met. She was about ten feet from me and turned her head as I was watching her. She froze. I froze. We stood entranced for at least a full minute. People walked between us. Still we stood. I began to feel awkward and a goofy causing an uncomfortable smile to cross my lips. When she saw that, she cried. Two tears, back to back, fell down her cheek. My heart burst into flames.

I had expected us to be cordial, say hellos, etc. I had planned on just walking up and shaking her hand. This was so different than I had imagined. This was raw, real, unpredictable, and true. Could it be possible that she was craving me as deeply as I was craving her? We walked toward each other and then clasped on to one another in one of the truest, most meaningful hugs that I have ever been privy to. No words were spoken. Instead, we stood there, hand in hand, waiting for her bag.

We grabbed the bag then hopped in the car. The silence continued on. Her hand rested in mine, both sweating profusely even though the A/C was cranked to high. Both staring out the windows lost in our own thoughts, occasionally we would glance at the other and catch eyes. It was wild and wonderful. Each time I would feel a new surge of love and happiness in my heart. For a moment, I forgot about my pain.

The sun had gone down just after we had left the airport and we were now driving along on a lovely Missouri summers night. We could see the stars in the sky and the air smelt fresh and full of possibilities. As we neared the halfway point in the drive I felt a surge of cravings. I felt a need within me that had to be satisfied. A hunger that was bursting through every pore in my body. I believe she was feeling it too by the way she was caressing my hand and how her breathing had changed.

We were in a remote part of Missouri. Nothing but cows, fields, and farms. I noticed a little gravel road just up ahead that lead to a barn. I felt compelled to take it. We had still not spoken a single word, yet she didn't protest to my executive decision. I pulled my car up along the barn and turned off the lights. I went around to the trunk and pulled out a blanket that I had put in there a month ago for a picnic. I closed the trunk and laid the blanket out on the ground. She walked over and lay down on the blanket. I joined her.

Initially, we started kissing slowly. Our hands beginning to search out those places that we remembered from touching so many times before. The passion overcame us and we became rabid for each other. Our kisses became deeper, our touching became increasingly stronger. In swift motion I yanked her sweatshirt up and over her head.

A soft summer breeze enveloped us as we made love with so much passion I was afraid someone would hear us. The stars above our heads provided the light for us to see each other's bodies. The crickets played their music, setting the tone for our moment. All five of our senses were elated. It wasn't long before I reached the point that I couldn't hold on any longer. For the first time since we had seen each other at the airport, she spoke.

In my ear she whispered, "When you lose control tell me you love me."

At that exact moment I did. I squeaked out, "I love you."

This caused her to lose control as well. For a few seconds she was rigid and tense. My body went completely limp and she lay down beside me. She curled her tight tanned body up next to mine and laid her head on my shoulder. We stayed there, staring at the stars in silence, letting the events of what had just happened sink in. It was as if words weren't needed. Our hearts, bodies and minds understood more than words could ever express. After an hour or so we dressed, loaded up the car, and got back on the road. Soon we were home and curled up holding each other in bed.

The next morning we awoke to a room filled with sunshine. I could hear the sounds of cooking in the kitchen and the smell of bacon was enticing me awake. We threw on some comfy clothes and made our way upstairs to see what was up. Brad had awoken an hour earlier and had prepared Jennifer and I a hearty country breakfast. There were pancakes, sunny side up eggs, toast, bacon, jam, jelly, honeydew, and chocolate milk.

We made introductions and had small talk as we enjoyed breakfast. The events of last night running through both of our minds as we would catch each other's eyes and smile occasionally. The conversation with Brad was fluid and there were never awkward moments of silence. After breakfast we let Brad head off to work while we stayed and cleaned up. The whole while, we talked.

The conversation was always kept very PC. What had I been doing, what had she been doing, how the families were. The usual stuff. No mention of the past, or of current relationships. It was as if we had awoken at home and nothing had ever happened. Deep in the back of my mind I knew that it would not last that way, but I enjoyed it while it was. I wasn't hurting and right then that's all that mattered to me.

After cleaning, we showered together. I lit candles and put on soft music. We stood there in the water holding each other. I washed her, she washed me, we kissed softly. After the shower we got dressed for the lake and headed down to the dock. We spent an hour or so just sitting in the dock, the local top 40's radio station playing the latest Justin Timberlake and similar songs in the background. We talked about how life was living on the lake. I told her about working at the bars, building stuff around Brad's house, and then I told her about Jessie. She laughed at how excited I got talking about a jet ski that I had named. Her laugh, the way it caused her beautiful smile to show and incredible eyes to sparkle, caused my heart to feel it's first twinge of pain since she had arrived. I pushed it out of my mind and continued on.

I asked her to join me for a ride. We gassed up Jessie, packed some snacks in the storage compartment, threw on the lifejackets, and headed out. I took her slow through the cove, as I always do, respecting the neighbors. Once we hit the open waters of the main channel, I pushed the throttle all the way in. Within seconds we were flying across the lake. Other boats zipped by as she laughed, giggled, and squeezed me ever so tightly.

At one point I took us to a cove that had no houses, pulled around a corner where no other people could see us, and I made love to her right there on the jet ski. It was much softer than it had been the night before. We both still craved each other, but this time we let things happen naturally. The sun beat down on us as we rocked back and forth going with the motion of the lake waves.

Each time she reached the point of ecstasy she whispered in my ear, "I love you."

I don't remember how many times it was, but it was enough to make my heart sing with happiness. The way the words flew from her lips was magnetic. I felt myself drawn to make her get there over and over again. Then I lost my ability to control my own body and we enjoyed the final moment together. We laughed, plunged into the water, and swam around letting the lake cool our hot, sweaty bodies.

After our ride on Jessie we grabbed a shower then a quick nap on the couch under the A/C. That night, Brad and I took her out for a nice steak dinner on the lake. We laughed effortlessly and reminisced of good times. On multiple occasions, though, the subjects neared dangerous topics. Each time my face would get flush and I would feel that hint of anger build up inside of me. Each time I would push it back down and overcome it. I knew eventually it was going to win this battle.

After dinner we went home. Brad had to be up early, so he went to bed. Jennifer and I made our way down to the gazebo and we sat and talked. Again, the conversation started easily, but this time there were more pauses. There were more moments of awkward silence. At one point I realized that I had no idea when she was leaving.

"When is your flight home?" I asked, purely out of curiosity and the necessity to plan around it.

She responded, "Tomorrow night at 11 p.m. I'm taking the red eye."

This was the first time we had realized that there would be finality to this moment. It was the first time that I was forced to realize that we weren't still together and that all of those bad things happened. They happened and they weren't forgotten. The silence went on quite a while, allowing the anxiety and pain to build to a boiling point. She sat there, stewing in her own thoughts while twirling a straw in her hands that must have been left over from a recent gazebo party.

As any person knows, pain plus silence will generally bring sarcasm. This moment was of no exception. "How's Hayden?" I asked out of nowhere and with a condescending tone in my voice. I knew it had been a mistake the moment I had said it. I knew that I should have just held on to the happy times we were sharing as long as I possibly could. My heart would no longer stand for the pain it was feeling and it let that gem fly. As any person who has ever been in a relationship can tell you, if there is one thing you can count on it's that for every action there is an equal reaction.

"Fuck you, Chase!" was her quick yet appropriate response. We had broken the barrier to the pain. All at once she was flooded with tears. I felt bad, genuinely bad for bringing it up. It was my mistake. Even though she had wronged me before, I had been the one to hurt her this time and that was wrong. I chose to pick her up at the airport. I chose to bring her home. And I chose to say a hateful remark.

"I'm sorry. I'm hurting too and it's hanging over my head!" was all I could muster in my moment of shame.

She nodded at me. After a moment I got up from my bar stool and walked over to the hammock. I lit the citronella candles next to it, then reached into the watertight cupboard next to it and produced an old afghan style blanket. I lay down on the hammock and wrapped the blanket around me, leaving space for her to join. Without words, she did. We curled up next to each other and fell asleep watching the stars and listening to the sounds of the lake. We spoke no more words that night.

The next morning we awoke to the sounds of boats on the lake. The temperature was warming up and in the 70's already. We said good mornings, but kept it simple other than that. We ate breakfast (biscuits and gravy made by yours truly) and went back out to the gazebo. The conversation was less fluid and we spent more time in silence than talking. It was obvious that the elephant in the room was starting to grow larger and larger. My outburst the night before was evidence of that.

We spent time in the hammock swaying in the breeze. Staring up at the sky, looking at shapes in the clouds and watching jets fly by, miles above our heads. We took Jessie out and I showed Jennifer how to time the wakes of big boats to catch good air. We spent time just splashing around in the lake, anything to keep the words at a minimum. Both of us knew that words could lead to talk. Talk could lead to fights. And a fight would ruin what we were enjoying.

Soon we began watching the clock. The time to head toward St. Louis was fast approaching. Her flight was leaving at 11 p.m. We had to assume she would need an hour and a half for security and to get settled in at the gate, plus the two hours it would take to get there, plus a half an hour of "just in case" time. That meant we would have to be on the road by 7 p.m. It was already 5:30. We went inside, began the packing process, and hopped in the shower. This was a very different shower than the others we had that weekend. We stood there, in the candle lit darkness, holding each other. The only sounds coming from the water leaving the shower-head and then hitting the floor or our bodies. Neither of us used shampoo, conditioner or body wash. All that mattered in that shower was the feel of our bodies pressed against one another.

We could both feel that this was nearing the end of something. We had begun our lives together with light friendship and deep crushes. That evolved into an immense passion that led me to propose. Those feelings eventually changed to pain, hurt, and hatred as the events of that last week transpired. The past few months we had both gone through our own emotions and dealings with what we had to accept. Now here we were, holding each other in a shower, squeezing our bodies together so tight that our abdomens were probably still dry. The next transition was going to be what came next. Would this act as our final goodbye? A sort of closure to finally allow our hearts to fully heal?

Or...

I didn't dare finish that thought. Every time I began to let my mind wonder to "or" I was immediately reminded of Hayden. The idea of them making love in the bed that I had hand built for her made me sick to my stomach. I would then remember that Mom had always taught me to forget and forgive. Was this a forgivable thing? Could I let it go? No, I just didn't think so. My heart decided to let this be the last goodbye. I would drop her off at the airport and this stint of my life with Jennifer would come to a close.

The evening came and we loaded up the car. Brad had just arrived home from fishing and said goodbye to Jennifer with a hug. He had been very kind to her that entire weekend and I respected him a lot for that.

Within minutes we were on the road. The sun had begun its descent and, though it was still quite light outside, the mixtures of oranges, purples and yellows were beginning to show on the horizon as we drove toward the airport. We had the windows down letting the nice breeze fill the warm car.

She must have been thinking the same thing I was because, after a while, she said, "This is a much better closure than the one we had before."

"I agree. I'm actually glad you came." I told her, "I couldn't have said it better myself."

"And I'm glad you were at the airport. It made my heart leap when I saw you standing there," she said with a cute smile. Anyone could see that we both still had love for each other. There was just so much damage now. So many walls. So much pain. As a well-known song goes, 'Sometimes Love Just Ain't Enough'. This was the right thing to do. She leaned over the armrest, reached her left hand under my right and clasped our hands together. Then she laid her head on my shoulder and stayed that way for the rest of the drive.

We hadn't made love since the day before. Even our kisses had been less frequent. I think, though, this was evidence that what we had was so much deeper than just sexuality. Her hand wrapped in mine. Her head on my shoulder. That felt better than sex. I really believe that.

I knew that I wouldn't be able to walk her all the way to her gate, so I chose to just pull up to the curb and drop her off outside. Since it was such a late flight, the airport was fairly empty. We were able to find a spot right in front of the doors to pull up to. I parked, and then hopped out to help with luggage. It wasn't much, but it was still my duty to help. I set the bags on the curb where she could easily retrieve them and then gave her a hug; a long hug. I nuzzled her head under mine, breathing in her scent. Filling my nose so that I could remember that smell for as long as possible.

We pulled back and kissed. It wasn't overly passionate. It wasn't rushed. It was the kind of kiss that happens between two people who care deeply about one another, but one that is unabated by sexuality, sensuality, or any other distractions. It was just real. Real was right for that moment. Without another word, she spun around and headed toward the automatic doors. I leaned back against my car and watched her. For some reason I pulled my phone out of my pocket and snapped a pic just as she entered the doors. Right as I hit the button to take it, she took a last look back. Her eyes were caught in that moment forever in the pic. Then she was gone.

I got in and laid my head on the steering wheel. I would occasionally look at that picture, her incredible eyes telling me how much she still loved me without any words getting in the way. I sat like that, wondering how two people could love each other so much but not be able to make it work. I realized that, well, sometimes things just suck. There is no explanation or reason other than the obvious, it just sucks. With this thought in my head and a cop giving me the 'It's time to move' look, I headed home.

The drive home was filled with an influx of changing emotions. I was sad that she had gone after we had enjoyed so many good moments in such a short amount of time. I was happy that we had ended on such a better note than we had before. I was angry that I allowed myself to feel happy about seeing her, knowing how much pain she had caused me. I was confused that I could feel so many emotions at once, but there they all were, bubbling and fighting each other to be the one on the surface.

I got home, went to my room, tossed on some PJ's and passed out. The mixture of physical and emotional exhaustion had taken its toll. Things would be different now. I had my closure. Now I could wake up refreshed, and ready to take on the world.

I awoke the next day and got back into my routine. I was happier at work and people took notice. I spent less time trying to kill myself on Jessie and more time enjoying the sun on my face out in the open water. Weeks went by. The time allowed me to get settled into things being as they were. Brad and I had grown very close and we had a lot of fun. Whether we were bowling on the Wii or out at the bars looking at the ladies, I was single and flirting felt good for the first time, we were really enjoying ourselves.

I had lost a lot of self-esteem through the whole ordeal. Going out with Brad and speaking with girls again was nice. It felt good to see them flirting back with me. I even went on a few dates here and there. It was nothing more than just talking and fun. Every time things would seem like the girl wanted anything other than friendship my mind would immediately start comparing her to Jennifer. None of them compared to her. Not that they weren't amazing in their own way; they just weren't her.

After a few weeks, Jennifer texted. She just started sending messages asking how life was and if I was doing okay. I was hesitant at first, then began to enjoy our texts. We would chat back and forth. In the beginning it was a text or so a day. Then it went to a few texts a day. Soon we were acting like best friends, texting each other more than we talked to anyone else.

Eventually, cordialities turned to 'miss you's'. Before long we were saying 'I love you'. Even sooner we were flirting and speaking of her making another trip. Almost one month to the day, I flew her out again. The process was much the same as the first. By that I mean I picked her up, we made love on the way home, we made love a lot, we rode the jet ski, and we had a lot of fun. This time, however, there was less anxiety. There was less of the negative undertone that stemmed from my pain. My heart was more willing to just enjoy the moments.

Three nights and two full days went by with pretty much no incidents. The lovemaking was fluid and unforced. The passion, though less crazed than the first night, seemed to be going stronger with each touch. We were like two kids on the playground, running and pinching and teasing each other. Two birds twittering away in the breeze. Nipping at one another, then darting away playfully. It would be easy to assume that love was in the air, but we kept it very simple. We never spoke of the future or of 'what's next'. We just enjoyed the moments.

Soon I dropped her back off. There was no tear dropping moment this time. It was as if we both knew it wouldn't be the last time we saw each other. We hugged tight, said goodbye, and she was gone. I smiled. It had been a good visit. Within minutes I was on my way back home. This time the emotions I was feeling were less confusing. I was pretty much just happy. Maybe even a little hopeful, if I may be bold enough to admit.

I began to realize that we were acting as much like best friends as we were lovers. We told each other everything. We shared dreams and aspirations again. We would chat until the early hours of the morning only to nap and start it all over again. I should probably admit that I was distracted during this time. I was less engaged at both of my jobs. I would spend less time on Jessie and more time in the gazebo texting with Jennifer. I didn't work on Brad's house as much as I should have.

Soon the next trip was booked. She bought her tickets this time. It was six weeks after the last trip. As with each time before I drove and waited, picked her up, made love to her on the way home and spent the weekend doing our normal routine. It reminded me of the movie *Groundhogs Day*. In that movie Bill Murray re-lives Groundhogs Day over and over again.

Then she surprised me. I was just getting used to our little trip routine when she said, "I don't want to keep visiting you anymore."

I was really hurt by these words. Sure, we had made no promises or said anything about the future, but the way she said it was like daggers. She must have been able to tell that she had hurt me because she immediately corrected herself, "No, Chase, I mean, I want more."

Wow, there it was.

For a moment those words hung in the air. Floating. Hovering. Waiting to be told that they were excused. My mind was a whirl. I hadn't expected her to say anything like that. Hell, I never really expected us to ever get past what we were doing at the moment, but there it was. She had broken that barrier. It was Saturday night. She would be leaving in 24 hours and now we had much to discuss and not a lot of time.

She led me to the gazebo, hand in hand, nervously checking on me. She sat me down, looked me deep in the eyes, and started. "We have gone through hell and back. Both of us. We have felt more love and yet more pain than most people feel in a lifetime. We have faced obstacles and failed. Still, here we are, overcoming more. I guess, what I'm trying to say is, ummm, I need you."

Let me tell you something. When a woman looks into your eyes so deep you can see her staring into your soul and says 'I need you', I can assure you that you are going to feel something; I did. I was dumbfounded. My heart began pounding so hard. My mouth went dry and I got choked up.

She continued, "I know that I have wronged you, but I also know that you still love me as much as I love you. I know that you crave my heart, body, mind and soul. I can see it every time I look in your eyes. For your hazel eyes with their greenish/blue color with specs of gold have given you away. They have betrayed you."

She was so right. I was feeling everything she was saying. I didn't know what to say so I just sat there, nodding, listening, and enjoying hearing what she had to say.

"So, we can agree that we both love each other very much?" she asked and I nodded.

"We can agree that we want to be with each other more than anything else?" she asked and I nodded.

"We can agree that we belong together and that we are one another's best friend?" again she asked and I nodded.

"Then can we agree that you should immediately get your things and come home? Will you move back in with me and be my fiancé again?" She asked.

This time I stopped. I was dead cold.

You see, inside each of our fragile hearts we have what a lot of acting teachers call "triggers". These triggers are things that make us feel something immediately. An example that one of the greatest acting teachers of all time uses, Mister Sanford Meisner, is that of a group of young boys forcibly dragging a young girl behind a building. That is all one has to read to "feel" an emotion toward it. Maybe you didn't, but for me, that thought makes me angry and sad. I feel as though I wish I could save that girl even though I don't know what happens or could happen after that moment. For all we know is the immediate of the words and circumstances we are given.

Well, she had just found a trigger. A trigger that, up until that exact moment, I was unaware of. What had made me go so cold? What had made my face flush, my heart stop, and my fists ball up? The answer: come home. It was as simple as that. When she had said that my mind went 1000 miles in a second. It connected the word "home" to be her house. The image of her house led to the thought of her bedroom. The image of her bedroom led to the thought of her in her bedroom. The image of her in her bedroom led to the thought of Hayden in her bedroom. The image of Hayden in her bedroom led to the thought of them having sex in that bed. The image of that bed, OF MY BED, covered in their sweat made me so angry I wanted to vomit.

She must have seen the look in my eyes. She turned away, face red, and said, "I'm sorry. I didn't think you would take it that way."

How else could I take it? What was she expecting? The moment was ruined. I excused myself and walked out on the dock to think. I took off my sandals, put my feet in the water, lay back to look at the stars, and started thinking.

It didn't matter which way I imagined it. It didn't matter how much I analyzed or tried to justify it. My brain, my heart, my soul would never allow me to set foot in that house again. Ever.

I walked back over and explained it to her. I had calmed down. I had organized my thoughts into a direct, yet sweet phrasing. She let it all sink in. We sat there staring out at the lake for a while in silence. After a bit, she spoke again.

"I can't live here," she said in earnest. I knew that. I knew that the country life would never work for her. She hated the cold and, truth be told, so did I. I had already begun dreading winter.

Back to silence. We sat there for a longer time. Listening to the lake sounds. The music of the crickets. The splashes of a fish breaking the surface. We smelled the fresh lake air. Aromas such as fresh cut grass, pine trees, and wet wood wafted by us.

I was still a bit angry, but I was trying to calm myself. We may have been having a lot of fun and enjoying each other better, but my heart was unwilling to forget the events that had led us here. Nor was it willing to let me put myself in a place that could be a constant reminder of that pain.

At about two in the morning she looked at me and said, "I may have an idea." She began excitedly, "My idea would be a compromise. One that would require us both to give something up. Are you interested?"

"Yes, you know I am. What is this idea?" I asked her.

"My parents just bought four properties in Austin, Texas. They bought two lots of land, one good-sized house, and one really big house. They believe that Austin has one of the best real estate markets and they want to invest there as much as possible," she said in a child-like giggle.

"Okay," I responded, "so what it this leading you to?"

"I bet my parents would rent us the good sized house! Then, if we wanted, we could build on one of the lots they bought. We could buy it from them!"

She was so excited. It was actually quite cute, but the realist in me was a little hesitant and I asked, "Jennifer, what about your job? What about your house? What am I supposed to do? What would your parents say to us just taking over their investments?"

"Those are all things that I will have to find out. Let me

ask you this first; would you meet me in Austin if we could make this all work?" she asked seriously.

This was a big question. It would mean setting aside all of the pain and baggage to try again. It would also mean another move and more compromising, but it would mean being with her.

"Yes I would," I said.

She launched herself on top of me, knocking me off of the bar stool and we tumbled to the ground. We kissed and touched and hugged until we climbed up into the hammock and fell asleep. Tomorrow would be a day of change. I was going to need my strength.

We spent the next day in a state of excitement. Unable to make any plans at this point, but reveling in the idea that we had plans to make. As usual I took her to the airport where we hugged and kissed goodbye. I watched her go, then I headed home. What did all of this mean? What was my future going to bring? Would I really be moving again? So much to answer in such a short time. My answers would come quickly.

We texted a lot over the next couple of days. Finally she sent the important message: Too much to type, call me when you can. I was sitting in the gazebo, so now was as good a time as any.

"CHASE!" she exclaimed in her giggly excited voice. That was one of my more favorite things she did. I always did like that voice. "We have so much to talk about!" And thus began the conversation that would set in motion the next chapter of my life.

When Jennifer had returned home from this last trip she had sat her parents down to speak with them. She told them of our plans to move to Austin. She discussed her house, her job, our futures, and their thoughts, which she then shared with me.

"Okay, so, if you will agree, here is what we have come up with…" she started laying it all out. "School starts September 8th, that is one week away. If you leave immediately you can get to Austin, get settled in, get a job, and prepare to start classes back up for the X-ray program."

She hurriedly continued, "While you're doing that, I will be setting my house up to be sold, getting my job prepared and set to transfer me, and getting my belongings together to move to you." She had done a considerable amount of planning with this. Some of it I was leery about, but most of it sounded great in that moment.

"My dad is going to stay here in California and look after our stuff for a while. Mom has already taken a plane to Austin. They also want to live there and have decided to make the larger house they bought their home. Since my dad will still be here and we are worried about her being alone, we are asking that you live with her until I get there."

This part started to worry me. Questions began to arise in my mind. When would she be here? Why did I have to live with her mom? Would we still live with her parents once she arrived? I started to ask these, but figured I would let her finish before interrupting her train of thought.

"I should be able to move there by October. However, I have already booked a flight to visit in mid-September. So we won't be without each other for too long. My brother and his wife are also in Austin right now. They have decided to buy a house and are currently looking for the perfect one. They are staying in the good-sized house. Once they find the right one, they are going to move into it. I should be there by that point and you and I would then move into the good-sized house. We will stay there, paying rent, while we are having our dream home built. With the sale of my property we should have more than enough to build exactly what we want. Didn't you say you wanted a three car garage baby?" and she laughed as she delivered the last line.

This was so much to take in. So many decisions to be made. The biggest and most immediate being do I go? I loved her. If that meant dealing with all of this craziness, then I was willing to do so.

Here I was again, repeating a process that I had already done. I went to each of my jobs and quit on the spot. Apologizing profusely for leaving so suddenly and wishing them the best. I arranged for mom and everyone to come up for a BBQ. I wasn't calling it a going away party because I had had too many of those recently.

I sold off all of the new stuff I had bought to furnish my room at Brads. I spent as much time on Jessie as possible, knowing I would probably never get to do this much jet ski-ing ever again.

Lastly I packed my car with only what would fit into it. Then I started the drive from Lake of the Ozarks, Missouri to Austin, Texas. I had no reason for going to Austin other than Jennifer. I was hoping with all of my heart that it would turn out to be a good reason. Only time would tell.

16

Here I was, only months after my last time, driving a packed car for hours as I moved and changed my entire life. This whole process had begun to feel very repetitive. I would sometimes wonder if I was making another mistake. Then I would realize that exceptional things take exceptional chances. If there was a chance that Jennifer and I could be happy together for the rest of our lives, I wanted to find out.

The drive was without much excitement. This time there was no frantic phone calls. This time there was no hysterical crying or pleading. This time it was just the road, my thoughts, and I heading down from Missouri. I had never been to Austin and didn't know what to expect. I was scared. I was unsure of myself. One good thing, I knew I had overcome so much in my life that I could do this.

I pulled into the city on a Thursday. School was to begin on Monday. So I had precious little time to get settled in. Jennifer's Mother was already set up in her home and was expecting me. I admit to being a little skeptical about living with my ex/new fiancé's mom. Especially after everything that had happened over the past six months.

I found the right address and pulled up out front. I looked at the home I would now be staying in. It was incredible. It had a driveway that sloped slightly up hill meeting the three-car garage. The house was a two story made of large dark stones. The accents on the windows and around the roof were of a light color. It gave the appearance of elegance. The landscaping was tasteful and there was even a coy pond next to the steps that led up to the front door. I left my stuff in the car, walked up the driveway, and knocked on the door. Within moments the image of Jennifer's mom appeared through the ornate glass. She opened the door and greeted me with a big hug.

She led me in and gave me a tour of the house. As we walked in the foyer I could see a formal dining room to my right and a really well designed office on my left. We walked about ten steps into the main living room. It opened up into a great room. The ceilings went all the way up, about 40 feet tall with the back wall covered mostly in windows that overlooked the enormous back yard. Right in the middle of all the windows was a white brick fireplace. All of the couches and chairs were set in such a way so that all could see the fireplace and out into the yard. Oversized Art had been hung on the walls way up in the air.

To the right of the great room was the kitchen. Dark granite countertops, large tan travertine tiles, and all stainless steel appliances. There was a breakfast nook in the corner with dark colored table and chairs. On the opposite side from the kitchen was a set of double doors. She opened them outward and I looked into her master bedroom. It was one of the biggest I had seen. In the center against the back wall was a California King bed. There were nightstands, dressers, and even a large footboard with a hidden TV that would lift up into view with the touch of a button.

The master bathroom was exquisite. Light colored travertine tile lined the floors as well as the walls of the stand-up shower, which itself could hold ten people. The shower had a ceiling mounted shower-head as well as an eight head, full body massager/cleaner that was mounted on the center wall. The standing shower was open to the rest of the bathroom. It was so large that it didn't need walls. Instead it just had a little six-inch barrier to keep the water from flowing out. Next to it was a sunken in Jacuzzi tub. I could probably have made a small home in that bathroom.

We left the master bedroom and she led me to the side of the great room near the foyer. There was the stairs that led up to the rest of the house. The top of the stairs had a railing and walkway that went all the way around the great room, save for the back wall that had the fireplace and windows.

From up there you could look down on everything and see just how amazing this house was. The top level had three bedrooms, all of good size, two bathrooms that were lovely and also an entertainment room that had a ceiling mounted projector and a large screen for watching movies while you relaxed in the stadium seating recliners.

The house was fantastic. I chose the bedroom at the far end of the walk. I was to the right of the fireplace and directly above the kitchen, which seemed better than being above my soon to be mother in laws bedroom. I started carrying my meager amount of belongings into the room and getting myself set up for my new life while Jennifer's mom cooked me dinner. After eating, we curled up in the movie room and watched *Armageddon*. I was fast asleep in my recliner before the movie was even half over.

I got up at 8 a.m., dressed and got ready, then headed over to the school to set up my classes. This didn't go as I had expected. I was told, quite ceremoniously, that none of my credits would transfer from the school I had attended in Orange County. Not only would I be forced to repeat every single class that I had taken, but they also had three other classes that were required to complete in order to enter the x-ray program. I was infuriated. For an instant I felt my Irish blood boil up inside of me. It was like I was forced to meet obstacles every time I turned my head.

Yet again, her actions had caused me to take a set-back in my life. For that instant, I began to regret my decision to go back to her. Then I swallowed. I swallowed my anger. I swallowed my pride. I swallowed my doubts. And I signed the paperwork agreeing to pay out of state rates to re-take classes I had already excelled in. I took a deep breath, let it out, and laughed to myself. This journey wasn't easy, but it was the journey that I had to make work.

I was done by 10 a.m. and figured I should start the job search. I spent the entire rest of the day driving from restaurant to restaurant applying. Finally, about five hours into the day, I was given a break. A chain restaurant agreed to let me bartend and I was to start on Tuesday, after class was done for the day.

School started on Monday and was frustrating at first. I was older than most of the other kids in class and I was relearning something that I had just learned. Soon I settled back in to my routine and was excelling. Work at the bar was fairly simple. I got to know the regulars and tried to do a good job. Everything felt like a deja vu.

Time moved by at a steady pace and soon it was time for Jennifer's visit. I picked her up at Austin's airport. We didn't have our usual mid-drive rendezvous as the house was only a half hour drive from the airport and the area was a little too populated for that kind of fun. Instead we went home and enjoyed four days of cuddling, love making, and 'I love you's'. Her brother and his wife had found a home, which meant that the house we would be staying in was now empty. We went over and checked it out.

It was perfect for us. About 2,500 square feet, two car garage, three bedroom, two bathrooms, and quite lovely. Sure, compared to her mom's house, it wasn't nearly as fancy, but it would be perfect for us while we decided where to build our dream home and exactly what we wanted.

We talked a lot about when she would be moving to Austin. She had started the process of listing her house and had already begun speaking with her head of HR about transfer to a hospital in Austin. I admitted to her my feelings of living with her mom. How it was awkward for me, being a grown man, staying with my soon to be mother-in-law. She laughed. She hadn't seen it that way. To her it was me keeping an eye on her mom, making sure she was okay. She assured me that soon she would be there and life would be okay.

The time came to take her back to the airport. We realized that I would probably not see her again until she moved to Austin. That could be from one month to many more, depending on how long it took to get her house taken care of. That idea worried me, but I pushed those feelings aside, said goodbye, and watched her head into the airport. Yet again leaving me standing there watching her go. I had a ridiculous set of circumstances.

Life continued on. I worked hard in class and on my

homework. I did well at work easily becoming one of the management and crowd favorites. I helped Jennifer's mom around the house. I even helped her turn the corner of the backyard into a putting green for her husband. Her mom had been so excited to set it all up. I must admit, it turned out really well. Time seemed to move slowly waiting for Jennifer. Unfortunately, I would soon find out, some things just aren't worth the wait.

I opened the window to the bathroom to let in the fall air. It was late October and the smell of changing seasons wafted in. I closed my eyes and took a deep breath, filling my lungs with the fresh smell. I had just finished school for the day and now needed a quick shower before work. Steam began to billow, telling me it was time to hop in. The second I stepped into it, my phone went off. I looked at the caller ID and saw that it was Amanda calling. I thought about answering it, but figured she would call back if it was important. So I climbed into the shower.

One minute later, it rang again. Again it was Amanda. I thought to myself, *Okay, it's weird for her to seem so pushy with her calls.* So I dried off my hands and the side of my head and I answered. Standing there in the steam filled bathroom, naked, holding the phone to my head.

"Well, aren't you persistent." I said in a playful voice. I was immediately brought out of my playful mood when I heard the sound of her voice on the other end.

"You have to leave her, Chase. You can't stay with her any longer. She is trash and you deserve better, " she squeaked out to me in such a sad tone I was taken aback. I didn't know what to say. Why would Amanda be talking about her own cousin like this?

"Amanda, calm down. Are you okay? Jennifer and I are doing well. You know I'm in Austin living with her mom now. She was just here a few weeks ago. Things are going great actually," I said, trying to calm her down.

"Chase, you don't understand. There is something you

need to know," she blurted out.

Now my mind was whirling a thousand miles a minute. What could she be talking about? I had spoken with Jennifer every night since she left. There should be no problems that I didn't know about. Was this really happening again? Was I really being put in a position to feel scared and unsure again? I wasn't about to let it hang over my head. I needed to know.

"Amanda, you are like a sister to me. I appreciate you calling to warn me, but, damn it, I need to know what you know or what you think you know. "

She took a deep breath, composing herself. "I want you to know that this isn't easy for me. She is my cousin. She is blood. I do care about her very much. However, you're a good man and I have come to see you as a little brother, you know that. I'm very torn on what to do right now."

She was freaking me out. My mind couldn't grasp what was going on. I had to get to the bottom of what she was obsessing about.

"Amanda, tell me!" I almost shouted.

She paused, started talking, then stopped again. Moments went by with her collecting her thoughts. I patiently waited, listening to her breathing. Finally she began again.

"Okay, if I'm going to tell you this, you must agree to not hold anything against me. You must also understand that what I'm going to tell you could be devastating, so you must be ready to hear it. Agreed?"

"Yes, please continue," I said.

"Okay, let's start at the beginning," she began again, "Jennifer called me and asked if I wanted to go to dinner with her and some friends last night. She made me promise that anything I saw last night stay between us. At the moment, I laughed. I thought she must have planned on getting drunk, or silly, or something. So know that I'm breaking my promise to her right now."

She paused for a moment. I waited, letting her prepare herself.

"I got to the restaurant. That is when I realized that things were not what they seemed. At the table was Jennifer, two of Jennifer's best friends, Hayden, and Hayden's parents. I was very confused as to why he or they would be there, but I sat down and joined the group. We all had appetizers and a main course. Everyone was drinking and the mood was very light. After a few drinks the conversation turned to you. Everyone, including Jennifer, was talking about how you wouldn't leave her alone. How she had broken things off with you, but how you just kept trying to get her back. They asked where you were and she told them Missouri. She kept looking at me, wondering if I was going to tell them. I didn't, Chase. I'm so sorry that I didn't."

She had to pause. She had gotten choked up. I didn't know what to say. I was numb. I started to speak, but she cut me off.

"No, wait. There is more. You need to hear the rest of it before you say anything." She took a deep breath, then said, "Then, after they were done bashing you and how you won't leave her alone, his parents started asking about their engagement. Hayden had proposed and Jennifer had accepted. His parents were all a twitter with excitement and making plans for the wedding. The nerve she had to sit there and pretend that you aren't where you are. That you two aren't engaged. She is trash, Chase. TRASH! It gets worse. After all was said and done, she and Hayden left together and went to her house. I followed them over there and saw them both go inside. I can't believe she is doing this to you again. I won't let her. I won't let her do it. Even if that makes me the bad guy."

I think, for a moment, my heart actually died right there. Months ago I had regained my life back. I was in a better place. I was healing. Here I was, in an even worse predicament than I was before. The pain I had felt the last time didn't compare to this. That was heartbreak. This was an all-out destruction. I was broken, beaten, destroyed. I had nothing left. I thanked Amanda for the information and hung up the phone. There I stood, still naked, alone in a bathroom that belonged to the parents of the woman that I now hated. I wasn't just alone in the bathroom. I was alone in my own world.

I had no money saved up because I was paying every cent to school, out of state tuition had bled me dry. I had no place to go because I had been living with her mom. I had no possessions. I had no hope. I was lost.

I called her. She answered in a chippy voice.

"Hi, baby!" she said.

I hadn't expected her to be nice. I was beyond being sad. I was beyond being angry. I could feel gravel in my voice as I spoke, "I know about last night. I know about Hayden. I know about your engagement. Since you apparently are tired of me bothering you, I'm giving you your wish and I will never speak to you again. You don't deserve to hear my voice. You don't deserve to see my face."

She was silent. The moment of angry fire began to grow between us. "Chase, what did Amanda tell you?"

"Everything," I shot back in a voice as cold as ice.

"I'm sorry!" she responded, "I'm sorry that this is happening. He came to my house the other day telling me how in love with me he was. He proposed right there on my doorstep. You weren't here. You don't know how lonely I get when you aren't around."

Was she really trying to justify her actions with me? Was she really trying to make it like I'm the bad guy here? Did she really just say that I don't know how lonely it gets?

"I'm confused! You know how much I love you. You also know that I love him. Now you both have proposed to me. I don't know what to do. Can't you give me a little bit of time to figure it out? Can't you respect that this is hard for me?"

That was the last straw for me. For me to be in that house, in that town, in that school, FOR HER and for her to put this back on me. For her to think, for one second, that her actions were okay. The anger had reached a fever pitch and I lost my ability to control words, emotions, and outbursts.

"YOU ARE TRASH!" I shouted. "You're trash. You are the feces that gets stuck to someone's shoe. You are the lowest form of cockroach. You're a bad person, Jennifer. YOU ARE A BAD PERSON! No, I won't give you time to figure it out. I thought you had it figured out when you talked me into moving to a state where I don't belong!" I was screaming. My heart was pumping so fast that my fingers went numb. I started stammering because I didn't know what to say. My mind was going too fast for my words to keep up.

Realizing I was barely using real words I ended it with, "You don't need to choose. I have chosen for you. Bye!" I hung up.

My words had been harsh. They had flown out of me before I could make sure that they were okay. I didn't care. She tried calling, I ignored her. I heard her mom's phone ring downstairs. I prepared myself for a fight as I began packing my stuff. I had almost everything tossed back in the bags they had come in, so I headed down the stairs to the car with the first load to pack. I saw her mom head to the bottom of the stairs to meet me. I took a deep breath and got ready.

She stopped me, tears in her eyes, and said, " I'm so sorry that my daughter did this to you."

Then, she hugged me. I wasn't expecting that. I was expecting her to yell at me or argue. I dropped what I was holding and hugged her back. She cried on my chest as I cried into her hair. I will never forget that moment. It was one of the sweetest moments I have ever been a part of. The moment ended and I packed the car. It took less than thirty minutes and I was on the road.

I had nowhere to go. I had nowhere to live. I was in a haze. A fog. I knew not what I should do. The next thing I knew I looked up and I was at work. I had instinctually gone to work. I parked, put on my work clothes, then went inside. I clocked in and began working as I normally would. The only difference, I couldn't speak. I just worked, nodded, and forced a smile.

At about 10:30 p.m., a couple of regulars came in. They were Vietnam Vets. He was the older guy who would sit up late at night with a glass of Jack Daniels and talk about Charlie. She was in a wheel chair as she had lost the use of her legs from a mortar round.

They had been in the bar for about half an hour when they pulled me aside and asked what was wrong. I couldn't hold it in any longer. So, I broke it down into a quick five minute synopsis. The last thing I said, something that hit me even more than it hit them, "And now I'm homeless." I was. I was homeless. I hadn't even thought of it like that until that moment. I didn't have enough money to stay in a hotel more than a few days. I was worried. I was really worried.

We closed the bar down at 2 a.m. At that point we made everyone finish their drinks, then shooed them out the doors. The War couple hung around till the very last second. I walked over to them to remind them that they had to leave too. The gentleman, Gary, extended his hand as if to shake. I reached my hand out to take his. When we clasped hands as gentlemen do, I felt something cold and metallic in my hand. I looked down and saw a key ring with two keys. I looked up at him confused. Marianne, his other half, smiled from her wheelchair and handed me a piece of paper with an address.

"This will be your new home as you get on your feet, Chase. It isn't much, but it's yours. We will charge you no rent, but would sure appreciate any help you could offer as work on the house while we convert it to more wheelchair friendly."

Just like that I had a place to live. Without ever having to ask. Though I was about to enter the darkest part of my life, I was still shown a bit of kindness. A small candle in my world or darkness. May God bless that couple and those out there that act in a similar manner.

They told me to drive over there and they would be by shortly after. I followed their directions to the house, which resided in North Austin. It was a cute little two bedroom, one bath house with a small garage. There was a basketball hoop in the driveway, which I found to be a good sign. The inside looked like something out of a horror film. The carpeting was gone and the floor had been taken down all the way to the concrete, but the glue from the carpeting still remained. Leaving these eerie swirls of white and black against the backdrop of the gray concrete. All of the walls had been re-moved of all coverings. So the entire interior was open, save for fishbone look of the structures of the walls. I could see the wiring that would normally be contained within, dangling, waiting to be put to use. At first glance, it was a haunting looking place. However, it had four exterior walls, a roof, a working bathroom, and air conditioning. As far as I was concerned, it was a castle. I was so grateful for their kindness and hospitality.

They showed up about half an hour after I did. I had already unloaded all of my stuff into the smaller of the two bedrooms and had set myself up. My only concern, I had no idea how I was going to sleep. There was absolutely no furniture in the house. I figured I would just sleep on a pile of my clothes. However, they had thought about this problem already and produced four couch cushions from their couch. A bed was made.

That first night, I can say with no hesitation, was the worst night of my life. I pushed my cushions up against the wall, laid my sheet on them, turned off the light, then curled up in the darkness. The events of Amanda's phone call and then Jennifer's played through my mind. Darkness was all around me. The only light came from my phone, as I would continually turn it on. Searching for something. Waiting for something. Hoping for something. Something never came.

I lay there, deflated and destroyed, contemplating life. There were moments of hopelessness where I considered alternative options to living. I fought through them. Suicide is never the answer. The pain was just so deep it would occasionally let my mind wander. In those moments, as a person's mind runs wild with thoughts, it takes a lot to hold on. Pain that is unaffected by pills explodes from inside. It is an inconsolable feeling that makes one feel lost.

The fishbone look of the house mixed with the occasional cars headlights driving by only added a more eerie feel to my already dark world. I opened up one of the bags, pulled out a bottle of her Gucci perfume that she had left at her mom's, sprayed a pillow, then fell asleep hugging and crying into it

This is where I lived for the next six months. Each night I would curl up on my bed of couch cushions and cry myself to sleep. A man crying. It was sad. It was pathetic. Looking back I wish I could have slapped myself out of my depression. The way she had treated me, the way she had made me feel like I was so easily disposable, the way she had made me feel so low; it had just caused me to lose so much of myself.

I still got up and went to school. I still went to work. And I still worked hard to help build the Vet's house into something that was both beautiful and functional. I did what I was supposed to do. I did what was expected of me. I continued to live, but living a half-life.

I found out that Jennifer's parents and brother all decided to move back to California. Their reason? They couldn't leave Jennifer behind. She had changed so many people's plans with her own selfish, uncaring decisions. Though I really didn't want to ever see her family again because she was connected to them; them leaving made me feel even more alone.

Sure, I had made friends at school and work. They were more like acquaintances, though. These weren't people that I had known for very long. They weren't someone I would confide in or share my pain with. None of them knew what I was going through. To them I was just the happy go lucky guy. Because that was the persona I wanted them to see. I held the pain inside. It was my burden to bear, and bear it I did.

Each day consisted of getting up around 8 a.m. and studying for an hour. I would sit on my couch cushions, books in hand, working hard. Then I would shower and head to school. I would usually be at school for three to five hours, depending on how many classes I had and how much time I could spend studying at the library. Then I would head to work, changing from school clothes into my bar uniform in my car. I would work until about three in the morning, only stopping for a quick bite to eat. Afterwards I would head home and pass out on my little make shift bed.

This became my routine. Having a routine is what kept me sane. The only time I had that was free was late at night. That is when my mind would wander. I would lay there, surrounded by darkness and pain, and think of the choices I had made that had got me to this moment. From a boy with a paper plate on his face, entertaining the masses, to a man laying on a bed of cushions alone and scared.

I would, of course, have two days off from school and two days off from work each week. I would usually spend that time studying or helping work on the house. However, on the rare occasion that I was off of both on the same day, I would sometimes go by myself out to Mount Bonnell. Mount Bonnell is a little mountain in Austin that has parks with beautiful views of the lake. I would park along the road, walk the steps to the top, and wind my way down the path that led to a secret little spot nestled in among the trees. This spot overlooked Lake Austin.

I would sit on a little rock that jutted out over the cliff. There was no railing to protect me, so a mere foot in front of me was a drop off of over a hundred feet. If I were to slip it would be the end, which felt freeing. I would sit up there for hours sometimes, seeing the beauty of life around me, even if I didn't feel the beauty within myself. I would just sit up there letting the sun warm my face, watching the boaters criss-crossing the lake. Though I couldn't join their happiness, I was grateful to live vicariously through them from afar.

I was doing very well in school. So well, in fact, that one of my professors asked me to teach study classes for those students who were falling behind. I agreed. It gave me something to do to fill my time. The more time I filled, the less I felt the pain. I would never have people over to my place though, as I didn't want anyone to know how I was living. I wasn't ashamed of the house. It was actually coming along quite nicely. I was ashamed of myself that I let my life get to this point. I was ashamed at how sad I had allowed myself to become.

There was a time when anger began to join sadness. Twinges of something dark that grew inside of me, trying to take hold. I never let it control me, but could always feel its presence.

Something that made me very angry was the fact that she had the engagement ring again. I had given it back to her the last time she visited me at the Lake. The more I thought about it, the angrier I became. I did some research and found out that, according to California Laws, the ring was the property of the man until the marriage paper was signed. Since she and I had obviously never signed the papers, the ring was still my property. That ring had cost more than some of my friend's cars. To make matters worse, I was still making payments on it. I grew more and more furious as I thought about it.

One day, after sitting and steaming about it for a few hours, I texted her mom. In the text I said, "Jennifer still has my ring. That is my rightful property and I would appreciate if it was returned, quickly, and safely."

I expected an immediate response, but nothing came. All day long I kept checking the phone, waiting to see a message. By the time I went to bed that night I was so angry I could barely stand it. It took an act of supreme willpower to keep from calling her and yelling, however I knew it was better to keep that anger buried inside, so I calmed myself and went to sleep.

When I awoke the following morning I found a simple text displayed on my phone.

"You're right. I am flying in this weekend to give keys to a new renter on the small house. I will bring you the ring. I am sorry."

The message was both kind and comforting. I would get the ring back.

I thought that would make me feel better, but it didn't. The weekend came and went and I became the owner of a cursed ring. A ring that was nothing more than an expensive reminder of something I had failed at. Sure, it was she who had done all the bad things, but it was I who had allowed it to get this far. I had allowed myself to fall, to move, to build, to fail. It was eating me up inside.

I bought a little safe and put the ring inside of it. I found myself taking it out and staring at it. Each time reliving the pain and memories that were burned into my mind. Sometimes, ring in hand, I would pull up her Facebook page online. I would see her smiling and having fun, kissing Hayden. Living the life with him that we were supposed to be living together. All the while I was doing this I was sitting on my couch cushions in the corner of my dark room, the only light coming from the screen of my phone. This felt like a metaphor of my life. Living in darkness, concealing my pain. Hiding my feelings.

My day-to-day life began to get a little better after those first six months. My bank account was actually keeping more money in it than what it was costing me to pay for school, which I was excelling at again. Work was going well and it was apparent from the management and from the customers that I was one of the favorites. The house I was staying in was nearly ready for the couple to move in, and I had been a big part of that. It wasn't big or extravagant, but it was very nice.

Slowly I began helping them move things from the apartment to their home. I knew soon that they would want their home to themselves, yet was aware that they weren't the kind of people to ask me to leave. This knowledge in hand, I began to try and figure out what I was going to do when the time came for them to fully move in. The answer to that question came as an unexpected, but happy surprise. Well, not happy for everyone, but a little bit of happiness for me.

One early spring morning while sitting in the library at school, I got a text from a great friend of mine that I grew up with in Missouri. His name was Denny, but we all called him Lil' Den. Long story short, his dad was named Denny and his stepbrother also happened to be a Denny. Since he was the smallest of the three Denny's, he got Lil' attached to his name.

The text I had received from him said, "Please call when you can."

I packed up my books and study equipment, headed outside, and called him while walking to my car.

"What's up brotha'," I said in our normal greeting.

He responded in a sad voice, "Chase, she cheated on me man. She fucking cheated on me."

I could hear the hurt when he spoke. I knew all too well what he was feeling and that he needed me not to joke around. Instead he needed me to be the supportive friend. The kind of friend I had needed for the past six months but found.

"Shit, LD, I'm sorry. Are you sure? And if so, are you going to break off the engagement?" I was trying to get him to open up and let some of his steam off.

"Fuck yes I'm sure, I walked in on them. It was one of my buddies man. One of the guys on my crew. There is no way I'm marrying that bitch."

His crew. Dang. He had left St. Louis and moved to Phoenix to work with a crew of guys that were tasked by the electric company to switch out old house meters and install more efficient ones. It paid well and he liked doing it, save for the occasional angry dog that chased him over a fence.

"Are you still sleeping on couch cushions on a concrete floor?" His question was sincere, rather than sarcastic.

"Yeah man, unfortunately, and school costs so much it has been hard to buy a bed. So, instead, I have been saving up my money to get my own place. These guys have been so kind in letting me stay in their home, but it's time for me to move on. Why do you ask?"

"I know you're going through a tough time, man. Hell, we all know. Even though you try to hide it. We all worry about you being stuck out there in Austin alone. Now, with this new shit..." He cussed some more, took a second to compose himself, then continued, "I have to get out of here. If you want a roommate, I'll be there tomorrow morning."

Whoa, had I just heard what I thought I heard? Was he really thinking of moving here? I'm not going to lie; I immediately thought, *Hell Yes!* I was in dire need of a good friend. A confidant. Lil' Den and I knew each other. We could tell each other anything. This would be perfect, but I had to slow myself down. I had to make sure he wasn't just overreacting and making a bad decision.

"Are you sure you want to do that, man? Are you sure? Trust me, it's a big step. Once you leave her, there may be no going back," I said, trying to sound wise but also empathetic.

"No way, man! Not ever. Not after seeing some chubby guys sweaty back as he pounded away on her. If you want me there, say it. I just don't' want to drive all that way if you don't want me to."

"Hell yes, I want you to! Get your ass here! I'll spend the rest of the day looking at apartments and we will get one tomorrow. I think I can get you a job at the bar as well." I felt a sudden rush of hope build inside of me. A feeling that something amazing had just happened.

True to his word, he arrived just after 11:30 the next morning. His faded green Hyundai Santa Fe packed to the gills with his stuff. He told me he had taken a page out of my book and just sold or gave away everything he had. A 'clean break' he had called it. We went over to the apartment complex that I had chosen. It was a huge place with two swimming pools, two hot tubs, racquetball and basketball courts and covered parking for both of our vehicles. The apartment itself was nothing special. Two bedroom, two bathroom, living room, dining nook, kitchen and patio. The biggest bonuses were that the bedrooms were separated by the living room, so it added more privacy, and it had a really nice fireplace.

We signed paperwork that day and I blew what little savings I had on our deposit. Thirty minutes was all it took to put everything we owned into our new place. It was pitiful. In his room was a blow up mattress and clothes, while mine had couch cushions, clothes and my DVD collection of course. The rest of the place was completely empty.

The next day I got him a job at the bar. They were actually quite happy to hire another guy that acted like me. Getting the matching set, they would say. A week later we went and bought mattresses as a celebratory present to ourselves. It's quite amazing how something as simple as a mattress can bring joy to your life; sunshine on a dark day.

Things continued that way. We would save up money, then buy the next piece for our home. With each piece we added, a part of my sadness seemed to go away. We added a 60" TV in the living room, bad memories faded. We got couches and chairs, pain subsided. We bought beds to put the mattresses on, tears turned to smiles. Our friendship grew strong in those months. We really needed each other as we both still had a lot of pain. Though we were growing stronger, there would still be moments where we would be overcome by all of it, unable to hold it in. Anytime that would happen, the other would be there; standing by their side, holding strong until the moment subsided. I'll never forget the last episode I had.

It was late November and Lil' Den was set on us getting a tree before Thanksgiving. I find that to be nonsense as it is my belief that you shouldn't skip holidays. Decorating for Christmas before Thanksgiving was disrespectful to Thanksgiving. We argued and laughed, but eventually I gave in and it was decided that we would get a real tree.

We drove to one of the local lots, excited to see what we could find. As we arrived, the scent of the trees permeated the air. The pine smell was wonderful, inducing memories of opening presents as a child. As we walked up and down each aisle, looking at each type of tree, I began to feel overwhelmed. The smell of the pine reminded me so much of Christmas in years gone by, that my last Christmas with Jennifer came back so vividly in my mind. It brought back memories of building the bed and her excitement when she saw it. More memories flooded in. I started fighting back tears. Out of nowhere, I remembered my last Christmas. I had spent it huddled in a corner of a dark house, shadows caressing my body as I lay curled up on couch cushions, more depressed than I had ever been in my life. Only one year ago I had considered giving up. From one of my most fond holiday memories ever to the worst one in my life. From seeing the woman I would marry open up gifts, to seeing nothing but emptiness.

It was about 9 o'clock at night. The tree lot was bustling with people. Right there, in the midst of all their happiness, I lost my control. I fell down in a sobbing mess right in front of everyone. LD had gone up ahead to look at a tree he really liked and had become excited to show it to me so he started walking back. That's when he saw me, lying there on the straw covered ground, crying uncontrollably.

"Make it stop," I cried out to him as he came running up to me.

I was begging him to help me stop crying. I wanted it to end, but it wouldn't. I had lost control of my own emotions. Like a battlefield soldier grabbing a wounded man, he picked me up, leaned me on his shoulder, and drug me to the car as dozens of people looked on, whispering their thoughts and assumptions. He opened the door, put me in the seat, buckled me in, and drove me home. Once home he helped me to bed, put an action movie on the TV, drug a chair in from the dining room, and sat there while I cried. He never tried to say the old clichés "you're going to be okay" or "there are other fish in the sea" or "you're better off without her". He knew that I was aware of all of those things. He knew that, right now, I just needed to cry. To let go of something I had been holding inside. My body was releasing the years of pain, heartache, and sadness it had held in for too long.

I passed out from sheer exhaustion around 1 a.m. He turned the TV off, left the room, and went to bed. We never spoke of that night. He understood and I appreciated him for that. A true friend, one that sees to the heart of you, never has to have big moments explained. They live them with you.

That was the last time I ever cried for Jennifer. Sure, I thought about her from time to time. Never like before, though. Now, only in passing. A light memory here and there. My heart had let go. My soul had moved on.

I was free.

17

Sometimes the places that you love change. Sometimes the people that you respect change. These changes aren't always for the best. If there is one thing I have learned and can pass on it's this: Change happens. Always. You can't stop it. What you can do, though, is adjust to it and change yourself to continue on.

I really liked my job at the restaurant. The customers were very nice and it had paid my bills decently for over a year. Unfortunately, the managers weren't as happy. Not with me, but with the people above their heads, so they began stealing. Each night they would take home a bottle of liquor. Soon that turned into a couple of bottles and a six-pack. Before long corporate was on our butts about liquor costs and why the bartenders were giving away too many drinks. The managers, trying to save their butts, came down hard on us bartenders. Yelling at us for giving away free drinks when the truth was they were stealing.

I knew the truth. I had witnessed it on multiple occasions. So I was unhappy with the amount of negativity I was facing for no reason. One day they called a meeting. I went in, happy as usual, and sat down. After a little bit of cordialities, they told us that if the liquor costs didn't change that they were going to fire someone. This infuriated me. I have always lived by the Golden Rule, and for a thief to tell me that my job was on the line, well, that wasn't going to sit right. So I told them where they could shove the liquor, waved goodbye with my middle finger, and quit right there on the spot.

There are a few jobs in my life that I wish I had left in a

better accord. This was not one of them. And I'm still proud to this day that I didn't continue to stand by and let them treat me that way.

I applied to restaurants, though secretly hoped I would not get a call back. Restaurants, except for ones like I had been at, generally won't hire bartenders straight out. They want you to be servers first. I was a bartender, so serving would only be a last resort.

I applied to West Sixth Street. That is where the higher end bars for the more mature were. I would have been okay if one of these called. Though it was pretty far from school, the money would have been good.

I also applied to the Warehouse District, also known as Boys Town. It's called Boys Town because it's mostly gay bars. I have no problem working in a gay bar. While I was applying at one of the gay bars downtown, a guy asked me if I had applied at a place called It's About Time. I told him that I hadn't.

"I'm a regular there. I go there at least three times a week. It really is a fun little bar up in North Austin, and I think they would love you there," he said.

I thanked him for the heads up and thought to myself, *Well, it's in North Austin, which is a lot closer to home and school than these places are. I should go check it out.*

It's funny how life has a way of working out. How a random guy in a random bar can mention a random place that would change your life. With that thought in mind, I drove north and arrived at It's About Time. It was in a very unassuming building along the freeway. It had a large gravel parking lot, a giant red door, and a sign that read "It's About Time for some Cocktails and Pool."

I knocked. Nothing. I knocked again. Nothing. I began to knock a final time when the door opened and a man of average height, bald head, and a happy face said to me in a voice that sounded like a little boy trying to use a man's voice, "Sweet Jesus, young man, we ain't open yet."

I smiled. Sometimes you just meet someone and you get a feeling about them. I got that feeling with this guy. I said, "Hello, sir. My name is Chase. I heard from a regular of yours that you may be hiring and I'm here to apply."

He looked me over, opened the door wide, and told me to come in. As I entered the little foyer area I was greeted by two large stuffed toys, people not animals, sitting atop a table and holding pamphlets and flyers of upcoming bar promotions and deals. I thought it odd, yet smiled at how they added to the charm of this little bar.

As we rounded the corner, I got a glimpse of the rest of the bar. It wasn't very big. In the middle of the space was one long rectangular bar that had two stations for serving drinks, one at each end. On the right side of the bar was a pool table, a couple of tall drink tables, a tiny dance floor, a couple of old televisions, and the beer cooler. On the left side were two small bathrooms, another pool table, a super tiny DJ booth, an office, and a door that led outside. That was about it.

The bar itself had what looked to be about 40 stools lined around it. The bar top was made of old wood, which had a lacquer finish that was peeling, and millions of tiny dents from the drinks that must have banged into it over the years. Hanging randomly from the ceiling and on the walls were a few neon signs and beer promotions all trying to sell their wares.

This was a bar straight out of *Roadhouse*. It was old and abused. The carpet was worn, the dance floor was faded, and the beer coolers refrigeration unit was so old I could hear it. To a fancy person, this bar probably seemed terrible. To a country boy like me, it was perfect. If the people that came here had half as much charm as the bar, I knew I was going to be okay.

The bald man introduced himself as Trevor. He asked a few questions about my bartending experience, my living situation, and my car. We chatted about why I left my last job and what my plans were. I told him of my schooling and working toward the hospital job. He asked about my love life, and I briefly mentioned what I had gone through. That's when things got awkward for a moment.

"Oh, she was a real girl?" he asked confused.

"Yes," I responded, even more confused than he sounded.

"You are aware that this is a gay bar, yes?" he asked

slowly while looking intently at me.

I totally hadn't put two and two together. I would never have thought that a bar that looked like this could be a gay bar. I was assuming it was a biker bar.

I laughed and said, "No, I was not. That being said, it doesn't bother me."

I was telling the truth. It really didn't bother me. I respect people's decisions. I told him of my hippy upbringing and of my love for all people. I told him of my respect and how I feel about life. I suppose I did a good job because he told me I was to start the following day, after school.

"You wanna' see the best part about the bar?" he asked in a giddy voice.

Feeling relieved, I responded, "Of course."

He led me out the door by the office and to the side of the building. There, fenced in and surrounded by seating, some covered, was a full sized sand volleyball court; complete with beach quality sand, a nice net provided by an energy drink company, as was proudly emblazoned across the net, and a tall judges stand at the center. I would never have known that this was there. It was awesome. I had never seen a bar with a volleyball court connected to it.

"Do people play here?" I asked, hoping that they did.

"Well, yes and no. Yes they do, but not like they used to. The bar has needed someone to run the volleyball tournaments, which bring in a huge crowd. No one has done it in a long time, because it is a lot of work. Sadly, the court sits empty most of the time."

I made a mental note of that. I didn't want to promise too many things when I hadn't even had my first day of work, yet I was excited. A bar like this was the kind that one might like to go to work. Trevor and I shook hands, signed a couple of papers, and I became the newest edition to It's About Time.

Sometimes you just know when something fits and It's About Time fit me. There was something about that small, dark, old, bar that seemed to be calling my name. I politely declined the other options, finished up school, and headed to work. It felt good to say work again.

Once at the bar I tried the door, locked. I knocked and it was immediately answered by a different guy. He was a shorter, rounder, Latin man. He said, "You must be the new guy. I'm Harmony."

He must have seen the confused look on my face because he laughed and clarified, "I do drag sometimes and my drag name is Harmony. It's kind of stuck and crossed over to my non-drag days now."

I smiled, thanked him, introduced myself and walked inside.

Trevor waved hello and told me that Harmony would show me the ropes for the day. I spent the next hour following him around, learning what it took to set the bar up and prepare it for the day. It was pretty simple: Fill the ice bins, cut the fruit, set up the tables and chairs, prepare the pool tables, and count the money. On most days I would open by myself, so it would just be the customers and me. I liked that. Luckily though, Harmony would stay with me for the first couple of days to make sure I was comfortable with the computer system, where things were located, and if anything crazy came up.

There is a lot that you could say about that little bar. One time I heard a young gay boy, which I later learned was referred to as a 'twink' because he was so effeminate, refer to It's About Time as the place where drag queens go to die. I laughed. Working there you understand that it's not known as the pretty bar. We were okay with that. The customers we had were established, happy, fun, and a more caring bunch. I would grow to learn just how caring during my four year stint there.

What I would say about that bar was this: You will never find another place with a more caring, happy, kind group of people all in one spot. I was blessed to stumble upon this magical bar.

There was a whole cast of characters that I grew to know and love. Within weeks I knew every person that walked through the doors. I knew what they drank, how many they would drink, and how much they would tip. They were almost all very generous. Very soon, I was able to start spending more money furnishing the house. Lil' Den and I actually got to go out and have fun versus staying in all the time to conserve our cash. I was even able to put a little back each week for a future day. Life was beginning to look better.

As time went on I began to know the customers on a more personal level. Each day they would come in, sit down, and drink for hours, doing so more for the socialization than for the alcohol. During those hours we would sit and talk. Sometimes they would just spend a large amount of time making fun of me. This was actually one of their favorite past times.

I took it in stride, which they appreciated. A group of them, all 50 years old and up, would come in at least five days a week. They would take up the back corner of the bar and refer to themselves as The Bitch Corner. Each day they were in I was the recipient of a lot of silly abuse. They weren't being mean. They just liked to pick on me and I actually grew to like it. The days they didn't come in seemed quieter, less fun.

There were guys who came in to play pool all day. On slow days, when no one needed a drink, they would challenge me to a game. I was terrible at first. Slowly they taught me how to shoot better. How to set up moves and even trick shots. However, the better I got, the more drinks I had to buy when I lost. I began to accept fewer challenges to save my wallet.

Some people came in purely to talk. They would come in, grab a drink and someone's ear, and they would spend the entire day just chatting away. My favorite of the talking crew was Kiwi. He was a New Zealand native that always wore super short jean shorts, steel toed work boots, and an open shirt that showed his overflowing amount of gray chest hair. He would talk about anything and everything for hours. Anyone who was within five feet of him was stuck in a black hole of unending chatter. He was awesome. I wouldn't have wanted him any other way.

We had drag queens that would come in, and like the twink said, these weren't the beauties that could easily pass as women. These were six foot tall men with full beards in a dress and high heels. These were 250 pound people whose boobs couldn't stay in their blouses. These 'ladies' were hilarious. They would act all ladylike, drinking their wine, and prance round the bar, the light twinkling off their sequins as they went.

Actual women also came in. Most of them were lesbians. I learned that lesbians came in all shapes and sizes. There were the beautiful ones that had pretty faces and great bodies. They were known as lipstick lesbians. There were normal women who liked to build things and wear flannel (That is not a stereotype, those girls loved their flannel!). There were big girls with super short hair that referred to themselves as dikes. I would never call them that, as I was afraid they would beat me up. All of them, though, were fun and sweet. I have heard it said that lesbians and gays don't get along well in the same bars. That was never a problem at It's About Time. Everyone knew everyone and the fights were rare.

The fights were really rare actually. That was another reason I loved working at that bar. Coming from bartending in crazy straight bars, I was used to having to throw at least one drunk person out a night. I was used to having to jump the bar and drag a guy out for breaking things or peeing in a corner. I had been punched, kicked, bitten and even pepper sprayed. Let me tell you, being pepper sprayed is one of my least favorite things that I have ever had happen to me. It's hard to breathe, it burns your eyes, and it takes hours to get over.

None of that happened at the gay bar. In fact, in the four years I worked there, I threw three people out. Three. One was so drunk he peed on the side of the bar, later telling me he thought he was in the bathroom. One kept using derogatory terms and making my favorite customers uncomfortable. And one, a new guy, had the nerve to reach behind the bar and steal my tip bucket. I jumped the bar and dragged his sorry ass out front. The best part was after I threw him out I looked behind me and 20 people from the bar were standing there. When he tried to come at me they all appre-hended him and reminded him whose bar it really was. So many great moments were had there.

I had friends, from time to time, give me a hard time for working in a gay bar.

They would question me, "Are you sure you aren't gay? How can you work in a gay bar, don't they try to take you to the bathroom and bang you?"

These were all things I had to hear over and over. Each time, though, I had to remind myself that not everyone had my open upbringing. Not everyone had the same opinions and beliefs that I do. Another great thing about mom was that she taught me to respect others opinions, so long as they weren't derogatory. I took that to heart. So I never got of-fended when people asked questions or gave their opinions.

That is, unless they chose to be mean. Occasionally someone would say something negative about gays. Now, if someone were to say, "I don't agree with a man being with another man." I respect that. It is an opinion based on someone's upbringing, religion, or surroundings. We are all entitled to our opinions, and I respected theirs. However, if someone called me the "F" word or was directly derogatory toward a group of people that they knew nothing about, I found that I would become very defensive.

Another group that would come into the bar was straight girls. Not a lot of straight guys know this, but straight girls love gay bars. They LOVE THEM. They meet a fun gay guy and become friends with him. They go shopping together and enjoy manicures and that sort of thing. Eventually the gay guy will bring them to the gay bar. Then their eyes are opened to a whole new world. In a gay bar the girl isn't objectified. In a gay bar a girl isn't constantly being hit on by guys who have no chance. They can dance without hav-ing guys grind on them and get 'happy'. They can drink without worry of getting drugged and they can talk to their friends without the constant interruption of a drunk, horny, hopeful guy.

This brings me to another benefit of being a straight bar-tender in a gay bar. Sure, gays tip better than straights, fight less than straights, and the music is better in a gay bar than straight bars. Sure, I laugh a lot more in a gay bar, but, we can't forget one of the best bonuses of all. When the straight girls find out that you, the bartender, are straight, they go crazy. For the first time in my life, I was the one getting hit on. No longer did I have to ask for the phone number or buy the drinks. Instead, every night, girls were flirting with me.

You see, in a bar like that, I have no competition. The girls aren't annoyed at all the guys hitting on them. They aren't frustrated and unwilling to get to know an actual decent guy. Instead, after a few hours, they get frustrated that no guys are hitting on them, and inevitably they will mention to their gay friend that they wish there was a straight guy in the bar. The friend would mention that I was straight, and the flirting would begin. In the beginning, it was still too soon after Jennifer to date. I was focused on school and getting my finances straight.

Even though I wasn't ready to date, their flirting started bringing back my confidence. I started feeling attractive again. The damage that Jennifer had done began to lessen. I had been over the hurt and pain for a while, but the emotional damage to my self-esteem was still apparent. These girls, sweet and flirty, made me feel better. Each night I would tell them that I wasn't interested in dating yet, but each night they made me feel a little stronger.

After a while I began to go on dates, but nothing really clicked. We would have a great time and they would even show me parts of Austin I knew nothing about, such as Eeyore's Birthday. Yep, the city of Austin shuts down to celebrate the character from Winnie the Pooh because, apparently, he never had a birthday. It was fun. It was freeing. I appreciated it all, but no one compared to her. Until I found someone that did, I couldn't imagine getting involved with anyone else. I even found myself looking to where my car was parked when I would get off work. Half wondering, half hoping that she would surprise me like she did that night so long ago. I would walk to my car and she would be there, begging me to forgive her.

Something else I was feeling inside, without forcing or

control, was happiness. I was feeling happy again. A huge contributing factor was that bar. Lil' Den, the support from my mom, friends I had made, and flirting girls all helped. It was the security, kindness, and fun I was getting from the bar that really helped give me back my smile.

I was also happy to start playing volleyball. Now, truth be told, I had never really played before. I was an athlete and had always been pretty good at sports. Basketball was my forte. So I figured I would be an ace at volleyball. I just hit the ball over the net as hard as possible, right? Wrong. I was soon to learn that my preconceived notions of some sports were factually inaccurate, I can thank a certain Mike from It's About Time for giving me that quote. Factually inaccurate means wrong, but said in a much cooler fashion.

Now, during the initial start at the bar, the volleyball court wasn't used much. Occasionally a group of people would go out and hit the ball around. I wanted something more than that. I wanted competition. That is when I met Donnie. Donnie was a black man, mid 40's, with an over the top personality. Donnie was also the foremost guru at getting volleyball games together. However, long ago, Donnie and the rest of the volleyball players had moved to a local straight bar to play. When I prodded him about why, he told me, "It's About Time doesn't care to have us here. They don't set up tournaments or offer drink specials for players. If they did, we would come back."

The next day I was in Trevor's office nailing out the details for a volleyball tournament. The court was too nice not to use. This could mean more business for the bar and more fun for me. I contacted Donnie and told him that I would personally be running the tournament and that we would offer drink specials for volleyball players on days that they came to practice and also on game days. My love for that crazy little bar was about to increase tenfold.

Donnie brought a few players in that week for a practice and asked if I wanted to play. It was about 8 p.m. and the sun was setting. I flipped on the lights for them, finished my shift, I got off at 9 p.m. on the days I worked Happy Hour, and headed out to play. They told me which side to go to.

I walked over, stood right in the middle, and prepared for battle.

"What the hell are you doing," burst out Shonda.

Shonda was a very athletic, lesbian, Jewish girl. She was almost my height and almost my build, but not in fat. She had three awesome kids and more spunk than a pit bull.

"We are in 3-2, so you're the setter right now," she told me.

I had no idea what she was saying to me, but she had motioned for me to move up, right in front of the net. I did as I was told. The other team served the ball. It went over my head and about six feet behind me. I dove to hit it, almost taking out Chris. Chris was a tall skinny guy who also happened to be an actor. One of the nicest guys I had ever met. However, Chris was none too happy about me almost taking out his ankles.

"Chase, what the hell are you doing?" he barked.

That was becoming a recurring phrase for me to hear.

For a half an hour it continued that way. They would serve and I would make a crazy dive to hit the ball. When I did get to the ball, I hit it right back to them. As far as I knew, the idea of volleyball was get the ball over the net.

Donnie pulled me aside, laughing, and said, "Have you ever played volleyball before?"

"No I haven't," I admitted, "but I'm pretty athletic."

"We have no doubt that you're athletic, as was proven by your ability to run around the entire court with reckless abandon. That being said, would you like to include your teammates? And, if so, would you like to learn the correct way to play?" Donnie asked.

I didn't know that there was a correct way. I was intrigued. Donnie made me sit out the next round and watch them play. A miraculous discovery happened while I sat there; they were following a pattern. The server would send the ball over, someone would hit the ball to the middle person, the middle person would push the ball gently in the air to one of the people on either side of them, and then one of them would get a monstrous hit. This didn't happen every time, however it happened often. When it did happen, it was enjoyable to watch. Sometimes these patterns would go back and forth for a while before someone would make a mistake. I knew right then that I wanted to be able to play like they did.

After that set, I asked Donnie to explain the game to me. I learned that the server sends the ball over, obviously trying to get a point. As the ball comes over it is everyone's job to 'bump' the ball. Bumping the ball means simply to keep the ball from hitting the ground and trying to hit it in a way that it goes to the middle person by the net. That middle person is called the setter. The second hit, the set, would almost always be their hit so that they can 'set' someone to get a good hit. The third hit, the maximum number your side gets, is ideally the 'spike'. That is when the setter puts the ball in just a spot so that one of the players on either side can jump up and hit the ball really hard. This process is called 'bump, set, spike' and I found out that it is the correct structure. Now, not every time the ball comes over the net will it go that way. That is the perfection that you strive for. He also made me aware that my job, in any position, was only within my area. If the ball was closer to someone else, it was theirs to handle. The setter, of course, had a little more leeway with this.

The next round I jumped in and began playing more correctly. I was still bad and my sets were useless to anyone within the confines of the court. It didn't matter, I was having a blast. It helped that they were so patient in my learning process. We played all the way until the bar closed at 2am. I helped clean up the outdoor area, turned off the lights, then headed home. It was the most fun that I had enjoyed in a long time. I had a smile plastered to my face. Lil' Den even noticed it when I got home. He was so curious of my happiness that he started joining me to play as well.

I continued to practice as much as possible. I wanted to be good. I realized that this sport, this connection of likeminded individuals, this grouping of friends offered me the meaning with life that I needed at the moment. I needed to feel something like a kinship with people. I felt it on that court.

Soon the teams were picked. Each team had to consist of four to six players. We played by the new collegiate rules, which meant that a point is awarded every time the ball is served. So the games are more exciting and could sometimes go very quickly. The tournaments were every Sunday from 2 p.m. until about 10 p.m. Afterward we would all head in and have fun.

It got to be so busy I even talked the bar into setting up a DJ outside. Then things really got fun. Most of the players, about 80%, were gay. So everyone danced and played when the ball wasn't in motion. Even the straight people, including yours truly, couldn't resist the fun and eventually joined in. That was such a great time in my life. To think that I had gone through so much pain recently. I had slept on couch cushions wondering if I would ever be happy again; now I couldn't stop smiling.

In the midst of one Sunday's festivities I climbed the tall line judge tower. I stood there for a moment, enjoying the sun as it added more to the tan I was getting from playing. I looked down around me and felt that tug of content in my heart. Beneath me were dozens of people from all walks of life, playing and dancing to the rhythm of their own beats, sharing in the joy of the moment. I thought about it, smiled, and added another notch in my moments that took my breath away.

Life is sure funny sometimes.

18

Volleyball season came and went. My team took second place, which I was quite happy with. I had actually become a great spiker Once I got my timing right, my jumping abilities from basketball actually paid off. I would jump so high in the air that I would get above the ball. That vantage allowed me a really great downward angle. Throw in the fact that I could hit with pretty good force and, well, we got a lot of points when I was a hitter. That being said, we lost a lot of points when I was the setter. Man, I was bad at setting. I think I actually set the other team more than my own.

School also came to a close. I had finished the first semester and a heavy load during summer school. Once that was done I realized I had finished all of my prerequisites, again. I was added to the waiting list. Though I attended the extra lectures and kissed all the right butt, it would be at least a year before I could start the actual program. That realization was the first seed of doubt to enter my mind.

I had been going to school and working hard because it was what I believed I was supposed to do. After being told I would have to wait, things began stirring inside of me. I never wanted to go into the medical field. I only did it because Jennifer told me to. I only stayed in it because that's what you're supposed to do; finish what you start, but I wasn't doing it for me. I didn't love it. Sure, I was good at it. My grades were high, I was respected by my teachers, and looked up to by my classmates. Being good at something doesn't mean it's what you were meant to do. These thoughts began to weigh heavily on my mind. Couple that with the fact that I had tons of extra time now that school was over and I found myself getting lost in a swirling confusing mixture of thoughts.

Luckily, amidst all of the confusion, I had my friends. Lil' Den and I had been going out a lot around that time. If I wasn't playing pick-up volleyball games or working, he and I were making our rounds about the town. Whether we were floating the river on the Comal during the day, eating at local restaurants in the evening, or hitting up the clubs at night, we constantly had a great gathering of friends everywhere we went.

I awoke to a pounding on my bedroom door one morning. I barely opened my eyes when I saw about twelve people come rushing into my room and jump onto my bed! My immediate thought was that I was being robbed. I went on the defensive and prepared for a fight. Then I saw Lil' Den and a few other friends' faces mixed in with the people jumping on top of me. They had decided to be my alarm clock.

"I'm awaaaaaake!" I yelled, laughing as I rolled and fell out of bed.

"Grab your shorts and the speaker cooler, it's river floating time!" Lil' Den said with more excitement than I'd heard from him in a while.

I hopped up, rinsed off in the shower real quick, then dressed and packed for the day.

Floating the river is one of the favorite past times of the people who live in and around Austin. It's simple: every weekend thousands of people pack up their cars, drive the hour south to the different tube launches, rent an inner tube, and hop in the river. Then they float. That's it. They just float, for hours.

Within 30 minutes we were on the road and headed south. We had five people in my recently acquired Jeep and there were three other cars behind us. During the ride I sent texts inviting more of our friends. By the time we had parked we had another fifteen people driving down to join us. A group of almost 30, just like we liked it.

LD and I were always great at organizing big events. We loved getting large groups of our friends together and enjoying the day, seeing what trouble we could get into. Today was no different.

We parked the Jeep in a church parking lot that doubled as parking for the floaters on Saturdays. Surrounded by thousands of other water enthusiasts, we made our way over to the pick-up location. Though we would wait for the others to arrive, we preferred to wait in the covered tent area. In that tent were dozens of people milling around and hanging out with one another. A lot of them were from our group, which I recognized and said hello to. Soon we were on the bus and headed to the tube rental place.

The bus pulled up to the rental place and we unloaded. Since our group took up more than half of the bus, it took us over half an hour to all get our tubes. Once we did, though, it was on. We walked the little path through the park that led down to the water. The park was filled with people, all enjoying the beautiful summer day.

The rocks at the base of the tube launch were covered in moss, causing the footing to be very slippery. One by one I helped everyone in. As our group was large, this was no simple feat. The guys all went running and jumped in, causing a ruckus for those who were enjoying the calmness of the slow moving water.

Laughing, I helped the women, keeping them from slipping on the moss and helping them each get situated into their tubes. Once they were all in, I handed them the cooler tubes. We had three tubes that had coolers built into the middle of them. Two of the coolers were filled with beer, bag wine (yes, bag wine… it's a river floating delicacy), my energy drinks, and ice. The third cooler held lunchmeat, veggies, fruit, and snacks. The last thing I helped in was my speaker cooler. I was quite proud of it.

I spent $400 to make a boombox. Common sense would say that I was ripped off. However, this was like no normal boombox. It was a speaker cooler built for the river. I took a large cooler and installed a six inch speaker on each of the four sides. Then I hooked up an amplifier, water proof boat battery, and a couple of other necessary parts within the cooler. Once that was done I added a cable that could plug into an iPod. Lastly, I made it waterproof so that it could only be opened if I removed the entire top for battery recharging. This gave me a very loud stereo on the water. We liked the idea of that.

Once the speaker cooler was in the water, I stepped down in to join everyone. Wouldn't you know it, I was rewarded for helping everyone else in by slipping and falling myself. I fell hard, slipping on the moss, and landed right on my butt.

I started to stand, then slipped and fell again. I was in a little bit of pain physically, but it was my ego that was more hurt than anything. I was sitting in five inches of water on a rock coated in green moss, frustrated at my lack of balance. Out of nowhere a little hand reached down to help me up. I spun myself around to face the person that was offering to be my hero.

She was standing at the edge of the water, directly in front of the sun, which caused a halo like appearance to form behind her shiny black hair. She looked like an angel; an angel sent to save me from my watery predicament. I kept staring, almost confused by the sight that was right in front of me. I couldn't make out her face, but I was grateful for the hand. I accepted it and allowed her to help pull me up. Once I was standing I finally got to look at her.

For a moment, everything froze.

I looked out at my friends, all still in the same positions they had been when I had fallen. The group of them, 30 or so, were in one giant misshapen circle, floating on the dark blue water that supported them. Each with giant smiles and laughter on their faces.

I looked out to my left, which is where the park was that sat next to the boat launch. Nestled in the park were dozens of picnic tables, each full of families eating, sharing, laughing with one another. Next to each table were bar-b-cue pits with fathers huddled over them, cooking the wares for the families.

I glanced out to my right where men were throwing Frisbees for their dogs. At that moment one of the dogs was stuck in mid-air, waiting to wrap his teeth around the large plastic disc that continued to elude him.

I looked at the sky, enjoying the way the wisps of white clouds looked against the stunning blue backdrop. I closed my eyes and felt the warmth of the sun. The sun that had been there for me so many times. There was no sound. The world had gone silent. Keeping my eyes closed I listened intently to hear anything, but I was alone. I inhaled the fresh air, filling my lungs with the smell of oak trees and crisp water.

Then I looked at her.

My heart quit beating. There was an electricity in that moment, as if it was unnecessary for me to ever breath again. Goosebumps formed on my skin as I saw her standing, arm outstretched, offering her help to me.

She was an Asian woman that looked to be in her mid-20's. She only stood about 5'1"; just a tiny little thing. Her dark tan skin reflecting the rays of the sun as they shone their light over her body, which was covered in short jean shorts and a blue bikini top. Her long, jet black hair, frozen in movement as the wind had tossed it before the world had stopped.

Her smile, visible now because her beautiful thick lips had parted, made me feel inclinations inside that hadn't stirred in years. Tingles, butterflies, eruptions all were happening within me. It was her eyes, though, that changed my life. Those eyes told me, in that millisecond, that the world was full of possibilities again and that life would be ok from then on. I don't know how to explain it. There was just a child-like wonderment within them that made me feel hope, made me feel alive. I didn't know her name. I didn't know her story. I didn't know who she was, but I needed to. I knew, in that moment, that something would be different.

We were still holding hands when I felt a spark move from her body into mine and from my body back into hers. I looked down, staring at our clenched connection for a moment, as if our two bodies were now one; joined by the extensions of ourselves. What was this that was happening? Was I dreaming? Had I fallen down so hard that I was actually meeting my guardian angel?

The tingle grew stronger and I looked back up into her eyes. This time they were staring back into mine as intently as I was into them. We were lost together. Two souls searching for a doorway to the others.

A tap on my shoulder brought me back to reality. I jumped about a foot and nearly fell down again. I had been so lost that I hadn't notice LD come up to me.

"You want to introduce us to your new friend?" he asked with a giant smile.

Realizing that I was still holding her hand, I turned bright red.

She was actually standing with three other friends, all cute Caucasian girls, that were looking at me like I might be a bit of a creeper. Considering how I had been staring so long and awkwardly holding her hand, I didn't blame them.

"Hi, there, um, I'm Chase," I said as I smiled at her. Had my awkward staring moment scared her away? Would she now tell me to get lost? I must have looked so stupid falling down.

"Hello, Chase, I'm Autumn," she said while smiling back at me, still looking deep in my eyes.

Was I seeing what I felt like I was seeing? Was she looking at me the same way? No!

There is no way that was possible! Was it?

Realizing that my best bet to continue to see her was to get her friends to join our group, I offered, "Hey, we have drinks and a giant boombox. Any chance you ladies want to float down with us? "

The four of them talked it over, then it was agreed that they would join.

We connected to the rest of the group, plugged my iPod in, hit play, and off we went. The first song, which I had picked on purpose, was "Baby Got Back." There is no better way to start any party than with some 90's Hip Hop or R&B. As if on cue, all of the girls started giggling and singing along.

Within minutes we went through the man-built chute that took us from the slow moving pool of water at the landing zone out onto the faster moving river water. All around us people started singing along to the music. As each little group would hear the music they would join in with the singing and connect to our group. In no time at all we had gone from a group of about 30 to nearly a hundred. A rolling fortress of people singing sexual music and Boy Band Songs.

Yes, we sang Boy Band Songs. I played 'N Sync, Backstreet Boys, 98 Degrees, and all of the others. I played Montel Jordan and All for One. I played the music that got people dancing, even if that dancing was silly rocking on an inner tube in a river.

I would sink down in my tube sometimes, just to eye level, and watch her from behind my dark Ray Bans. When she and her friends played, she would laugh. Not just any laugh. A laugh that sounded more genuine, more real, more pure than any I had heard in a long time. Each time she did, I found myself smiling like a giddy school boy. She was incredible.

She wasn't sexy in the way you think of when you envision women on the covers of magazines. Rather, she was beautiful in the way that can only be described as adorable. So many women hate the term adorable when being used to describe them. It isn't a bad term. In fact, it is my absolute favorite kind of girl. My definition of adorable is the perfect combination of looks and personality. This girl had both. That kind of beauty was so much more real. The kind of beauty that you can get lost in. Knowing that she might be a whole person, not a front like so many women put on .

Her eyes are what I kept feeling drawn to, though. Those eyes had that perfect almond shape that squinted when she smiled; which was something she never stopped doing. There was a childlike innocence that exuded from her. A pure happiness that seemed untouched by the darkness of the world. I couldn't explain it. I didn't understand it. Regardless, I liked it. I paused there, treading water, staring at her for as long as I could. Sometimes, she would glance my way. And though I was lost in a sea of other bodies, I would become embarrassed.

I had met so many girls since Jennifer. So many had hit on me. The few I had gone on dates with, none had caused me to act this way. None had me swooning. What had she done to me? I felt something in that moment. I felt like she was the type of person I could see sitting across from and getting to know over dinners. Not just babbling about the same old routine questions that people ask on dates. Rather, really getting to know one another. I was enamored with her, yet I knew nothing about her. She was someone I could see spending time with, growing with, and I didn't even know her name.

I have heard it said that there are two types of girls you meet: the ones you want to go to bed with, and the ones you want to wake up next to. She was the kind I could imagine waking up next to, watching her sleep, kissing her forehead. Thinking about this made me smile.

I had been lost in thought and hadn't realized that she'd left her friends. I looked around trying to find her, but didn't see her anywhere. Then ripples began to form on the water right in front of my tube. I almost pulled back, fearing there might be something there that I should be worried about, yet also intrigued to find out what it could possibly be.

A head slowly emerged from the water, lines of clear liquid draining from the shiny black hair as the head rose inch by inch. Eventually a face took shape. The dark hair, the almond eyes closed to protect themselves, her rose colored lips pressed tightly together hiding her smile, all came bursting forth from the water in one incredible fluid motion.

She opened her eyes and we locked in a deep stare again. Without words. Without material items. Without trying we were telling each other so much by searching each other out. Then she smiled her big smile and dove back under water.

She had been right in front of me. So close that I had a chance to talk to her, to get to know her, to say hello. In a flash she was gone then reemerged with her friends. I thought about chasing after her, but held myself.

I paused for a moment, contemplating what to do. There really was something different about this girl and I was intrigued. However, I didn't feel right just going over and interrupting her while she was with her friends. If she had wanted to talk she would have when she was closer. I resigned myself to going back to enjoying the music.

A little over an hour later we were nearing the end, which was a large gravel bar with people helping get the tubes out of the river and up on land. I could see that it was only about ten minutes of floating and then we would be there. I looked around, hoping to spot her. At first I couldn't find her. I assumed that she must have detached from our group and set out with her friends on their own. Then, out of sheer luck, I noticed that she and her friends had attached to the very back of our group.

I could hear her and her friends laughing. I strained to make out what they were saying. I heard one friend say, "How can you like Taylor Swift? She is just music for kids."

To which she responded, "No way! Taylor writes music that we can connect to! I love Taylor! How can you not?" Then she squealed with silly joy.

In a flash I grabbed my iPod, opened up my artists file, grabbed the Taylor Swift section and hit play. In a millisecond Taylor Swift was blaring from my speaker cooler. I looked to where she was sitting, this angel with the big smile, to see her reaction. For a moment she just sat there, looking slightly confused, then she jumped up and began singing along to the song. She was laughing so hard she could barely sing the words. Her eyes caught mine and we stopped, both lost. Lost in the moment again. Lost in time. Lost in each other's eyes. I couldn't believe how easy it was for us to do that. How it happened every time. She turned red, smiled that incredible smile, and I melted.

WHAM! We ran aground. I hadn't been paying attention to how close we were getting, which caused us to run our entire caravan into the gravel bar. Half laughing, half shook up, I stood and looked over to her, but she was gone, again. I felt defeated. I had thought, for a moment, that we had found each other again for a reason. I swallowed the frog in my throat and guessed some things just weren't meant to be.

I helped pull the others out of the water, drug in the beer and speaker coolers, and helped load up the bus. Shortly, we were headed back to the parking lot and back to our cars. We had enjoyed a wonderful day that was full of sunshine, friends, and happiness. Yet, I was sad. I felt like I had missed a wonderful opportunity. I felt like I was cheated a moment to find something more. I was walking toward the car, arms loaded down, and I felt a tiny little tap on my shoulder.

I turned around to yell at LD, but found her instead. She was standing there, now covered in short khaki shorts and a Rolling Stones T-shirt, smiling from ear to ear.

"I think you dropped this," she said with a giggle. She stuck what I had dropped into my hand, giggled a little more, then bounded off. I was left speechless, again. This girl had an uncanny ability to pop up and then just leave me hanging. I shook my head and opened my hand to see what she'd found.

It was a folded piece of paper. A note. I was confused. I opened the note. It read:

Well played, sir. I'm a sucker for Taylor Swift. 310-555-0981
Autumn.

Autumn! Her name was Autumn. It was interesting that her number started with 310, which was a Hollywood area code. I knew that because I also had a 310 number. Why did she have a Hollywood number, but lived here in Austin? I was even more intrigued.

I couldn't stop smiling. The way she had playfully flirted without acting like a flirt. I couldn't get over the childlike sensibility about her. I was overcome with thoughts, ideas and possibilities. I had no idea why, but things felt different this time. For the first time in many years, I felt hope.

I walked to the car, got inside, leaned the seat back, and stared at the note. There are all kinds of opinions when it comes to the "Right Time To Call" question. Some say you should wait until the following morning. Some say you should wait at least 24 hours. Some say you should wait at least two days. There are even some that say you should wait a week, keeping them guessing. However, they all agree on one thing, you should never text immediately. I failed miserably at listening to those opinions. I had looked at the note for all of two minutes and I was already texting.

I wanted to say the right thing. I wanted to sum up, in one short text, how good of a guy I was and how she should let me take her out soon. So I wrote, "I'm Chase. I love cars, sports, acting, and making people smile. If you would allow, I'd love to take you out." Then sent it.

I sat there smiling at my wit, then I read what I had written. It dawned on me that my text sounded like something written by a fifth grade boy who was in heat. It was about the least witty thing I had ever written. I groaned to myself and sent a follow up text, " I'm aware of how corny that sounded. I assure you that I'm much less of a spazz in person." That made me feel better. Now was the waiting game.

And wait I did. I patiently hoped for a response, but none came that night. None also came the next morning or afternoon. I became keenly aware that this girl might just have given me her number with no real interest in talking to me. Yes, that has happened before. Alas, the life of a man.

I must admit to being a little disappointed. Sure, I knew nothing about this girl. She could have turned out to be a mean person who spit on homeless people. There was just something about her, though. Something that kept making me wonder. Kept making me think that we could enjoy each other's company.

At about 7:30 p.m. I finally got a text. I pulled out my phone and read the message. I got excited. It was from her! It read, "Chase, thanks for the sweet messages, both of them. I rather like corny. Sorry I haven't responded. My phone was dead yesterday, then I had school all day today." I was curious about the school part.

What a person is in school for can say a lot about them. It doesn't define them, by any means, but it can definitely be a small gauge for who they are. A girl in school to become a chef will probably be very interested in food. A girl who majors in business will probably not like a guy who wants to be an actor. A girl who wants to become a lawyer probably expects to put relationships on hold for a few years. Things like that. Though these aren't the rules, they do tend to have merit.

I was curious, so I asked, "what are you in school for?"
She quickly texted back, "Film."

I couldn't believe what I just read. She was going to school for film. A woman who understood the business. A woman with passions like mine.

"Why do you have a Hollywood number?" I posed out of a mixture of excitement and curiosity.

She wrote back, "I moved from Vietnam to Hollywood five years ago. I didn't like the Hollywood scene at first, so I decided to choose to go to school outside of California, then go back when I was finished."

She too had been there. She too had dealt with adversity then chose to come to Texas. Admittedly, my reasons were less of a choice, but nonetheless. I learned that she was to graduate school after three more semesters. Afterward, she planned on heading back to L.A. to get her career going. For a career, she really wanted to make documentaries. She found something human in them. A sense of reality untainted by storyline, explosions, romance, or writers. She had a passion for something. I knew all too well what it was like to feel a passion. What it was to dream. To chase your dream. To work so hard on it, and for people to constantly negate you for it, telling you it's wrong.

In getting to know her, one thing became apparent above all others, this girl had heart. More heart than anyone I had ever met in my life. She had a genuine quality that made me ask more questions. I felt myself listening to her talk rather than forcing her to listen while I talked. With her, I needed to know more.

We learned more about the other in that short night than most people probably do in an entire relationship. We shared the parts of us that were most dark, most secretive, most painful. I told her of my relationship with Jennifer. She told me of the way men picked on her when she was growing up in Vietnam. She comforted me, assuring me that not all women were like that. I felt defensive for her, wishing I could meet those men, face to face, so I could have stopped them from trying to hurt her.

I remember the last text I sent that first night. I wrote, "I dressed in drag once. It was for a benefit at a bar I was working at. All of the bartenders dressed in drag and lip-synced to a song. The customers all threw money at us, which we donated to charity. I couldn't walk right in the heels and I fell down, breaking the heel. Then I had to finish my song with one broken shoe."

No text back. Usually the texts were quick in response. Had this admittance of silliness been too much for her?

My phone rang.

I answered it, knowing it was her, and said, "Hello."

All I received for an answer was laughter. Lots and lots of laugher. She was laughing so hard she could barely breathe. I started laughing too. She snorted. This made me laugh even harder.

"Don't laugh at me," she squealed, laughing even more, causing her to snort again.

Quite possibly the greatest first phone call I had ever had. I was laying in bed, The Daily Show with Jon Stewart playing on the TV, and I was enamored with the voice of this girl.

Oddly enough, if you had never met her and only heard her voice, you would have sworn she was a white girl from the Valley. She had the cutest, silliest, happiest voice. When she spoke, she spoke with optimism and heart. I could imagine her big smile and squinting eyes every time she'd laugh. It felt so good laying there talking to her. Here was this girl, pure of heart, intelligent, and caring; laughing and making me smile. If her intention was to make me swoon, she had succeeded greatly.

"How about a movie on Friday night?" I posed to her.

"I would love that! That is the perfect first date for us!" she announced.

I knew, in most cases, that going to the movies on a first date is a bad idea. With her it was different, though. She was in the film industry, just like I was and she loved going to see films as much as I did. Though we saw the movies through different eyes, mine from in front of the camera and hers from behind, we were able to enjoy them evenly.

Our first date. I was so excited. I remembered with Jennifer that I'd had to plan an extensive date. Sure, it had been a lot of fun. Looking back, though, I realized that it was forced. I spent all of that time and money because I felt a need to impress her. I had to get her to like me.

I began seeing a pattern of that when I would look back on my relationship with her. More often than not I was doing everything I could to show her that I loved her. Rarely was she reciprocating. I believe a great relationship is 50/50. If both people put in 100%, then they are both putting in their half, meeting in the middle. With Jennifer, it was like 90/10. I put in way more than she did, and I got burned in the process. I was just oblivious to it because I loved her so much.

With Autumn, it was different. Sure, I wanted to impress her. Sure, I wanted her to like me, but this time I felt the same yearning from her. I could tell that she wanted to impress me too. She wanted me to like her. We were two people on the same path heading toward one another, rather than one chasing the other. In our scenario, we would eventually (hopefully) run into each other's arms versus constantly chasing as I had been before. This realization hit me in my chest one day. I now understood why Jennifer and my relationship was always doomed to fail. For any relationship to work (business, romantic, family, or other) it must be based on a mutual need for both to gain something from the effort that each put in. If any side is putting in more or either side is offering less, the relationship will probably fail. A relationship that is based on mutual effort will bloom into a beautiful one.

That is what I was getting with Autumn. We both wanted to feel something. We both needed for this to be more real than what we had dealt with in the past. Though our paths were very different, the end results had been similar. We had both been hurt. Badly. We had less trust, less self-confidence, more anxiety about relationships. Luckily, we both didn't care about the past now. We both knew there was something special right in front of us. We hadn't even gone on our first date yet were feeling this way.

Friday night arrived in no time. We had already picked out the movie *Flight*. All I had to do was swing by, pick her up, then head to the theater. At about 8:15 p.m. I pulled down the street of her apartment building. I found an open spot in the guest parking section, hopped out of the car, then walked over to her apartment. I didn't see a doorbell so I knocked three quick knocks with my knuckles. After only a minute she was there, standing in front of me.

It was dark in her apartment and the sun had already gone down for the night. The only light was coming from a wall sconce hung about three feet from her door. That was all the light I needed to see her. That angelic face, that happy smile, and those amazing eyes. She had chosen to wear cute little cowgirl boots that went almost all the way to her knee. A pair of white shorts that were just short enough to show me the curves of her legs, without giving away too much, covered her lower half.

Her top was form fitted all the way from her neck down to her waist, then flared out a little to add dimension. She wore a thin silver necklace that had a tiny moon hanging from it. Her smile was in place and already grinning, but it was those eyes that had my fullest attention. Those deep dark eyes, already searching out mine. I think I could have stood there, in that doorway, all night and been happy.

"You still want to see this movie?" she asked me in earnest.

I had zoned out staring at her again. I really needed to get better control of that.

I laughed, "Yes, sorry. Let's go."

I offered my arm, she took it, and I walked her to my car. I stopped and opened the trunk, where there was a bouquet of daisies that had been tucked in, waiting for her.

"Oh, Chase, they are so beautiful!" came her response to my gesture. I could see in her eyes that she was genuinely happy.

I walked around, opened her door, then held her hand as she got in.

"I could have gotten my door," she giggled at me.

"I cannot promise that I will always get your door, but I promise to be a gentleman as often as possible," I responded back.

Her cheeks turned ever so slightly pink and she smiled.

During the drive to the theater we talked a lot. We had such a great stream of open conversation going. A recurring topic, one that we kept coming back to, was that we each felt like we had known the other for years. I told her that I felt like she was my best friend. She told me that she had been feeling the same way. She told me how she called or texted me first anytime she had something she needed to share with someone. I admitted that I did the same thing.

At one point I told her, "I don't really know how I feel about reincarnation, but if there is such a thing, I think that you and I have known each other before."

"Oh, my gosh, I have been feeling the same way!" came her ecstatic response.

We were on the same wavelength with each other. Two minds connected by similar

thought. We kept coming back to how comfortable we felt with each other; how the conversation was so easy. It was as if we had been friends and lovers before. That conversation would soon come about again.

Let me interject this right here. I know I have said it before, but I will say it again, the universe will sometimes work in mysterious ways. Things will happen, in what seems like random or coincidental ways, which set different actions and effects in to motion. With how much it was happening with she and I, well I began to wonder if it was coincidental at all. Or maybe, just maybe, the universe was helping me see what I was really meant for. That the pain of Jennifer was only to set me up for the good of Autumn. The signs kept presenting themselves.

The ticket booth person told us how sorry he was, but that *Flight* was only offered as a preview showing that day. Those that came to see it, at 7:30, were given a short survey after. Otherwise, it wasn't actually in theaters until the following weekend. We were both bummed. It was our first date, and we had already hit a snag. It looked like the only really good movie that was out. Nothing else really appealed to us, plus we were looking forward to seeing it.

"Is there another movie you would recommend?" I asked in a defeated voice.

"Well, *Cloud Atlas* is supposed to be pretty interesting," he replied.

"*Cloud Atlas*?" I asked her.

She looked at me and shrugged her shoulders.

Neither of us had any idea what it was. We looked over the rest of the movies, but none seemed to be any good. We talked it over, then agreed to grab tickets to it. The movie wasn't for an hour, so we decided to grab food at a restaurant nearby.

We chose a cute little sandwich/salad shop just around the corner from the theater. It was the kind of place where you ordered your food at the counter and then went and sat down. Kind of like the middle stage between fast food and normal restaurant. I liked that. We weren't really in the mood for a sit down place, but also didn't want a greasy fast food burger. This was perfect.

We stood in line, laughing at our misfortune, and being playful with one another. I would poke her, she would poke me, we would giggle. Like two kids on the playground, playing pinch tag. The connection was real and unaffected by the beating down of life.

We ordered our sandwiches and stood to the side to wait for them, both munching on Sea Salt and Vinegar Kettle chips. At one point I bent down to whisper in her ear. I was going to tell her how much I loved her hair in a ponytail. I leaned my head in just as she turned her face at the last second. Without thinking, we kissed. Surprised, yet happy, I kissed back gently, for a long moment.

I pulled away and said, "Wow, I wasn't expecting that."

She looked at me confused and laughed while she said, "Then why did you try?"

She thought I had been leaning in for a kiss. She had decided at the last second to accept my kiss; only to find out I was going to tell her something in her ear. She became super embarrassed.

"I can't believe I did that!" she exclaimed. "Now you think I'm ea...,"

Before she could finish I cut her off by grabbing her and kissing her much deeper than we had kissed before. We explored each other's mouths, hearts, and souls in that kiss. When we pulled apart I said to her, "No, I don't think you're easy. I think you're fantastic. I'm glad that we broke that barrier."

From that moment on, the touch barrier was never a problem again. We held hands, hugged, and kissed whenever we felt. Granted, we kept the PDA to a minimum after that first kiss, but we still refused to let go of each other's hand. The need to keep our skin touching outweighed anything else. To not feel her hand felt wrong.

We took our sandwiches to the benches in front of the theater to eat, which had a big circular area with lots of landscaping. The landscaping was encompassed by nice footpaths. Each of these paths eventually led out of the theater front and into another part of the outdoor mall. Above our heads were strands of lights. They were the kind that all faced down with the big bulbs. It added a touch of class and a hint of romance. We sat there, laughing and flirting, as we enjoyed our food.

"Tell me something about you that you're proud of," I said while munching away on my sandwich.

"Don't put me on the spot like that," she hissed in a shy tone.

"I'm curious," I said with playful puppy dog eyes.

She sat there, thinking, figuring out something that she was proud of, then said, "Well, I'm actually really proud of the film I made recently. It is a documentary about undocumented immigrants coming to America for the chance at the American Dream."

She continued on, telling me how she had driven to the border and filmed the fence. She told of finding undocumented people and interviewing them, letting them tell her their story in their own words.

At the end she said, "Making this film is when I realized who I am as a filmmaker. Letting people tell their stories is what I want to do. Showing the world the side of things that they may not know or choose to turn a blind eye to. That is what makes me proud."

I was blown away. To her, she was just telling me what had happened. To me, though, it was so much more. In her voice I could hear the passion that she had for her career and for life. In her story I could hear about her compassion and her thirst for learning about people. In her eyes, while she spoke, I could see the wonderment within, excited to show the world what she saw through them. I felt something stir within me. A feeling of understanding. Understanding of one's passion. Understanding of a drive within that is stronger than time, pain, or heartache. Something about her passion made me feel mine again. I shook my head to bring myself back to the present moment and smiled at her.

We went inside and grabbed a seat just before show time. I was so happy to find out she also preferred the very back row. We both agreed that it meant no one putting their feet on your chair, bumping your seat, throwing popcorn, or spilling soda.

It turned out that *Cloud Atlas* is a story about a few people and their interactions throughout time. Yes, through reincarnation they bump into each other many times. Sometimes they are in different forms. Sometimes they are men, then the next time they are women. Sometimes they are the heroes; sometimes they are the bad guys, but each time they play an integral role within each other's lives. I will, right now, say that the acting in the movie was fantastic. For those actors to each play three or more roles, and in such believable ways, was amazing to watch for another actor. From the filmmaking perspective, Autumn agreed that the film was exquisitely shot and edited. However, it wasn't the mechanics of the film that caused she and I to begin freaking out after it finished.

We each had spent the past couple of days thinking about how much we felt that we had known each other in another life. We had spent the past couple of hours before the movie telling each other how much it felt like reincarnation. Then, out of the blue and not what we planned, we spent 2 and 1/2 hours watching a movie about people being reincarnated and finding each other. All while on our first date.

As the credits began flowing, sitting there in the dark theater I kissed her. I squeezed her, held her, hugged her as tightly as I could. She reciprocated everything I was doing.

She whispered in my ear, "I can't get enough of you."

My temperature raised ten degrees when she said that. I don't know if I fell in love with her in that exact moment, but

I do know that was when it started to grow. I knew, without a doubt, that I wanted to make it work with this woman. It really was as if we had known each other for an eternity of lives. I can only imagine in what forms we had met before. What situations had we endured? What lives had we built? Had we always found each other? Now we had the opportunity to build again.

I had never met anyone else in my life that was so real. She didn't play games. She meant what she said when she spoke. I don't know if it was because she was born in another country or because of the hard times she had gone through, but there was an innocence to her soul. She was a strong, independent woman, yet mixed with the light happiness of a child. I still don't fully know how to explain it. What I could explain is that I knew I needed her every time I looked in her eyes.

She'd look at me and I would melt. Sure, I had felt similar things with Jennifer, but this time I could see her staring back, getting lost in my eyes, looking into my soul. I couldn't believe that I might possibly have found something so strong. This time the other person wanted it as badly as I did. This time she was as involved as I.

We left the theater around midnight. I asked, "What should we do next?"

She responded, "It's late, let's just go back."

I knew it was late too. I was hoping that we would spend a little more time together, but I didn't want to rush her. If she thought it best to end the night where we were, I would respect that.

I drove to her place and pulled up out front.

She looked at me, confused, and said, "Park silly."

We walked inside her place. It was a cute little two-bedroom, two-bathroom apartment. There was very little furniture. Her roommate, I learned, was one of the very few gay men on the planet that didn't have decorating sense. There wasn't any living room furniture except for two plastic lawn chairs, one TV dinner folding table, and a 60" LCD TV sitting on the floor. I laughed, which prompted her to hit me for laughing.

I have never been a materialistic person. After dating Jennifer, I realized that was a quality in a woman that I would no longer want to have to deal with in a relationship. So to see Autumn's place, confirming what she had told me about not being materialistic, well it made me happy.

She led me over to her room which was simply decorated. A tall birch dresser in the far corner with a little TV on it that wasn't even plugged in. Her bed was a box spring and mattress sitting on the floor. In the corner on my right was another dresser, this one of a non-matching wood color to the first. Her small closet was open and overflowing with clothes, most of which looked to be of the T-shirt and jeans variety. There were schoolbooks, video cameras, and miscellaneous items strewn about the floor.

She sat on her bed and I sat on the floor while we talked. Seeing her cameras got me asking questions about her wants in the business. We talked of doing projects together and of pushing each other toward our dreams. This was so much different than the conversations I'd had with Jennifer. Jennifer had always wanted to me to get a real job. Autumn wanted me to follow my passion, as she wanted someone to push her to follow her own.

She showed me the projects that she had made while in school. Including one that had been entered and won at her schools film festival. It had won first place in the short film category. Seeing this, watching her footage, made me feel a sense of pride toward her. Proud that she was as talented as she was driven.

We Googled some of my work on YouTube, so she could see me as an actor. One in particular had me singing and dancing to a popular 70's song. It had been for a national TV show, which she had never seen.

"TURN IT OFF!" she screamed, laughing so hard tears were falling from her eyes. I knocked her off the bed, held her down, and forced her to watch.

"This is cruel and unusual punishment" she cried between laughs.

Besides my mom, brother, sisters, and my theater director from high school, I hadn't ever met anyone that made me proud to be who I was. I felt that with her, a new confidence building inside me, a motivation beginning to grow. I started to feel like me again.

It was well past 3 a.m. when I said I should go home. She lifted her covers, smiled at me, and motioned toward the bed. I joined her, reached over, turned out the light, and pulled the covers up. She gave me a long kiss then rolled over to sleep. I wrapped my arms around her, gladly accepting my position as big spoon. We hadn't needed to have conversations about sex. We hadn't needed to talk about how we would sleep. We had a mutual connection and understanding. Without saying it, we knew things would happen when they were supposed to.

19

I couldn't believe that I had found a woman who had even more heart than beauty and was willing to put in as much effort as I. Those first few months with her were magic. They were the medicine my soul had needed. The pain from Jennifer faded more and more with each smile from Autumn. I was falling in love. I had found the woman that I was truly meant to be with.

We had decided one night that we should sit out on the patio and watch the sun go down. We headed out there while there was still a bit of light in the sky, with our blankets and pillows. Engulfed in those blankets, bodies wrapped together tightly, we watched the sun set over the horizon. Each second that passed brought new colors and shapes for our eyes to see. Mother Nature showing us the beauty that is always around us, but that we rarely open our eyes long enough to see.

She took my right hand and placed it upon her cheek while looking at me. I closed my eyes and ran my hand up and down that cheek, slowly, taking in every millimeter of skin. Then her hands were on my body.

The blankets offered the perfect protection for our exploits. Cloaked in the darkness of night, covered by the cloth, we made love. This love was more soft and more sensual than any I had ever experienced. We took our time, exploring each other's nature. Letting our sense of touch be the guide to our ecstasy.

Eventually, after many hours and much perspiration, we collapsed upon ourselves , panting in a heap of sweaty mess. We straightened ourselves up, looked around, and realized the sun was already coming up. This brought laughter and playfulness.

"How in the world did we go from sundown to sunup?" She had asked.

I shrugged my shoulders and laughed. It didn't matter how it happened, only that we could now watch the day come upon us, then fall asleep in each other's arms. Content with our lives exactly as they were in that moment.

We spent the whole next day repeating the process. When Lil' Den was home we spent the time in the bedroom, only leaving to replenish our bodies with water or Apple Jacks, my favorite post sex food. When he would leave we explored the apartment almost as much as we explored each other's bodies. Though we left LD's bedroom alone, there wasn't a corner, nook, or closet we left unturned. We both agreed that the patio was our favorite, and that is where we ended the second night as well. Admittedly, we were both so exhausted that we didn't make it to sun up again. It didn't matter. Sleeping there on the patio with her curled up on me was better than any sunrise could have been.

We had fallen in love. Deep love. Unconditional love. The kind of love that I had been searching for so long ago, but hadn't found. Her pain from her past was mostly eradicated, as was mine. We were best friends, lovers, partners, family.

Time came and went. Summer, spring, winter, fall all showed us the beauty of changing seasons. Soon, school was done for her and the decisions of what next began to arise. I spent a few days trying to decide how I felt about things, then I called her.

"Autumn, I love you. I love you stronger than I have ever loved someone before. You treat me better than anyone has ever treated me. We understand each other's paths, goals, and dreams. I want us to continue to work on our dreams, but I want to do it together. Will you move to Austin and be with me? Will you move in with me?" I asked her.

It was a big decision for me. I knew it was a big one for her as well.

"I don't want to be a burden for you baby," came her response.

She was worried that she would burden me. How could that be possible? Having her by my side could do nothing but lift me up, not bring me down. I explained to her that she wouldn't burden me. That she would help become my motivator, pushing me back to following my dreams. We discussed it over the course of a few days, and then the decision was made. She would move in.

At the same time, LD and I had been outgrowing our apartment. Add to that the fact that I had met another friend, Jerome, and he had become a big impact on my life. He was a gay guy that worked with me at the bar. He was so much like me in every way, save for the fact that he liked boys and I liked girls. We became great friends very fast and I considered him to be my other best friend in Austin, besides LD. We all talked and decided that the best idea was for the four of us to get a big house to rent. We spent a good amount of time searching around Austin, then found the perfect place.

It was a four bedroom, three bath house in Pflugerville. Pflugerville was a town that resided just above Austin. It would put Jerome and I closer to the bar, LD closer to his work, and give us a lot more room. It also had a huge back yard and a two-car garage. It was perfect. The three of us guys spent the next three days moving all of our stuff inside. Autumn and I took the master, LD and Jerome the two second biggest rooms, and we turned the fourth bedroom into an office/studio. Things were really coming along.

Autumn immediately began working as an unpaid intern for production companies. She was weary about doing this at first, stating how badly she felt about not being able to contribute financially for rent and things. We all agreed that she should pursue her career. Money would come when it did. I loved how LD, Jerome, and I all understood life and how trivial the small things are. We were like a little family. A single guy, a gay guy, and an unmarried couple living together. The most dysfunctional family ever, but family nonetheless.

So much had happened those past couple of years. My

home had gone from being couch cushions on a floor to now living in a beautiful house. In the beginning I was alone, living in the darkness of my soul, now loving people that I considered to be family surrounded me. I worked at a restaurant bar to start; now I was running the volleyball tournaments at a bar I loved to work at. I went from having customers to having lots of friends. I had gone from a broken heart to a man that was madly in love.

Love. In love. It felt odd to think those things again. I had been worried, during my dark time, that people might only find powerful love once in their lives. Thinking that I had failed with mine made me sad. Autumn had shown me that was wrong. I knew that anything was possible again. I knew I wanted to be with this woman. In every way.

It soon became apparent that I was not the only person to see how great Autumn was. The longer she spent with the production companies, the more they loved her. Soon she had gone from being an unpaid intern to being a paid production assistant. She had even been given a producer credit on one of the projects she had worked on. As she became more engrained in her work, she began pushing me back toward mine. I had pretty much just devoted myself to the bar and the house. Working hard to make good money, run volleyball, have fun, and make the house look nice. Every day I would tell Autumn how jealous I was that she was back on set, jealous that she was working toward her dream.

"Chase, I think you should pick yourself up, dust yourself off, and get back into it. You won't know until you try," she told me one day.

She was right. She had called me out on it. It was easy for me to complain and be jealous, yet I did nothing about it. A switch flipped within me and I set out the next day to restart my career.

I met with a few agents around Austin and found one that seemed to fit me. I got my headshots done again, set my accounts back up, and prepared for my auditions to come.

This, unfortunately, was to not be the case. I would get maybe one audition every 3-4 weeks. The few I did get were mostly for commercials. The few films that were filming in Austin were mostly cast in L.A. and flown here. I had been out of the business for years. Now that I was trying to get back in, I felt like I was being pushed up against more walls than ever before. It was like all of my training and hard work was for nothing. It broke my heart. Autumn was incredibly supportive. She pushed me hard to continue. Each day reminding me, "Walls aren't infinite. You just have to find a way around, over, or through them."

Always the optimist. Having her on my side was a great advantage.

Unfortunately, one day I finally reached my breaking point. I went to audition for a commercial for a local restaurant chain. It was the first audition that I had been called for in over a month. It was held in one of the meeting rooms at a local hotel. I remember thinking how different this was from the professional process in L.A. I walked in and saw that it was an unorganized cattle call of about 30 guys that all looked similar to me. It was a first come, first serve style audition. This wasn't even legal according to the laws of my union, SAG. What choice did I have? I auditioned and hated myself for it.

It wasn't that I felt that I was above doing a local commercial. It wasn't that I felt that I was better than the other actors there, like me, trying to further their career. It wasn't that I was confronted with something so unprofessional. It wasn't because it was my first audition in a month. It was the feeling that I wasn't supposed to be here. I had already worked my way past this spot on the chain.

I drove to the bar, parked, and walked in. It was just a little after three, so the bar had just opened. There were no customers yet and Jerome was putting his finishing touches on setting up. I walked behind the bar, grabbed my energy drink that I had hidden in the cooler, and gave Jerome a hug.

"How was your audition?" he asked casually.

"Shitty. Same silly nonsense. I don't like it," I responded. He knew I was upset. So he nodded and went about his business.

I went over to one of the tall tables in the corner of the bar. I sat there contemplating what I was doing. Trying to figure out if I was making a mistake.

"Autumn, I feel like nothing is happening. I feel like I'm going nowhere," I texted her.

"Then make something happen," came her quick reply.

Jerome had just walked up behind me with a bowl full of Chex Mix to nibble on when her text came though. He saw her words.

"I agree, Chase. Make something happen." He said to me as he dropped off the snacks and walked away.

For a moment I felt like arguing. For a moment I felt that twinge of self-pity and doubt that we all experience when we are facing a setback. I felt defensive and upset. I looked around me. I looked at my life, my surroundings, my circumstances, and it hit me. It hit me like a ton of bricks right in my face.

I launched up and ran to the office. I grabbed a stack of plain white paper from the printer, a few different pens, and ran back to the table. At the top of one of the pieces of paper I wrote: Metro, The Story Of Me.

I sat there staring at it for a second. It sounded good, but something wasn't quite right. For no reason, I scratched out the last three words. I looked again, Metro was left. I scratched it out as well, then rewrote it on a different piece of paper, and in all caps, "METRO."

The second my pen hit the paper it went wild. I started writing a summary for a short film. I figured if I could write something maybe a few minutes long, I could film it and put it on YouTube. At least get my face seen a little bit. I could never have known what sitting there at that table, in that bar, writing those words, was going to do for my life.

Within 30 minutes I had the summary. It was a short story about a guy who was straight, but who was always mistaken for being gay. The reason for this was that he was metrosexual. That is where the METRO came from. Metrosexual was a term made up to describe the straight men that lived in metropolitan areas. These men had as much concern for their hygiene, personal appearance, and fashion as gay men, but were in fact heterosexual. Metrosexual was born.

As a young man in school, I had experienced prejudice and was even beaten up for being mistaken as being gay. I used these experiences. I used the experiences from working in the bar, playing volleyball, living with a gay guy. I took these, put them together, and built a summary.

Once it was done I sat back and read what I had written. I smiled. There was something good in my hands. This was step one of a thousand that I needed to make. I took the next piece of paper and broke down the summary into an outline that could be made into a screenplay. This took me over an hour. The next time I looked up, the bar had 15 people in it, all drinking and having a good time. I hadn't even noticed them come in. I had been so lost in what I was doing.

My next step was to take the outline, and make a first draft of the screenplay. My pen went crazy as it streaked across the pages in a possessed form. Lines became letters, letters became words, and words became sentences. After three hours of anxiety fueled writing, I held 17 pages of something. I didn't know what it was at that time. All I knew was that it wasn't going to be able to just be a three minute sketch for YouTube, which is what my original thought had been before I started writing.

I went home that night a renewed man. I told Autumn of my idea and had her read the script.

"I'm so proud of you. I think this is a great start. If you would allow, I would be honored to work on the project with you," she beamed at me.

Yet again she was showing me why she was the right one for me. Not only did she support who I was as a person, but she also wanted to be a part of what it was that made me the happiest.

Night after night we sat down together. Editing, rewriting, changing, sculpting the script. Though I had done a good job of making the first draft, it was very rough. Over and over again we combed through it. We looked for moments to make the audience feel something. We removed parts that lagged or didn't seem pertinent.

One of the great things about making a film in Austin is that one could do it much cheaper. You wouldn't have to pay for the types of fees, permits, and taxes that Los Angeles charges to make films. Plus, the city hadn't been inundated with people overusing every business and person that the industry could find. I figured I might find a little bit more help from people. I had no idea how right I was.

One day I was working at It's About Time and I was so excited about the film that I told one of my regulars, Joey. Joey was an older gentleman, late 50's, who was a gay man from New York. He loved film and theater and absolutely loved the idea of my film.

"Chase, how much would I have to chip in to be a producer?" he asked.

"I hadn't thought about anything like that," I told him.

He responded, "It's something you're going to need to think about. You are going to need money because you're going to need a lot of things. I would love to be a part of this project. It is beautiful, special, and has heart to it."

I decided right then, money or not, that he'd be one of the executive producers.

Joey proved to be invaluable. I saw things from the creative side of the film. I saw the writing, the acting, and the shooting. He saw the business side. He saw to the money, the insurances, the permits. He would come into the bar each day I worked, as soon as we opened. He would sit there with his Grey Goose and soda, sipping slowly, working with me all day long, helping me learn the parts I didn't know. Soon we had a budget and a plan. First problem, I was going to need about $6,000 to make the film correctly.

Even though we knew we could find local actors and crew who would work for free (they would work for no pay, but accept credit in the film and copy instead. A deal which I myself have done countless times) there would still be a lot of expenses.

Joey suggested that we offer people incentives to invest in our little project. I went home that night, sat down with Autumn, and tried to figure out what to do. I came up with a system of incentives that increased per amount that was donated. To be honest, I doubted very much that anyone would want to invest.

The breakdown for incentives went as follows:

#1. $20: Get your name listed in the credits under the Thanks Section at the very end of the film.

#2. $50: Get your name listed in the Special Thanks Section which came earlier and had larger type so your name would be seen better.

#3 $100: Get your name listed as a Producer in large type. Also got a free copy of the DVD once completed.

#4 $500: Get your name listed as Executive Producer after Cast and Crew. Also got a free copy of the DVD. Also got a free ticket to the Premier of the Film.

#5 $1,000: Get all of #4, plus an autographed copy of the poster for the film, plus you got to ride in a limo to the premier with Chase.

I looked over this list dozens of times. I couldn't imagine people caring enough about my little film to want to put money into it. I knew it was a pipe dream to think that we would reach our goal of $6,000. To start it off, though, I went ahead and put the first thousand into it.

Joey loved my incentive set up and made me fliers to hand out. Over the next few weeks I passed out the fliers, describing the film as I did. Nothing happened at first. Then I got a letter in the mail from my mom. The letter was wrapped around something. It was a check for $100. The letter read,

"Dear Chase,
As you know, I don't have a lot of extra money to throw around. That being said, I believe in you and I believe in your project. I believe that you are worth putting money toward. I want to see my name in the credits. If you make this happen, I promise to be there for the premier.

With all my love,
Mom"

I burst into tears. Chalk another mark up in my book of moments that took my breath away. Not only was she the first to donate to the film, but she did so with so much heart.

Shortly after that letter, the money started pouring in. I had many $20 investments, many $100 investments, some $50, and even a couple of $500 investments. I couldn't believe the amount of people who wanted to support this project. Three of my regulars from the bar (Joey, Tommy, and Miles) all came in together one day to surprise me at work.

They had a gift bag with crepe paper sticking out of it and "Happy Birthday" emblazoned across the side.

"It's not my birthday guys," I said laughing.

"Shut up and open it!" Tommy responded.

I did. And I gasped. Inside were three separate checks. All three made out for $1,000 and each one had the word "METRO" written in the memo line. I was so taken aback I could barely breath.

Why had people been so accepting of my project? What had I done to affect so many? I felt so surreal. Me, Chase, just a simple guy, being shone kindness and generosity by all who surrounded me. I couldn't believe the outpouring of support. The most surprising of all, 85% of the donations had come from regulars of the bar. Each saying things like "We believe in you Chase" or "Hell yeah, I want to be a part of anything you work on." It was inspiring and humbling at the same time. I felt surges of anxiety and pride. Things were happening.

I totaled up the investments and opened a bank account in the movies name. The total I deposited was $9, 080 More than $3,000 over my initial budget. Over and over again I looked at the deposit slip receipt, watching it turn from a taught piece of paper to a crumpled mess. More than $9,000 donated for my little film. $9,000. I was dumbfounded. These people didn't owe me this. Autumn had pushed me to follow my heart. Now others were showing me their heart so I could follow mine.

The next step was to begin the pre-production of the film. That meant getting all permits, finding all of the locations, nailing down crew, and finding the right cast. I, of course, was going to play the lead. I wrote the film as a way of getting my face seen. Though the film had grown, I still intended for it to serve its original purpose.

I found a local company that would handle the insurance for the production of the film. Since we would be filming on a street, and because we would be renting expensive equipment, I was required to obtain a $1 million dollar production insurance. Just seeing that number blew my mind. Paying the insurance on it took up a large chunk of the budget, but it was worth it. I was now insured and ready to go.

I began working with SAG. I wanted to make a film that followed the SAG rules, but didn't have the budget to pay the actors. Then I stumbled on their ultra-low budget contract. It stated that I could find union actors to work on the film, so long as I paid them IF the film made money. If it made money I would be more than happy to pay them! Since I was a SAG union member, I had to work with SAG in order to be in my own film.

I had to find the right locations. I needed a gym, a club, a bar, a volleyball court, a bedroom, a bathroom, a kitchen, and a place with a good view of the city. Again I was confronted with generosity and kindness.

One of the regulars from the bar owned a house not too far away. He told me that he thought I might be able to use it to film a couple of the scenes. He showed me around and I fell in love. His house had a stylish bedroom, a very nice updated kitchen, a large bathroom, and a pool in the back yard. His house alone would make up three different locations and five different scenes in the film.

Then I had another regular tell me that he had connections at one of the dance clubs downtown. I met the owner and he was gracious enough to let us film. We discussed when I could film, what I would need, and what rules I would need to follow.

One of my regulars belonged to a private gym call Anytime Fitness. It wasn't the kind of gym that had a person at the front desk and hundreds of members. Instead, it was more expensive. That made it have fewer members and instead of checking in, when a person wanted to work out they had a key card that unlocked the door for them. This allowed them use of the facility whenever they chose and with less distraction. A place like this would be perfect for me. I spoke with the owner and, yet again, I was given such amazing response and kindness. As with the club, the hours I could film were a bit unusual, but it was perfect for what I needed.

I now had the gym, all of the house locations, and the club. But I needed a bar and a volleyball court. It's About Time had both of those. I sat down with the manager, Trevor, one day to talk about it. Admittedly, he was not keen on the idea at first. Truth be told, the owners of that bar worked him to death. And something like this meant he'd have to be there even longer. That being said, he knew me. He knew my work ethic. He knew I would make sure everything was taken care of. After a little bit of pleading, plus the promise to have the premier after party there, I had the rest of my locations.

Next up was to find a crew. I spoke with Autumn first. She punched me in the arm when I asked her if she would direct the film.

"Ouch, why are you hitting me with your ineffectual fists?" I laughed at her.

"I can't believe you asked me now, and so causally. You knew damn well I was going to. For you to ask me, cordially, ugh, I can't believe that." She laughed and hit me again.

I did already know she'd say yes. Together we were such a great team.

The rest of the crew came from a Craigslist ad that I ran. I was up front in admitting that there would be no pay, but that I would give them due credit, copies, and VIP seating at the premier. My email inbox was overwhelmed with people willing to be a part. I chose a couple of guys, James and Tristan, who claimed to be good filmmakers and a woman named Carrie who wanted to be the lead PA (Production Assistant).

I met the three of them at a coffee shop one day that

week. I wanted to get to know them in person before agreeing to take them on the crew. The two guys asked about my camera and sound. I told them that I planned to rent some at the film equipment rental store.

"We would like to change your mind. We actually have a very good Canon DSLR camera and the separate sound equipment needed to make a good quality film. We would only charge you the same price it would cost to rent them, plus we will work on your film with you," James said.

I was very unsure at first. I had no idea what at DSLR was, nor if these guys would be worth the risk. Luckily, they saw my worry.

"We have brought some footage to show you of the last job we worked on," said Tristan as he pulled out his Power-Book, opened up a file, and hit play.

I was completely blown away. The footage was incredible. The image was crisp. It even had night footage that gave so much more for the eye to see than a normal camera would.

"Did you really film this?" I said astounded.

"Yes, sir, we did and we could do the same for you," James responded with a smile.

I hired the two men right there on the spot and, after a brief interview, hired Carrie as well. Without those three, my project would not have become what it did.

I also found a make-up artist. She was one of those curvy girls that carried themselves really well. She looked like a pin up from the 1950's. A curvy pin up girl. Her portfolio was amazing. If she had been living in L.A. there would be no way that I could get her to work for free. She would easily have been worth $300 or more a day. Since we were in Austin, she was willing to do it for just the cost of make-up. Sold!

I asked my local hairstylist if they wanted to be a part of the film. Since there wouldn't be any crazy things needed with hair, someone just to make sure everyone looked their best would be fine. He was good at making me look my best.

We held the casting for the parts other than mine at the bar one morning before it opened. Though I knew it would have been more professional to do so in an office setting, I didn't want to waste any of the budget renting a space just to cast. Many actors, people just like myself, showed up to audition. In the end, I chose a few of the actors, but also a few people from the bar.

Cast, check. Crew, check. Budget, check. Locations, insurance, permits, check check check. I hired a catering company for both weekends of filming, you can hire actors and crew to work for free, but you should NEVER let them work without feeding them on set. That stuff makes me so angry. I knew that catering would eat a huge chunk of the budget, but that was what the budget was for: to make a movie the right way.

We were to begin filming the next Friday night. It was going to be a crazy couple of weeks. I would work full time at the bar from Monday through Friday, then film from Friday through Monday. Then repeat the process the following week. That first week felt like an eternity. I was distracted; constantly adding more and more to my lists of things to get done.

Finally, Friday morning arrived. I packed my bags full of everything I would need, including the film equipment that I had to rent. I got ready for work and headed in.

It's funny. That day would start the count-down clock to when I would leave Austin.

I was under no false impression of what I was doing. I was only making a short film. I knew that the finished product would be seventeen minutes or less. The way to estimate the length of a movie is to assume one minute of film for every page of script and it generally works out pretty close. That being said, it felt like I was the head of a major film studio, and this was to be the studios record breaking film.

The excitement inside of me was dying to explode out. I finished my shift at the bar at around 9:15 that night and by 9:30 I was driving to Anytime Fitness Gym for my first night of filming. We were allowed to film from 10 p.m. until 5 a.m. as the cleaning crew would be there to set up for the next day. That gave us a seven hour window to film an entire scene. To say that was optimistic is an understatement. However, it was what we had and I was grateful for it.

I pulled into the parking lot and saw 12 other cars. A smile crossed my face. All three of the crew were already there as well as Andy, a few other actors, Autumn, hair and makeup, and a few extras. An extra is someone in a scene that doesn't have lines. Though they don't speak they are integral as they make the scene more real. More tangible. The only thing that makes me sad about being an actor and the making of movies is that extras don't get their names in the movies they work on. Everyone else does. The person who puts bananas on the cart during the day does, but not the extras. It is sad. Not in my film though. They earned the right to watch their name scroll along the screen with everyone else.

I carried my bags up to the door while the crew started grabbing the rest of the equipment. I used the key card that the owner had given me, flipped on the lights, and got to work. The gym had a very nice, yet simple layout. Directly in front of the door to the left was the cardio area, which was about ten feet above the rest. To my right was the rope and ball fitness area. Down the steps in front of the cardio area was all of the free weights, machine weights, etc. Nothing was cluttered. Since it was a private gym it had very nice equipment that was laid out in a very clean and comfortable way.

We had about five shots to set up. There were three purposes to this scene. One was to show the playful friendship that Andy and I had. One was to have us speaking about volleyball. And one was to have two actors talking about us while we worked out. The idea was to have one trainer say how we were a gay couple and for the other, a female, to say she knew for sure that was untrue. I wanted the feeling of ambiguity to be a recurring theme throughout the film.

Within half an hour the crew was all ready for the first shot. We filmed a few takes. Then James and Tristan showed me what the footage looked like. It looked like I was filming with an extremely expensive camera. There was no grainy texture. It was beautiful footage. Autumn came over and watched as well. She was looking at it differently, though. She was seeing things through the directors eyes. She immediately set to work, moving around extras, filling in gaps, removing unnecessary set clutter. Back to shooting we went.

Catering showed up around 1 a.m. with a full taco bar set up. We paused for half an hour to relax and enjoy the meal. I really do believe in feeding a cast and crew, and feeding them well. I even worked better after eating, and it was my own project.

Once eating was finished, we got back to work and the night went on right up until 4:30 a.m. Autumn was such a good director that she kept us on schedule. By the time the cleaning crew showed up we had already removed all of the equipment and cleaned up any mess we had left. It was impressive watching this group work. To think that I had found a crew this professional willing to work for almost nothing. It was a powerful realization.

I gathered everyone and thanked them all for their amazing work. I gave them the following days shooting schedule and direction sheet. We now had time for a four-hour nap, then we would spend the next day filming the house scenes.

Autumn and I collapsed in bed, still wearing our clothes. It had been a long day, but worth it. It was all so surreal. I had been working so hard I hadn't taken a moment to realize that I was doing it. I was doing what I loved to do; acting. By the sweat and tears of my hands, Autumns' hands, and my friends' hands, I was able to bring life to my creation.

The alarm buzzed way too soon, awaking me from my deep slumber. I gathered all of the clothes and props I would need that day. Though we were filming in one house, it was three different locations and five different scenes. A lot of changes would be necessary. After a cup of coffee, Autumn's producing mind kicked in, which made her organizational skills into perfectionist style. She darted around the house, checking things off her list, making sure I didn't move or forget anything.

We drove over to the filming location for the day, the house that had been loaned to us. We were the first to arrive. It was 11 a.m. and we would be filming until at least midnight. I immediately began setting up the hair and make-up area in the garage. Then I went around the house with Autumn, organizing the different rooms to be what I would need.

Quickly, cast and crew began arriving. By 11:30 we had more than 20 people, all ready to go. The hair and make-up area became an assembly line of getting people ready. Stormy, the make-up artist, was incredible. The way she was able to sit someone down, get a sense of what they would be needed for, then bust them out in no time was something to behold. She even gave me a perfect black eye and cut up face, which I would need for my first scene to film.

Since we had kids for the shoot, we figured it would be the smartest to shoot their scenes first. At noon we were already filming in the backyard and pool area. The kids were all great. They were so willing to do what was needed, plus looking natural doing so. I stood out there, watching the crew work, filming them as they played. I remembered my own childhood and thought, *Had I been that carefree? Was I like that little boy; running around with reckless abandon?*

I wasn't needed in that scene, as one of the kids was actually playing me as a child, so while they were filming in the back yard I went to set up the second scene. We rehearsed with the actress to make sure she had an idea of what she would be doing, set up the lighting, laid down the camera tracks and were ready by the time they were done in the backyard. I thanked the kids and the parents for their hard work, sent them home, and then set about the next scene.

Autumn worked tirelessly. The way she organized every scene so that the next was ready by the time the previous was finished was incredible. She saved us hours in set up and break down time. She even had one of our friends as the clean-up crew. They would be the last to leave any part of the house. They had pictures of what the room looked like before we started filming, and they put it back exactly as it was. All of which had been Autumn's idea.

"We can't very well use this house for free all day, then expect them to clean up after us when we leave. That is just ludicrous," she had told the rest of the crew.

I had catering set up two meals that day, since we would be filming for over twelve hours. For lunch they made thick burgers with bacon and waffle fries. For late dinner we had pork steaks and mashed potatoes. I knew that every dollar I was giving them was well spent as the food was always so delicious. I always had a happy crew.

The day went on almost perfectly as scheduled. From the kitchen we went to the living room to film a couple of shots. Afterward we moved to the bathroom in the master bedroom. Then the bedroom itself, where we used a dolly on tracks and the jib arm for an amazing shot of me waking up from sleep.

The bathroom scene was the hardest of the day. It was the scene that required me to feel emotion. I had to get into the moment and feel what my character was feeling. It took longer than normal for me to get to that place. I realized the reason was because I was doing too many things. I was trying to help direct, produce, set up, and prepare all while also doing my acting. I took a deep breath, gave myself the time needed to be real, and then did my scene.

We finished all of our shooting around 11 p.m. Autumn had kept us so perfectly on schedule that we were done earlier than I expected, and with great footage. We had to be at the next location at 5am. That meant we had very little time to rest. We rushed home, deciding against unloading the vehicles, and passed out.

What felt like minutes later the alarm brought us back to consciousness. Let me tell you, making a movie is no easy feat. Especially on a tough time schedule. Three cups of coffee and some stretching later got us back on the road and driving to the next location.

It was Sunday morning. I had been given permission to film at the downtown club that day. The deal was that we could film in the club, with full run of anything we needed, but we would only be able to film from 5 a.m. until 11 a.m. The bar would open at noon and the bartenders would need that extra hour to set up. It was an extremely optimistic shooting schedule. With Autumn's help, though, I believed we could do it.

We arrived at 5:10 in the morning. The owner was there for us. He opened up, showed me where to find anything that I may need, then told me he would be in the office napping if we needed him.

The cast and crew were all there by 5:30. Well, what cast there was. This was where we encountered our first problem. We were filming in a club. Though we were filming at 5 in the morning, we needed it to look like it was late at night. We needed it to look like a fun, packed club. To get enough people to be in the movie I had run an ad in the local paper looking for extras for the scene. I had put ads on craigslist. And I had asked many of my friends. Of the 200 I was hoping would show up, I got 20. 20 of 200.

I was freaking out.

Yet again, Autumn was my saving grace. She pulled me aside and said, "Chase, I know how we can make this work. We won't do any wide shots. We get rid of the opening shot that shows the entire club. We focus on staying close up on you and Andy. If we do it right, the club will look packed."

I sent my thanks up to the clouds, then headed in to film a scene of Andy and I at the bar taking shots. Since it was inside the club, it required a lot more lighting. This took much more time to set up, but also gave a chance for the caterers to get their food prepared.

I felt as if everything was moving around me at hyper speeds. Here I was, standing in the middle of a bar lit with movie lighting. I was surrounded by people all using the sounds I loved to hear; film jargon. "Quiet on set" someone quipped. "Extras to places" I heard. "Back to one" was repeated. "Cut" and "Action". I was in heaven. Autumn by my side, Peanut butter pancake in my mouth, making a movie. This was everything I wanted.

One by one we knocked the shots down. By 10 a.m. we only had one shot left, the dancing scene. The dancing scene would be our most tricky scene. We had a DJ set up, a pole for dancing, two go-go girls, and a very big dance floor to make look busy. Autumn set to work. She turned the house lights all down very low, turned all the dancing/disco lights on high, and started positioning the extras. Within minutes she had it designed. Then she had the cameraman walking around the dance floor. Wherever he walked she would send extras to fill in spots and spaces. He even got great footage of the DJ and the go-go girls. While all of this was happening, I was doing what I loved to do; act.

11 a.m. came and we wrapped for the day. I was so grateful to everyone for their hard work that I bought a round of drinks at the bar. The owner was so happy with how we had taken care of everything that he bought a second round. We were all cheering and having a blast, yet I was too exhausted to keep partying with everyone. So, I excused myself and told the crew that I would see them on Friday night.

We went home, crawled into bed, and slept until the following morning. A glorious sleep it was. She had to work at 9 a.m., but I didn't have to be at work until 1 p.m.. So I went to the gym, then spent a little bit of time going over the footage from the weekend.

The footage was unbelievable. Every shot was so crisp. The actors were all in focus when they were supposed to be. Each scene looked full of life. The extras all moving and entwining with each other in the scenes with lots of people, adding texture to the background. Each take looked seamless, and I knew why. Autumn. So many times already that weekend it was Autumn who was coming through for me. Autumn who was supporting me. Autumn who was working like crazy for me.

I worked the next five days straight. Each day I would go in at 1pm to bartend, but would spend all day talking and having fun, occasionally serving a drink or two. The patrons of the bar were just as excited about the film as I was, so they asked tons of questions and celebrated each bit of good news. Every one of them wanted to be a part of it in some way. I was so blessed to have found that hole in the wall bar. So blessed.

The week passed quickly and soon Friday was upon us again. The time we had to film were going to make us work like crazy. We didn't mind. You never mind working when you love what you do.

I finished work at 9 p.m., but couldn't start filming until

2 a.m.. Our next shoot was at the bar. We were going to film the volleyball tournament portion of the film on the sand volleyball court of the bar. The benefit of doing this meant we wouldn't have tons of people interrupting us or making noise at a public place. The drawback was that we would have to film at night.

I had all of the extras, which were all the volleyball players from the tournaments we had done at the bar, the cast, and the crew all meet at the bar at 1:30. I bought a round of shots for everyone, just to get the energy up. I owed these people something as they were staying at a bar after close until the sun came up. And stay they did.

By 2 a.m. we already had the first shot set up and ready to go. Autumn had set the filmmakers up on the roof of the bar, overlooking the volleyball court. This would give a great wide-angle shot to cut back and forth to. Once the patrons of the bar who weren't staying in the movie were gone, things got serious.

The number of people willing to work until sunrise blew me away that night. We had nine crewmembers, six cast with lines, 20 extras for volleyball players, and another 12 extras to hang out on the sidelines as spectators for the shots. Almost 50 people, for my little film. It brought tears to my eyes looking at all that was happening.

At 2:15 we started filming the first shot. By three we were off the roof and filming close ups of the action shots. By four we were doing the intricate shots, including the one that gave me the black eye that we had filmed the previous week. Darkness receded to light as we were getting the last of the pick-up shots of the announcer, crowd excitement, and scoreboard. Almost as if on cue, the night gave way to light just as we got the last one. We couldn't film any more after that because those shots wouldn't have matched the night shots. Everything had worked out wonderfully.

I fed the extras a little bit more, then bid them all farewell. The crew and I, however, had only just begun. We moved all of the film equipment into the bar to set up for the next scene. We had until 1 pm, to get this bar shot. I began to get worried because it was already 6 a.m. by the time we were set up, but not a lot of cast had arrived. That included the band that was supposed to be in the bar playing. I sent a quick text out, reminding them, but knew if they were sleeping, the text would not do enough.

My fears soon subsided as cars began filling the parking lot. By 6:30 the entire cast was there, the band, and almost all of the extras. Since it was a scene in It's About Time, I didn't need a lot of extras. Just a few to play pool and be scattered here and there. Hair and make-up did their amazing work, Autumn took charge, and things got underway.

We did the shots of the band first. We had them play their song four times in a row so we could get lots of different shots of them. Within thirty minutes they were already done and on their way home.

Then we went around filming the different shots in the bar. These took longer as we had to reset the lighting for each new shot. Even with the slow-down, we were still done over an hour early thanks to the shot-list and impeccable planning of Autumn. I wanted to stay around and celebrate another great shooting day with everyone, but I was wiped out. I had been up for almost 30 hours. In that time I had worked a full shift at the bar, organized and filmed an entire scene, let those people go then organized and filmed another scene. That was all I had in me. By the look on Autumns face, I could tell that she was done too.

We headed home, grabbed a much needed shower, then took a nap on the couch with *Pawn Stars* on the TV. Autumn curled up with me after a bit and passed out laying on my shoulder. We slept from Saturday afternoon all the way to Sunday morning. It was one of the most restful sleeps I had ever had. Then it was time to get back to work.

Sunday was our last day of filming. We were grateful to get to sleep in, but were eager to meet up with Andy, James, Tristan, and Storm. This last bit of filming was all of the exterior shots and extra pick up shots. We drove around town with a camera strapped to the hood of my Jeep. Then we drove around with a camera strapped to the hood of the car. Then we did shots from far away watching me drive this way and that. Then we got shots of Andy and I entering the gym, the club, and the bar.

It was about 10 p.m. when we were finishing up. We were parked in an old warehouse parking lot unhooking the camera from the hood of the car and going over footage. The parking lot was right up against the freeway in downtown Austin. I noticed, out of the corner of my eye, a good place to go pee. At the far edge of the parking lot was what looked like a wooded area. I had needed to go for a few hours and it was becoming a necessity. I jogged over to the wooded area to find my spot.

Once I got past the first set of trees I realized it was a hill. I thought to myself, *Why not?* Then traipsed my way to the top. It wasn't too tall and I was at the crest within five minutes. On the left of me were some high end condos. I stood there looking at them, wondering how much they must have cost sitting up on that hill, then I looked to my right.

If I hadn't of held my pee, I wouldn't of had the need to pee. If I didn't have the need to pee, I wouldn't have gone to the woods. If I didn't go to the woods, I wouldn't have climbed the hill. And if I didn't climb the hill, I wouldn't have seen what lay to my right.

I was standing near the edge of a low cliff. I was maybe 50 feet up in the air, but those 50 feet were enough to give one of the most beautiful views of downtown Austin. I mean, it was unbelievable what I had stumbled on. My mouth was hanging open while I stood there, taking it all in. I had wanted to find a shot to use to connect parts of the film. This view, this amazing view, was perfect. I couldn't believe I had stumbled on it.

My phone went off. I looked at it. "Where are you?" shown across my screen in a text. It was Autumn.

"You aren't going to f'n believe this when I tell you!" was my hasty response. Then I tore off down the hill to go get everyone. I wanted that shot. No, I needed that shot.

We packed everything in the car that we wouldn't need, then took the Jeep up into the woods. I admit to a bit of satisfaction at the fact that I got to take the Jeep off-road in the middle of filming my movie. She climbed the hill effortlessly. Soon we were at the top and were setting up the shot. We filmed some of me driving the Jeep to and from the spot, then some of me in the spot, acting. All the while with the nighttime back drop of the colorful city of Austin. Simply amazing.

As quickly as it had begun, it was over. The months of planning. The fundraising. The casting and hair pulling. It was done. I had successfully filmed my first ultra-low budget independent short film.

Autumn and I went home, grabbed our blankets and pillows, curled up on the patio chairs, and passed out under the stars holding each other, grateful that it was done being filmed. Sure, we still had to edit it. Sure, we were far from a completed product.. Sure, it was just a short film. However, we had accomplished so much. This new found feeling of motivation burned inside of me like a silent driving force. I felt renewed of my life purpose.

Next up was editing. How hard could that be?

20

Somewhere, in a dark cubicle huddled in the corner of an office space on a cold winters night, someone invented Final Cut. I don't have proof of these circumstances, but only someone in that dark of an environment could have invented something so sinister.

Final Cut is a program that allows someone to edit digital footage. In the right hands it is an incredible tool. Final Cut gives you the ability to cut your footage, add your audio, edit the video, and so much more. You can change colors. You can change the speed, giving it the slow motion effect or speed it up. You can add transitions, graphics, letters, you name it. It truly is an amazing program… in the right hands.

When Final Cut is in the wrong hands, it acts as though it was invented by Satan himself sent to Earth only to temp one into going mad. I should preface this with the fact that I had never had any training to use this program. I'm a smart guy. I just figured I could learn it on my own. I figured wrong.

In truth, Final Cut is just a really intricate software program written so that the person using it could do everything they needed to edit a film. This was one of the programs the professionals that work on big budget films even used, the other primary one is AVID. Most that use it either go to classes to learn or they work under professionals to get enough experience to use it. I did neither. I opened the program and dove in headfirst.

I YouTubed a lot of the questions I had at first. That seemed to work. I learned how to import the footage and file it away. I learned how to add the sound that was filmed separately and how to connect it to the video correctly. I learned quickly that I was a bad editor.

After about four weeks of sitting at my computer every minute that I wasn't at work, I became very aggravated. I felt like I was being cruelly punished for wanting to do it myself. I had wanted to prove that I could make it work. Autumn had offered to help, but her experience was barely more than mine. I was at a loss. Every time I moved video the program told me to "render" it. Rendering was basically the Final Cut program making the video that I had edited into a code it could continue to work with. Rendering took hours to do sometimes. It was obvious I was doing something wrong and I couldn't figure out how to fix it.

I finally broke down and found someone to help me. His name was Mark and he was willing to train Autumn how to edit. This would allow me to make pretty good use of the budget while also getting Autumn the training she would need to do it herself. I figured having her learn was better than me since I knew I would never, ever, want to edit another project as long as I lived.

The three of us sat down one night when they said they were done, and watched it on my big screen. We had a final product and I was impressed. When it was over I felt myself wishing there was more to see. I realized that I was feeling compelled to learn more about the story, which is exactly what a movie is supposed to do. I had done it. I had made a product worth watching. I had received a lot of invaluable help along the way to make it happen and now it was finished.

I felt a wave of relief wash over me. So much stress. So much planning. So many days, hours, minutes spent working on something. What made it most rewarding, though, was that I was working for me. It was my project. Its success and failures were directly related to what I had done. That is what made me the most proud. I suppose it's what a father must feel, watching his son play a great game of football.

I knew what my next two moves were. The first, and foremost, was to set up the premier of the film. The premier was mostly for the cast, crew, and investors who had helped make the film a possibility. Without them it would just have been me standing in front of a camera on a tripod. Instead I was given a fourteen-minute movie to share with the world. The second was to start submitting *METRO* to film festivals. My main objective was to get my face seen, but the idea of selling the film and making money was a good reason as well. Besides, I owed a lot of friends that invested in the film. They knew they were only going to make money if the film did, so I wanted to try my hardest to make it work for them.

The first part of setting up the premier was to find the right venue. I knew that I would need at least 100 seats. That would give enough seats for the cast, crew, and investors that I owed a seat to. It also would allow them to each bring someone with them. I preferred for it to be a midday showing so that we could all go back to the bar for a fun after party, without it being too late.

The showing of a film to a cast and crew is very important. These people gave their time to be a part of something special. They donated time and money because they believed in something. They deserved to see what they helped make. They deserve to be there the first time it their project is shown on the big screen. I was honored to be the one to help make that happen.

Figuring out how to submit for film festivals seemed like a daunting feat. We all hear of the big ones, Cannes and Sundance, but there are hundreds more. At first, I got a little overwhelmed. I bought a book that listed them all. I started from the beginning, trying to learn about them. Trying to understand how to submit, where to submit, what it cost, what was the best way to go. It just wasn't organized enough. Then, by a stroke of luck, I stumbled across an incredible website: withoutabox.com.

Withoutabox.com is a website that lists all film festivals in the world. Not only does it list them, but it allows you to narrow your search for the right festival for your film, and gives you the option to submit right from the website. I was blown away. I had spent so many hours researching through the book and on the internet. Now, in front of me, was a way to be more focused on exactly what it was that I needed. I began perusing over the site and realized something very quickly. I needed to be very selective in my submissions.

Each film festival charges a fee for each film that is submitted to it. Paying the fee and submitting does not guarantee that the film will be chosen to play. A great example of this is Cannes. They get more than 5,000 submissions, but show less than 100 films.

I spoke to many theaters in the Austin area about showing my premier at their location. Each had benefits and drawbacks. One theater was beautiful, had over 1,000 seats, and was stadium seating. The problem is I knew there was no way I would fill 1,000 seats, but I had to rent the whole thing. It was the most expensive of all the theaters I looked at. Another one I looked at was great, but didn't have a way to project DVD's, only film. It was definitely not in the budget to spend a few thousand dollars to do a digital to film transfer.

The fifth theater I looked at I was very unsure of to start with. It was in a complex. The complex had a bowling alley, skating rink, and the theater all housed in the same building. This worried me because I was unsure if there would be enough parking for the people who came to watch the film if the complex also had the bowling alley and skating rink going at the same time. The theater itself was pretty perfect. It had 200 seats, a very nice screen, a good sound system, the ability to play DVD's, and they had a microphone set up so that I could speak during the premier.

As I was going through the Festivals on withoutabox. com I found one that had to have been serendipitous. It was too much of a coincidence. I filled out the form, paid the fee, and submitted to The Austin Gay and Lesbian Film Festival or AGLFF for short. I had stumbled on a Festival that was not only in Austin, but the films had to have a gay theme, and the festival was only three months away. I couldn't believe it.

I knew there was no guarantee that my little film would be chosen, but I also knew it was my best chance. Four days after submitting, I received a phone call from a gentleman named Isaac.

"I'm looking for the Director of *METRO*," came his voice over the phone. Autumn was technically the director, but I knew he meant whoever was in charge of it.

"That is me, sir. How may I help you?" I responded.

"We have viewed your film and are proud to announce that you are being accepted into the short film competition of the Austin Gay and Lesbian Film Festival!" answered the voice on the phone.

I was speechless.

"I'll take no response to mean that you're excited as well," he laughed.

"Yes, sir," I stammered back, "I'm very excited. I don't know what to say."

"Just say that you will go over your film another time, work on any rough edges, and submit it again for us. We think you have a great product and it could be even better if looked at with fresh eyes. Since you're local, we really want your film to have that extra boost," he said.

I hadn't even thought about what it could mean for the festival to have a local film do well. I had only thought about it from my point of view. I now understood why I had received a personal phone call versus just an email.

I sat down with Charmaine, the lady who ran the complex that I was considering doing the premier at. The price was within budget, the amount of seating was great, the theater itself was nice, but I was worried about them having other events going on at the same time.

"That is a good point. Hmmm, let me think for a second," she said, while going over her calendar.

She looked over a few things, took a little bit of time, then said, "Okay, okay, this could work." She pointed at a Sunday about a month away.

"If you can have your premier on this Sunday, at 4 p.m. and be done by 6 p.m., I can make sure we don't book anything else that day until after you're finished. That will give you the entire parking lot and space for your premier. Will that work?" she asked.

It was exactly what I wanted. The right time. The right space. I was overjoyed when I said, "Yes. Very much yes. Thank you!"

The premier was booked.

I met with Isaac the following week to hand deliver the final copy of the film. Autumn, Mark, and I had combed through it frame by frame fixing any sound issues, making smoother transitions, and chopped out any parts that seemed to drag. The final product came out at twelve minutes in length. I stood with Isaac while he watched it on his laptop. Once it finished he turned to me and said, "Well done. Very well done."

My heart filled with pride as he said those words.

"Thank you so much for the kind words. I actually have a premier for the film in a couple of weeks. Will it be okay to announce its acceptance at that time?" I asked, hoping he would allow me to do so.

He smiled and said, "I'll do you one better. If you would like, I will come to the premier and personally announce it. That will allow me to get the word out not only about your film, but also of the great festival we have this year."

I couldn't believe it. I was willing to come and be the one to say that *METRO* had been accepted. Words couldn't describe how my heart was feeling.

I picked mom up from the airport the night before the premier. She, Autumn, and I stayed up almost all night making premier packets for everyone that came. The packet included a postcard sized picture of the film poster, a lanyard for them to wear around their neck, a questionnaire about their opinion of the film, a thank you letter from me, and information about the festival, but not the announcement that we had made it, just general info. We wanted everyone that came to remember his or her experience as much as I was going to.

We woke up bright and early that morning. Lil' Den had agreed to run to the theater early and set up. I gave him the packets and an idea of what I'd like to have done. Mom, Autumn and I all ate a hearty breakfast, got ready, then hopped in the limo. We headed to It's About Time to pick up the three guys that had been the biggest contributors, then we were headed to the premier. It was exciting being in that limo. The air was mixed with that of excitement, nervousness, and an overwhelming sense of pride.

We pulled onto the street where the theater complex was held. From afar I saw the first thing my made my heart explode with joy. The complex had a large marquee outside. The marquee was about 30 feet tall and blue. The digital portion of the sign that usually said the daily promotions was flashing *METRO* over and over again in giant red letters. Even from half a mile away I could clearly ready what it was saying.

The driver followed that sign and pulled into the parking lot. As we turned in I noticed two things immediately. The first, which I loved, has a full size movie poster hung in one of the light-up poster frames on the side of the building. The large bulbs that fully encircled it were dancing in rhythm, causing your eye to stare directly at *METRO*'s poster; of my face.

The second, which I did not like, was the fact that there was a line of people coming from inside the building, snaking out the front door, and wrapping around the corner. I felt hurt in my heart. I was hurt that Charmaine would rent that complex out to other groups when she had promised me she wouldn't. I was embarrassed that the people coming to see *METRO* would see this as a disorganized event. All of this made me upset.

The limo pulled up to the front door. I helped everyone out, then hastily headed to the office to ask Charmaine what was going on.

She popped her head out and said, "Hi there, Chase! Are you excited?"

She was such a sweet person, which made me immediately pull back on how upset I was. Calmly I said, "Charmaine, you promised me today would only be for my event, but there are so many people here. What happened?"

She looked at me for a second, confusion in her eyes, then finally said, "Chase, those are your people!"

It took a second for those words to fully register. *My People?* I thought to myself. I had been so hasty to come talk to her that I hadn't paid attention to who was in line. I looked out of the office and saw dozens of faces I recognized, all chatting with ones I didn't. Everyone was so well dressed and happy. I then realized that we were definitely going to have a problem: there were more than 200 people in that line!

I had chosen this theater because I had assumed 200 seats would be more than enough, but it was apparent that we had more like 350 people all waiting to get in. Charmaine looked at my worried face and said, "We already have guys grabbing folding chairs from the storage shed. We will get 'em all in there."

I thanked her and left her to make sure everything ran smoothly.

The line of people went all the up to the double doors that led to the theater. To the side of the doors was a six foot tall poster of my acting headshot. It had *METRO* emblazoned across the top. I laughed when I saw it.

Lil' Den was standing there with a camera. He told me that he wanted a picture of every group as they walked in. He had made this his photo op. Such cool gesture that and a fun way to make a memory. I snuck through the doors to make sure the theater was set up well.

On my way in I bumped into the projectionist, Max. He told me to just speak into the microphone anything that I needed and he would take care of it. I thanked him and snuck into the theater itself. They had hung streamers along the walls as well as cutouts of film cameras, clackers, and film reels. The chairs that would be considered the best seats had been roped off for cast, crew, VIPS, and their families. At the front, right in front of the screen, was a table with awards that I had given to Lil' Den to set up. Autumn was already there, organizing and fixing things. She had the microphone set up. She gave me a look, telling me that everything was going to be perfect.

Autumn. My angel, sent here from Heaven to save me. She really had. She had been the one to push me back to following my dreams. She had been the one there, night after night, putting in as many hours on the project as I did. She had been my partner as much as my lover. I felt that feeling, deep down inside, that told me I would never forget what she had done for me. A feeling that said, "Chase, this girl is something special."

As I headed back out the door to greet everyone I saw the crew bringing in stacks of folding chairs. They were going to line the aisles, add a row up front, in back, and in front of the screen. We were going to have a full house.

Once at the front, we opened the doors and started letting people inside. I shook everyone's hands and took pictures with those who wanted. I saw the entire cast who had acted in the film. I saw all of the crew who had made it work. I met families. I spoke to those who had put money toward it. The one thing everyone was saying, they were so proud to be a part of something special.

Finally everyone was in. We had every seat full plus about 20 people standing in the back. I took my place up front, grabbed the microphone, and began to speak.

"Thank you all so much for being a part of today. Many of you were in the film. Many of you worked on the film. And many more of you donated money to help make this film possible. Some of you, like my mom, are here to support your family or friends that were a part of something special. There are even some that I spoke to outside that are here purely to support an Austin production. No matter the reason, thank you. As you can tell by our overflowing capacity, I had no idea how many people were so interested in being a part of this," I began.

"This whole thing started out because of my frustration at not getting auditions. From that little start it has grown into something incredible. The final product is a twelve-minute short film. We are going to show that first. Then, I will speak to you again. Then, we will show a 20-minute version of the film. The reason the final product is twelve minutes is because we wanted to keep in very succinct for submitting for festivals. We cut out any parts that may have been good, but seemed to slow down the pacing of the film. However we want everyone to see him or herself, so we decided to show the long version as well. After that, I will speak again. Then we will show ten minutes of outtakes. Afterward, we will all head to It's About Time for the after party."

I explained the packages and the questionnaire for the film, then I told the projectionist to start the short film. For the next twelve minutes I feel my heart racing as I bounce back and forth from watching the movie to watching the crowd as they watched the movie. I was scared they wouldn't like it, but seeing them all react to moments made me feel better. I was overwhelmed with a feeling of accomplishment as it finished.

METRO showed in giant white letters across the screen and the credits began to play. The crowd erupted into applause, getting on their feet to show me they had enjoyed it. It had only been 12 minutes long, but those 12 minutes told a real story. A story that the crowd had enjoyed. I let the credits roll all the way to the end. Every person whose name was in the film deserved to see it play on the screen. So many had cried or were crying. So many had been affected.

I brought up Isaac from the festival. He announced the films admittance into the competition, which caused the crowd to cheer even harder. Then I showed the longer version of the film, allowing those whose parts had been cut from the original to see themselves. Afterward I brought up the cast and crew. I handed out awards, my favorite was the trophy to the caterer for best peanut butter pancakes ever, and I answered questions from the audience.

"What was your favorite part of making the film?" an older gentleman in the back asked. "My favorite part was shooting up on the hill with Austin as the backdrop. I love that scene and how it turned out," I answered.

"What was the hardest part of making the movie?" asked Brian, a guy who had been in classes with me.

"That is a tie between editing the film and shooting the emotional scene. I have now realized, after those two things, that I would much prefer to just stay in front of the camera. I'll let Autumn and those like her do the hard work behind the scenes," I laughed.

Next up was my mom, "So, when are you going back?"

I responded, "I think we are heading to the bar right after this."

She laughed, "No, silly. When are you going back to Hollywood? I haven't seen you smile the way you did today since you were a little boy, telling me you were going to be an actor. So, when are you going back?"

Momma knew me too well. Something had clicked that day. I just shook my head and shrugged my shoulders. I didn't know the answer. I felt things, different things, than I had in a while.

I answered a few more questions, showed the outtakes, then told everyone to meet us at the bar. Once they had all filed out I sat down in the empty theater to breathe.

I breathed a sigh of relief because it was over and I could relax. I breathed a breath of pride over how well it had done. I breathed for what this little film had just done for my life. I felt rejuvenated. I was ready for whatever came next.

Autumn and I went to the party for a while, but eventually snuck out and went home to sleep. It had been the most rewarding day of my life. If I died that night I would have died knowing I did what I had always dreamt of doing. I was not rich, I was not famous, and none of that mattered. What mattered was that I stood in front of a crowd and spoke while my face was on the big screen. I had my mom in the audience. I had the support of the woman I loved. I no longer had to feel like my passion was dumb and just a phase. I could now feel like I was doing what I was meant to do.

Sure, I wanted to do more of that. I wanted to do it over and over again. The bug had definitely bitten me, but I allowed myself to savor that exact moment. Next up was the festival. I was more nervous than excited about it.

METRO was included in a short film competition of other films, which I watched from beginning to end. Some of them were very good, some needed a lot of work, but I believed that METRO was the best.

In fact, when I left the theater at the festival, a woman walked up to me and told me she recognized me from the film. She also told me that METRO was the best one and that she was sure it would win. This boost of confidence made me feel really good.

It would be short lived though. I went to the closing ceremonies half expecting to hear its name called as the winner. It was not. Instead METRO took second place in the short film competition. It was beat be a comedy that was actually pretty well done. For a moment I sat there feeling sadness. I was so sure it was going to win. I believed in it. For a moment I felt a setback.

For a moment I felt the darkness of doubt creep up. Doubt in myself, doubt in my abilities, doubt in my life's path. Then a smile crossed my face. It had won. I had WON. I was exactly where I was supposed to be, sitting in a theater hoping that my name gets called. Even though I hadn't won first place, I had competed and I had done well. Time to make some decisions.

"If this is it...." she started, but paused to consider her words more carefully, "If this is it, if this is all we will ever have, it's enough. It's enough for me, Chase. The way you love me, the way you hold me, the way you show me the kind of a man you're ... it's enough."

We were laying in our closet floor, candlelight dancing off of the clothes, holding each other tightly. For some reason that night I felt like holding her. Not just holding her like I always did. Rather, I wanted to show her, with my arms, how I felt. I'm not sure how it happened, but for some reason I had chosen to make a pallet of covers in the closet floor. There was barely enough room for both of us to lay next to each other there in the darkness, but I suppose that may have been part of the reason. A way to bring her closer to me, subconsciously.

This woman, this incredible woman, had just done more for me than anyone else had in my life. She had worked, tirelessly, on a film that was meant for me. She had donated her time, her money, her sleep so that I would have a project to be proud of. Every minute of each day she was there next to me, pushing me to follow my passion, supporting me in my quest for meaning in my life.

In the beginning, thinking about being engaged again and even marriage really scared me. The worry of being hurt again. How I would feel if it didn't work out. Then, I would look into those eyes of hers, hear her sweet voice, and I knew it would all be okay. I believed, deep in my heart, that even if she and I didn't work out, that we would be okay. We would be friends for the rest of our lives, and possibly future lives, no matter what.

She had shown me, both through her words and her actions, that she was a good person. She made me feel a love that is true. True love. The meaning of being "In-love", when two people feel equally as strongly for one another; both hearts meeting in the middle. I was ready for what came next. Though I felt a twinge of that insecurity from the pain of before, I knew what was the right thing to do. It was time to talk to Momma.

She had made the drive down from Missouri to Austin for Thanksgiving that year.

Sitting out in the backyard of the house, she and I were chatting about many things.

"Mom, I think I might propose to Autumn," I paused looking at her, then added, "I'm worried that I'll fail again."

She took a moment, searching for the right thing to say, "Chase, you know I always support you no matter what. I have to say something this time, though. Autumn is real. She is the kind of girl you marry, hang on to, respect, and give your all to 'til the end of time."

"I guess I'm scared," was all that I could respond with.

"I know, baby boy. You had your heart hurt pretty badly, but someone like Autumn is rare. You are the luckiest man I know. I wish I could find your brother a woman like her. If you're asking for my blessing, the answer is a resounding yes. I'd kill you if you didn't marry her. I know I told you to marry Jennifer too. I feel bad about that, but this is different. I can see the kind of woman Autumn is. She cares about you Chase. She will be there for you, raise a family with you, and I believe she will never hurt you. In that same token, don't you ever hurt her either," she said.

It was weird having these feelings again. There were moments when I doubted myself. Moments when I was unsure if I should jump in again, head first, like I had before. Putting my heart in someone else's hand and trusting them to keep it safe. Then, I would lay there in bed, watching her sleep. Or I would think of how supportive she had been or I would look in her eyes. Any of these things brought me back to the reality that she wasn't Jennifer. She wouldn't treat me that way. The comment that I kept hearing from everyone I asked was that "She isn't Jennifer, Chase. She won't hurt you the way Jennifer did." I heard these over and over. It made me feel good. I loved that others saw Autumn the same way I did.

I took a drive one day up to Mount Bonnell. I hadn't been there in months, but I knew that day was a perfect day to go. I parked, walked those familiar stairs to the top, winded my way down to my favorite spot, then crawled out on the ledge. I felt tears fill my eyes. Tears releasing themselves as my gratefulness exploded out of me. I had found love again. I had found a reason to exist. Tears in my eyes, I gazed out over Lake Austin wondering to myself. Wondering about the proposal.

Where and how should I propose? I had done all of this before and I couldn't let the one that failed be better than the one that was meant to be. Yet, I knew Autumn wasn't like Jennifer. Material things, fancy things, trivial things weren't what was important to her. Effort was. Me showing her my love would mean more to her than the dollar signs of how much things cost.

The ring was going to be a tough one. I still had Jennifer's ring locked away in my safe. I knew that I couldn't keep that thing around. I believed in my heart that it held negative karma, and I wanted it gone. I thought about my options. I thought about giving away. I thought about selling it on eBay. I even considered bringing it up there with me, high above the world, and chucking it out as far as my arm could throw. The truth was, I needed to be smart. I needed to sell it so I would have more money for the new ring.

I went home and listed it on Craigslist. I had paid $12,000 for it and had taken three years to pay it off. After two days of nothing, I finally got an offer. A guy offered me $1,500. It broke my heart knowing how much I had spent on it, how much sweat and tears came from that ring. The economy had gotten so bad, used jewelry just had no market. I could have waited longer and tried for more money, but I accepted it.

The guy came by the next day to pay for it. He was a young guy, early 20's, and asked me why I had accepted such a low offer. I told him that I was going to be engaged again, and that I couldn't have my ex's ring in the same house as my current girls.

He was extremely grateful. He was madly in love with his girl. He stood there, for thirty minutes, detailing to me why she was so great. What it was about her that made her different than the others. I understood what he was saying, as I was feeling it too. He told me that he didn't have a lot of money and didn't think he would be able to give her the ring that she deserved. Then he saw mine on Craigslist. He knew that the ring was way out of his league, his words, not mine, but he threw out a number anyway. He couldn't believe that I accepted.

I tell you this right now. I don't care if someone would have walked up and offered me $8,000 right then, I would have told them no. When you can see that a man feels so much for his woman, maybe even the way you feel about yours, how could you not want to help him succeed in giving her the best that is possible? I'm not saying a $12,000 ring is the best ring on the planet. Of course not. It was the best that was possible for me to get Jennifer, and now that same ring was the best for him to give to his girl. I only hoped that the black karma from the ring would be gone since it was changing hands. This young couple deserved a shot at a long life of happiness.

I took that $1,500 and added it to some other money I had saved up for a down payment on a new ring. I didn't want to do the same thing as I had with Jennifer. I wanted this to be more special for Autumn, but also get her a better ring. My heart felt that the better girl deserved better things. It wasn't about the cost of it, it was about the thought of what she deserved. I thought long and hard about that. It was another one of those moments when the universe and fate have a way of jumping up and helping you out.

About that same time a friend of mine from L.A., Harry, was on a business trip to Austin. We hung out one night, catching up on all that I had missed while being gone. He was in the precious metals business as well as being really smart about real estate investments. I mentioned Autumn and my plans to propose.

He looked at me cross and said, "Chase, did you totally forget who I am?" Then, he laughed.

I looked at him confused and said nothing.

"Brother, I deal in precious metals. I have connections on jewelry across the entire U.S. I know the exact person you should contact," he said.

He set me up with a jeweler from Los Angeles. The jeweler was actually a wholesale jeweler with an office eight stories above the jewelry district in downtown L.A. Everyday he sent out hundreds of thousands of dollars in jewelry. When I told him my story of what I had gone through, he was more than willing to help.

"As Harry probably told you, I don't usually work with single items like this. I deal in bulk. That being said, I like you. I like your story you and I would like to design you a ring from scratch. Build it to be exactly what you would like," he said earnestly.

This sounded amazing, but, it also sounded very expensive.

"I would love that, but I'm assuming that you don't finance since you're a wholesaler. So, what would that cost me?" I asked in a worried tone. I would have loved to have Autumn a ring built that was a one of a kind, but I wasn't rich.

"Harry has been a really good customer for a long time, and he told me to take care of you. So, I'm going to build you a ring that would normally retail for over $20,000... buuuut... I will do it for $7,500. Yes, that would have to be cash. Can you make that happen?" he asked.

I already had $6,000 saved up. So that was incredible.

"YES!" I exclaimed. A little embarrassed, I added, "Yes, I would be grateful."

He laughed at my exuberance and said, "I'm glad to hear your excitement. I rarely actually get to see or hear the customers feedback to the jewelry that we make. It's refreshing. Call me tomorrow with details and we will get started on it."

I couldn't believe it. If I hadn't of run into Harry I

wouldn't have gotten this hook up. Yet again, I was smiled down upon. The $7,500 would barely cover the cost of the gold in the ring plus diamond. For him to basically make no money on the ring, Harry must have really given him good business! I made a mental note to pay for lunch next time he was in town. Now it was time to design it.

I perused over Tiffany's, Harry Winston, Bulgari, Ylang Ylang and others. One thing that I noticed right off was that a lot of the rings looked gaudy. Add to the fact that Autumn had really tiny fingers, so any stone over two and a half carats would be too big. I found ones that had too many diamonds and ones that looked too busy. I found ones that were too plain. I found ones that had colors and ones that were purely just about the main diamond. I spent so much time that my eyes watered from staring at the computer screen.

I looked through the pictures that she and I had taken together to find one where I could see her hands well. Then, I wrote down the types of designs I saw that I felt would fit her finger nicely. One design that I really began to like was simple and elegant, yet stylish. It had a two-carat princess cut diamond as the center stone. The band was exactly as wide as it was tall. It had a single row of smaller princess cut diamonds that circled 3/4 of the way around the ring on either side. This allowed for the main diamond to be the main focus of the ring while also allowing the band to have character. The more I looked at this style the more I fell in love with it. I imagined it being on her finger. I imagine her holding it up in the sun, watching it sparkle. And I knew it was the one.

I called the jeweler the next day to tell him of what I was looking for. I also emailed him a picture of the one I liked. Then I said what I wanted done to customize it to be one of a kind. The sides of the band were a slight bit taller than usual bands. They had to be to hold the diamonds inside. This allowed for a bit of engraving space. I told him that I had wanted to have him make the ring similar to the picture that I had emailed, but that I wanted the side of the band that would face her to be engraved with the words "First, Last, Only... Always and Forever."

He looked at the picture while we were on the phone. He said he loved the ring for a girl with hands like Autumn's. He would make sure to personally do the engraving as he wanted it to be perfect. He said it would be done, shipped, and in my hands before the proposal.

A part of me worried that I was merely setting myself up for failure again. Each time those thoughts crept in my mind, though, I would think of her laugh. I would think of her smile. I would think of the way she showed kindness to others and love for all. If I had a possibility of building a life with someone, she was the one to do it with. I had no doubt of that at all.

I wasn't going to let the idea of failing hold me back. I wanted a happy life. I wanted a strong relationship. I wanted a partner, a lover, a best friend. She was all of these things and I knew it. Now it was time to man up and ask.

21

Shoes off, pockets emptied, iPad in an open bin by itself, obligatory pat down. Just another day at an airport. Autumn and I were headed to Hawaii. I had told her that I wanted us to go on a romantic vacation. I hadn't told her why.

We were both very familiar with this process. She had flown internationally many times before coming to the U.S. for school. I flew all over the U.S. to visit family or for vacations. We were veterans of the security line. However, I was taking great care in keeping a sharp eye on my carry-on. The ring was tucked away in there. I didn't want it to disappear and I didn't want Autumn to see it. Walking through the giant x-ray machine got us nods of approval from the TSA, grateful they didn't have to remind to remove more clothes or metallic items.

Our flight was called, and we were soon sitting in our chairs, about to fly to Hawaii. We had picked our seats online and chose the exit row seats so we would have more leg room. It also put us in the middle of the plane, which meant less of a chance of smelling the lavatories. We snuggled up, she against the window, and put our movie back on. We were quite content in shutting out the rest of the world and just spending that time as if we were alone. Within minutes we were up in the air and on our way. In only a few hours we would arrive.

I suppose I should mention that we joined the Mile High Club. I had flown many times before that flight and always wondered what it would be like to do it on a plane. It intrigued and excited me. We got caught up in fits of laughter when we talked about doing it, then decided to try. I went to the lavatory first, she followed right after. I wish I could tell you that it was beautiful, passionate, or amazing experience, but it was not. It was awkward and uncomfortable.

We laughed more than we felt sexual. That being said, it was one of the most incredible experiences of my life. Only because it was with her. We were doing it together; doing something naughty. Sharing a moment that I may never have been able to experience without her. I don't believe either of us were sexually satisfied by the experience, but it did bond us even closer. Our love had blossomed.

We arrived in Hawaii in the early afternoon. A quick jaunt through the airport, pausing only to get our Leis, then we walked out into the beautiful Hawaiian air. We had decided to stay on the Island of Oahu. Though we had read that Maui was technically the more romantic of the Hawaiian islands, we felt that the amount of stuff to do on Oahu seemed more appealing. We could always bunny hop to the other islands should we choose to visit any of them.

I pulled the rented Jeep up to our rental home. The property owner met us outside to show us the house and give us the keys.

It was even better than the pictures had shown us. The front of the house was partially hidden by lush landscaping. Trees that had leaves the size of a surfboards created privacy from the front. It had a two-car garage, which would prove to be perfect, as we would leave the hard top of the Jeep on one side and park the jeep in the other.

There was a walking path that curled from the road, around some of the landscaping, and up to the front door. The house itself was painted a muted orange color. This scheme added just the right amount of color behind all of the green of the foliage. We opened the door and gasped.

The door opened up into the great room. It was obvious that they had renovated somewhat recently. They had chosen to rip out a lot of the walls and give it a really open feel. The great room, kitchen, and dining room all blended in together perfectly. As you walked into the great room to your right was a sunken in floor where the circular couch resided. On the far right wall was the large plasma TV. The only bit of dividing wall between the kitchen and great room was the fireplace, which had been updated and painted a dark chocolate color.

The kitchen had all stainless steel appliances with light wood countertops. I had never seen a wood counter top, but it looked gorgeous. There was a tall island in the middle that acted as a bar. The dining area had a tall, dark colored, circle wood table. Around it was four tall chairs.

The whole look of this open room was beautiful. It was obvious they had taken great care in designing and decorating. We checked out the smaller of the two bedrooms. It was nice; very simple with eggshell painted walls and light colored furnishings. The bathroom for that area was fairly plain too. Consisting of a basic bath/shower combo, a nice vanity, and simple decorations. Then we walked over to the opposite side of the house to look at the master bedroom and bathroom.

Autumn immediately fell in love. The room was designed and decorated with posh luxury in mind. The walls were painted a nice cream/tan color. The bed and furniture were all very dark chocolate wood. The floor was hardwood and had beautiful detail. Each wall had one piece of art on it and was lit to show its detail. We opened the closet door to reveal a giant walk in closet. It was the perfect bedroom for our trip.

We walked through the bedroom and into the master bathroom. They had kept the posh luxury feel going in there as well. The floor was done in large travertine tiles. The bathtub was actually a full spa tub built for two people and set up high against the window. Sitting in the tub allowed the view of the ocean. I knew for sure that I wanted to spend at least one night using that tub. Next to the tub was a huge stand up shower. The shower head was hidden in the ceiling. I turned the water on to see what happened and it was like rain began to fall.

The vanity had a single sink, but then a lower portion with extra lighting and a chair. It was set up so that the woman could sit down and prepare for her day. I could not have been happier with the home that we had chosen to rent. In all honesty, it was priced about as much as the resorts. I was proud of finding the right place.

We then walked out the sliding door in the dining room and out onto the lanai. That is when we really knew we had chosen correctly. The lanai had a small wrought iron table and chairs, and looked out to the ocean. The house was actually on the side of a small cliff. I'd say about 20 feet up above the ocean itself. This added height gave an extra amount of view. We could see houses dotting here and there along the shore on both sides of us. Below us we could see the ocean stretching as far as our eyes would allow. Best of all, we could hear the waves lapping the shore over and over again. A rhythmic beating of a beautiful drum. Adding peace and tranquility to the home.

That first day and even night we decided to just stay home. We did make a quick run to the local grocery store to stock up on bottled water, food to cook, and snacks. While the sun was out we sat on the lanai, talking about things we wanted to do and see while we were there. We talked of walking down to the oceanfront, but decided to save it for the next day. After the sun had gone down, a light chilly breeze came in from the ocean. We decided to head in at that point.

I found the woodpile hidden around the corner of the house near the shed. I brought in five medium sized logs, opened the door so we would get a nice cooling ocean breeze, and lit a fire in the fireplace.

We sat on that comfortable couch, fire going, breeze filling the air with the soft ocean scent, and talked of our love for each other. One thing about Autumn and I talking was that she allowed me to vent about the pain I held in my heart from Jennifer. She never wanted to hear full details, and frankly I couldn't blame her. No one wants to hear about their lovers past. Sometimes I had to vent, to get things off of my chest.

"I'm so sorry if I talk of the past too much. I know you aren't the one I'm supposed to share these things with, but I have to get them out of me," I told her while we were sitting there.

She took a moment, searching for the right words, took my hand in hers, and then said to me, "Baby, I'm your best friend as you are mine. If I'm not the person you're supposed to tell, then who?"

I hadn't thought about it that way. It was therapeutic to tell her my pains, my feelings, my thoughts. I believe it brought us closer. It showed her the me that was tucked inside versus just the me that resided on the surface. She accepted that me. She welcomed the me within. She was the woman I was supposed to spend my life with. All the while we were sitting there I knew that a certain ring was hidden in the closet, waiting for the right moment.

The next morning we awoke and decided it was a Pearl Harbor kind of day. I grew up a Navy brat and the idea of seeing something so powerful was exciting for me. I cooked us eggs while she got ready, keeping the sliding door open, enjoying the ocean air and letting it envelope me while I cooked.

Soon we were on the road. Using our iPhones for GPS, we took what looked to be the best route, while trying to avoid Honolulu traffic. We were in no hurry, but sitting in traffic is never fun. We had the top off of the Jeep and our hair, mostly her long perfect Asian hair, was flailing all over the place. Soon we arrived.

It is hard to describe the feelings one has about connecting to things from the past. Being here was both inspiring and heart breaking. On one hand, to see these ships and these artifacts, especially the USS Arizona, made you sad because you know that so many lost their lives that day. So many were hit with no idea that they were going to be fighting in a war that morning.

On the other hand, it was inspiring. It brought us together as a nation.

It was here, though, at Pearl Harbor, where I got a sense of what it must have been like for our military members that morning. My favorite part was viewing the USS Arizona. Seeing her there, still intact, holding on to her memories so that we, as a nation, can see what she stood for.

One must visit Pearl Harbor to understand the affect it

will have on your heart. The metal, though rusted with age, still standing strong; still trying to hold its ground. As if it's still fighting the war from that morning; trying to do the job it had been built for. The pictures of the young men who were there, wanting to defend our country, wanting to make their families proud. All of this is the midst of one of the most beautiful places on planet Earth.

Tears built up in my eyes standing there. Pride in my Country. Pride in my family who had served Navy. The love in my heart to be able to share that moment with this woman that I loved. I squeezed her so tight. She understood. Though the feeling must have been different for her being raised in Vietnam, I still think she grasped the levity of that moment and of the place itself. She had a way of connecting to people. Understanding the heart of them.

We drove home almost in full silence. Hand in hand, each staring out the Jeep, hair blowing in all directions, watching the setting sun. I don't know if we were changed that day. I don't know if we were different than before. If not, we were at least more full. Closer to being more human. I was so grateful that I had waited to go to Hawaii until she was with me. Waited to experience more of life until we had found each other.

It was still fairly early in the night when we arrived home. We repeated the steps of the night before, sitting on the lanai, talking and reveling in the moments of the day we liked the most. Then I excused myself, went to the bathroom, and started up the spa tub. I lit a few candles that I had found in the kitchen. Then I opened up the window to allow the ocean breeze to cool the room, save for the spa.

I walked back outside and escorted her into the master bath. She saw the candles and tub, which caused tears to well up in her eyes. She grabbed me tightly and began kissing me with so much passion she could barely contain herself. We hastily undressed each other. Only breaking our kissing for removal of shirts. We made love right there on the pile of clothes, protecting us from the cool tile. Afterward we giggled, and then climbed into the spa to relax. We stayed the rest of the night right there in the tub, surrounded by bubbles and cool air, staring out at the ocean that sprawled for an eternity before us. Once we had run out of energy we went off to bed, exhausted and happy.

The next day we decided to make a relaxing one. We awoke at the crack of noon and ordered some food to be delivered from a local restaurant. We ate on the lanai and enjoyed the crisp afternoon air. Once we were clean and full we trekked down to the beach. The owners of the house had built in a path that wound down the side of the little cliff to safely get you on the sandy shore below.

We got down to the beach in about ten minutes. The walk wasn't hard at all. The area of the beach was fairly secluded. Only the residents of the area must use it because it would be hard for tourists to get to. This meant that there weren't many people on the beach, which was all the better for us. We spent some time lying out, throwing the Frisbee, tossing the football, and playing in the water.

I knew that I would love the water. Especially after living in L.A. and hating the coastal water there, which is cold and dirty. The moment my feet touched it I knew I was in love. The water was warm. Perfectly warm, and I could see my feet. I was so excited that I went running in and dove head first into a giant wave.

Hours we spent swimming around. Sometimes we body surfed. Sometimes we used the body board. When we would get tired we would go lay out, relaxing in the sun. Then right back in the water we went. We stayed down there playing all the way until the sun started heading down. I never felt rushed with her. I never felt a need to impress. Rather, just the ability to share. To share the moments. To share our love.

We made our way back up to the lanai to watch the sun fully set. I don't know if I have ever seen a better sunset. Even of the others that we saw in Hawaii. That night was incredible. The sun, so big and powerful, sinking deep over the horizon. Watching the light fade from bright oranges to dark purples. Slowly darkness engulfed the land, bringing a calm with it. A quick shower and the rest of the night was spent on the couch resting after a fun day. In the back of my mind, I still had the idea whirring about when to pop the question.

I woke Autumn up early with pancakes in bed. I told her to get ready quickly that we had to head out soon. I had a surprise for her, but we had to get started. She showered and dressed fast after eating and we were quickly on our way. I drove us to Honolulu airport, where I had set us up a quick plane ride to the Big Island. The flight was very fast. Probably less than half an hour once we were wheels up. The plane was small. I have heard the term "puddle jumper" used to describe planes before. If that is a real term, this plane fit its description. It was nice, though.

And the staff that ran it was nice as well. I suppose living in Hawaii would make you a pretty happy person to begin with.

Upon landing on the Big Island we were greeted by a guy who referred to himself as Tiny. Tiny was a large Samoan man pushing over 300 pounds. He would be our tour guide for the rest of the day. I had heard that getting a guide to show you the best places to go was the right idea for the Big Island, especially if you were hoping to see lava flow. Tiny and I had spoken over the phone a few times, so he knew what we were looking for.

He loaded up our day bag into his Jeep while we got settled in. Then he jumped in and off we went. Tiny was a very talkative guy. It was easy to see how much he loved the islands and how proud he was of them. He told us of the Samoan heritage and history of the islands. He pointed out interesting locations and even mentioned spots we would recognize from movies, such as *50 First Dates*.

He drove us for a long while. Probably a couple of hours, before getting to the place he said we wanted to go first. We pulled into a small parking area to begin our journey. Tiny dug around and found us a little map that he had put together. He assured us that he would be right there, waiting in his Jeep eating pineapple, until we returned. He whispered in my ear that it would be a little over an hour hike each way.

Then she and I were off. I was grateful I had remembered to have us each put tennis shoes on that morning. Sandals would have been killer. I had planned us a hike to a very special place. We hiked through wooded areas, a grassy plain area, and rocky terrain. From the top of one of the hills we could see the ocean and so much land around us. The view was breathtaking. I knew that we were in an area that must have been a National Forrest, and therefore would not allow homes to be built. However, if I could have, right there is where I would have built my dream home. Every night I would have slept on my lanai, listening to the ocean and breathing the tropical air.

The color palette before me was astounding. The furthest colors were that of blues and greens with hints of white. The sky was a light blue with little wisps of clouds here and there. The ocean was a darker blue in the deeps and a lighter green closer to land. The tops of the waves as they crested were white with foam. The beaches were black from centuries of lava flow. The land just past the beaches was engulfed in green. The different trees, grasses, and plants all showing that the term green can be hundreds of things.

The flowers that jutted from, or around, these plants added the touch of color to everything. My eyes were inundated with reds, purples, violets, oranges, and pinks. Everywhere my head turned there were more colors to see.

Onward we marched. We reached our destination, a small waterfall, maybe only 30 feet tall with a mild water flow, in about forty-five minutes. The water landed in a small pool below. I dropped the backpack and stripped down to just my board shorts. Autumn followed suit and within seconds we were wading out to the waterfall.

It was deep enough that we had to tread water once we got close. We splashed each other, giggled and playing, yet still finding moments to kiss. There was a rainbow emanating from the mist, coming from the spray of waterfall hitting pool. The colors were blue, green, purple, and orange. They seemed to waver and move in unison with the spray.

The sun was a little past high noon, casting its rays all over us. The warmth was invigorating. We were surrounded by the most beautiful foliage one could dream of. It was so private. It was here that it hit me. This was it. This was the spot and the moment.

I knew I wanted to propose sometime that day. I knew

the right moment would present itself. Unlike with Jennifer, I didn't want to over plan it. I do believe that a man should put forth effort, and there is nothing wrong with a plan. I needed to do things differently with Autumn, though. I wanted to feel that it was right to do, not just expect it.

In the possibility that I may find the right moment at any time, I had been keeping my ring in my pocket. When I stripped down I had forgotten to take it out. I realized then, that the box would be drenched. It wasn't going to be perfect. That made me smile. I smiled because it reminded me of something Autumn always said.

I splashed her to get her attention, then started, "You know how you always tell me that we are imperfectly perfect for each other? How things never seem to work out the way we expect or plan, yet they turn out right anyway?"

Laughing at me, treading water, she said, "Of course! I fully believe that! You and I are so imperfectly perfect. Yet also perfectly imperfect. I wouldn't want it any other way."

"Good," I said back, feeling a little anxious, "because I have something to talk to you about." I took a deep breath, gathered up my courage, and began, "You have changed my life. It's because of you that I smile again; I'm strong again. Because of you I have found life to be worth living again. I'm happy when I wake up and happy when I go to sleep. I can't imagine my life without you. I can't imagine working on my career and celebrating any modicum of success without you by my side. What you did for me during *METRO*..."

I stopped. My thoughts went back, to just a few months earlier, to when she had helped with the film. When we had laid in the closet together. I smiled, feeling that welling up of gratitude build from within, then started again, "I see us working through the tough times and enjoying the great times. I need you with me. I love you. I will always love you. If you'll have me, I'd love to grow old with you. Will you, Miss Autumn, be my wife?"

As I said the last part I reached in my pocket, grabbed the soaking wet box, and brought it out. I hadn't even fully opened it before she responded.

She screamed so loud it startled me. Then she launched

herself out of the water and on top of me. I nearly lost the ring as I sank under the surface of the water. I slammed it shut and held on to it for dear life.

I fought my way back to the surface as she was kissing me over and over again while screaming, "Yes!" I couldn't tell because she was so wet, but I think she was crying.

We had drifted over and were now almost directly under the waterfall. For an instant, time slowed down. I glanced around me to memorize the moment exactly. The water falling on our heads from waterfall, as it did each individual drop moving gracefully through the air, showing off its wonder to the world. The rainbow above us, a multitude of wonderful colors all displayed in single file; like paint swatches. The crisp blue water we were floating in.

I smelled the air. Clean and sweet. Sweet from all of the flowers around the water. I took a mouth full of water in. It was cool, refreshing, calming. I looked at her. Her dark hair matted against her forehead and messy. Treading water with the ring box in one hand, holding on to me with the other. Her smile. That smile that made me melt. The eyes telling me what her heart was feeling.

I saw the spray of mist floating up around us that was water rebounding from the waterfall hitting the pool. I saw colorful birds fly in, chirping their approval of her answer. I turned my attention back to her and we kissed more deeply than before. I felt her soul entwine with mine. I had found the woman I would spend my life with. This time I knew it to be true. It was apparent, in that moment, that she wanted it as badly as I did.

I had a momentary flash of proposing to Jennifer, remembering her saying, "No, no, no," over and over again until she thought about it and said yes.

She had hesitated.

She wasn't sure, but Autumn was. She knew what I was worth. She knew how lucky she would be and how lucky I was. She knew that we had something special and she wanted to latch on to it for dear life.

After a bit we headed to shore to catch a breather. We sat down on a rock nearby and I properly presented her with the ring saying, "As I said, it is imperfectly perfect. The box is soaked. I hope that is okay."

I handed her the box. She looked at it then looked at me, her eyes welling with tears. I could feel her getting choked up. With the box firmly secured in her left hand, she reached her right hand down to open it up. She got it open enough for the sun to hit it so she could see what it looked like, and she gasped.

She lunged at me again, reaching her arms around me, hugging me so tight. I could tell that she didn't care how much it cost. She didn't care what the brand was or how I had obtained it. She cared that I had taken the time to find something that was right for her. The box was wet, so what, it was merely a covering holding the precious item that I had found for her.

I gratefully returned her hug. I loved her so very much. That moment was one of those moments that took my breath away. I could name at least five others right off of the top of my head that Autumn was directly responsible for before that day. This one outshone them all. The look of sheer gratitude and love on her face. The beauty of where we were. The tears in her eyes. It was picture perfect. It was as if Steven Spielberg himself was just behind the trees, directing the incredible scene.

She collected herself and took the ring out to inspect it.

"Chase. Chase, it is so… beautiful. Absolutely perfect. I can't imagine a better ring. You must have spent so much. You spent too much. Did you spend too much?" She was blabbering in her heat of happiness.

I just smiled and said, "No price could match what you're worth. I merely did what I was able to do."

She held it up in the sunlight, watching the way the big diamond glinted in the sun. The Jeweler had put an almost flawless diamond in it. It was a 2 and a 1/2 carat, VVS in clarity and B in color. Getting much better than that would have cost tens of thousands more. I was so lucky to have been put in contact with him.

Then she noticed the engraving. She read it out loud, "First, Last, Only… Always and Forever."

She let that sink in for a moment. Then turned to me with a look of concern and said, "But, Chase, I'm not your only and certainly not your first." She almost had a look of hurt on her face. I hadn't thought of it the way she was. I had thought of it in a completely different meaning.

I reached my hand over, slid the back of it down the right side of her face, trying to calm her. Then I said, "Autumn, please don't mistake it's meaning. Those are not mere words to me. They are what I mean to say to you. You're right in what you say, however, that is not what those words mean."

I paused, making sure to say what came next correctly, "You are the first woman I have ever met that made me feel the way that I do right now. You made me believe in myself again. Not just love, but a true love stemming from a kindred spirit. You are my lover and my best friend. My heart tells me, without a doubt, that you're the first. You are my last. I want no woman to come after you. I want to end my life with you. I want you by my side, holding my hand, soothing my soul as I cross on to the next plane when I grow old. You are my only. You're the only one who has ever believed in my dreams, my heart, and me as a person. You made choices to show me that you deserve me as much as I deserve you. You are the only one who could do that. I want this with you. The good, the bad, the ugly. The struggles and the joys. I want it always and forever. Baby, you're definitely my first. I want you to be my last. You have always been my only."

I thought for a moment more then said, "That is what those words mean. I would have needed a bigger ring to write all of that."

Tears streamed down her face as she looked back and forth from the ring to me. It fit her finger perfectly. The ring didn't look gaudy on her finger, but would catch anyone's eye that happened to look its way.

I had given the better ring to the better girl and proposed in the better spot. The country boy in me was happy in that realization. I would never have been able to live with the thought that Jennifer had got better from me than Autumn did. She deserved better. She deserved more. I was going to spend my life showing her that.

I drug her back into the water and made her follow me out to the waterfall. I swam under and back behind it. I found myself in a semi cave. It didn't go inside the hill, but curved enough to be able to hide from the outside world. She caught up to me and grabbed me. The middle of the day, sun shining bright, water spraying everywhere, we made love.

It was slow and passionate. I swam under water and kissed her over and over again. Back and forth we went like that. Taking turns kissing. Taking turns touching. Showing each other our love without words getting in the way. We were engaged.

Afterward, we made our way back down the trail to the Jeep where Tiny sat waiting, listening to the local radio station playing music I didn't recognize.

"Did you 'do' anything?" He asked me with a wink.

She produced her finger and showed him the ring.

"Damn, son! Now I KNOW I should have charged you more!" he exclaimed, wide-eyed.

We all laughed then headed further down the road.

Even though we had already had an incredible day, I really wanted to see lava flow. Tiny had told me that he knew of a great spot where we could for sure see it. He drove us all the way to the tip of the southern part of the island. We got out and followed him. He led the way this time. We had no need for privacy. After about a 30 minute walk we came upon an area of the beach with intense heat radiating. We could see plumes of hot gas emanating from the black substances further back from the water.

We could see steam exploding as the lava oozed into the ocean. We ran toward the location of the steam, being careful to mind anything that looked hot. We couldn't get too close as the lava was flowing enough to prevent us from doing so, but we saw enough. The molten hot lava was flowing incredibly slowly. You could see it moving, like liquid metal. It didn't look real. Liquid fire easing its way to the water. The beauty of it is hard to describe.

We stood there in that spot for nearly half an hour, holding each other, smiling and enjoying the moment. It was better than I could have dreamed. I had found my soul mate.

It had taken pain, wrong choices, and mistakes to find her, but it had all been worth it. If I hadn't gone to Austin I never would have met her.

Tiny took us back to the airport. I paid him and tipped him handsomely. He had delivered on his promises to show me lava flow and a waterfall. For that I was extremely grateful. We got back on the puddle jumper, settled ourselves in, and enjoyed the plane ride back the Oahu.

We arrived home at around 11 p.m. and went directly to the bedroom, undressed, curled up in each other's arms, and passed out. We had done so much that day. We were physically and emotionally drained. I couldn't have been happier with how it had turned out and that I had waited to find the right moment. I was even happier that she had accepted. It was obvious that she wanted it as much as I. My heart swelled with pride and happiness as I fell asleep that night.

The next day we kept it light again. We spent the whole day at the beach after a quick run to the grocery store. Autumn spent half of the day staring at the ring. Multiple times I caught her tearing up when she looked at it. Mostly, though, she had the biggest smile I had ever seen on her.

That night was spent on the lanai. We spent a little time in the pool. Once we were done we grabbed two of the pool lounge chairs and drug them over to the lanai. We found two extra blankets in the closet then curled up and fell asleep right there outside, listening to the sound of the waves as they crashed upon the shore.

We decided to spend the next day in Honolulu doing touristy stuff. We shopped at a lot of stores, grabbing trinkets and gifts for friends back home. We took pictures of ourselves in fun local spots, pictures to keep as memories of our amazing trip. We ate so much that we felt as though we could burst. We went surfing and enjoyed the water. We even went dancing as the night began to take over.

The best part, though, was when we went back to the beach and sat on the sand. Her body resting against mine, staring at the image of the moon reflecting off the ocean. Watching it move over and over again with the waves that it supposedly created. Moments like this reaffirm that I'm a man. For it is true that a man tends to not have the same emotional mind to put words to such beautiful things. For us, it is hard to describe. I can tell you that we were surrounded by a light breeze coming off of the ocean, but that we weren't cold. The air was salty. You would even taste it when you opened your mouth. The smells of the ocean mixed with all of the restaurants nearby made your mouth water, yet at the same time made you want to swim. Digging your hands in the sand felt grainy. The top layer was dry but only a few inches down it became wet.

Your eyes were overcome with sights. Too many to process them all. Thousands of lights in every direction. The moon and it's many mirrors. The waves. The beach. The other people going this way and that. Even though I cannot describe it as well as a woman might, I could feel it. I could feel what a place like this does to the heart and soul. I understood why I had waited to come here. I was glad that it was with her that I chosen to.

The last bit of the trip was much more relaxed. We ate out, spent time in the pool, enjoyed the ocean, and hung out. Mostly though, we just enjoyed being with each other. Taking the time to take each other in.

We didn't say much on the plane ride home. Most of the time was just spent holding each other. We also watched another movie on the IPad. I had reserved *The Notebook* for the flight back. I had a feeling it would be appropriate. I was right. Soon we were back in Austin after a short layover in L.A. Being in LAX, knowing how close I was to where I had always wanted to be, was tough. Autumn could sense it affecting me and asked what was wrong. I explained it to her. She fully understood. She felt similarly.

For she and I, one could not have planned a better vacation, a better proposal, and a better way to celebrate a new engagement. We were happy and in love. I didn't see how anything could change that. In fact, they got even better.

Life moved at the speed of light after the premier. Working at the bar was different. Going to the gym was different. Being at home was different. Nothing felt right. Everything felt as though I was just waiting for the next thing.

In my heart, I knew what that was. In my heart, I knew it was time. I was scared. I was scared to take the next step because of the failures from before, but Autumn was right there, by my side, supporting me. Every night before bed we would discuss over and over what we should do. I felt like I was stuck between two worlds.

It was a phone call with mom that changed everything. We had been talking for a while one afternoon when I brought the conversation up to her.

"Chase, you know I support you no matter what, but let me ask you this: Would you rather stay there in Austin where you can buy a house, raise a family, and live a 'normal' life or would you rather be in L.A., struggling to pay rent in a tiny apartment never knowing if you'll amount to anything all so you can chase a dream?" she asked me.

She patiently waited for me to answer. I took a moment, letting her question sink in, allowing the levity of the words she had just spoken settle in upon me.

"I'd rather be living in L.A., chasing my dream. Even if that meant I was broke and had nothing," I replied.

"That's what I thought you'd say. It sounds to me like you already know your decision. You're just being too big of a wuss to admit it to yourself!" she laughed.

She was right. I knew what I wanted. I knew how I felt.

She continued, "Son, life is too short to live for death. If you constantly worry about how you're going to pay your bills next year, well then you are already dead. The Good Lord did not put us on this planet to act as worker bees. I believe you need balance. Sure, you should also work hard to make sure you could pay your bills next year. But worrying about the future without being happy is a no brainer. Live, laugh, love. Change anything that goes against your happiness."

She was right. She's always right. I hung up with her and stood there for a moment. Was I really going to do this? Was I going to make this decision. A warm tingle ran down my spine. It hit me. Everything changed in that moment and I went bolting out to the patio where Autumn was tanning in the sunshine. "Um, so, let's move." I said to her in a fit of excitement.

"About time!" she said back, "I've been waiting forever for you to say that. Sheesh, you sure do take your time to make up your mind."

She was ready. My fiancé was ready to join me on the next adventure. The two of us against the world out to chase down our elusive dreams.

The next day I put in my two week notice at work and told all of my regulars that I was leaving. Not my boss, my regulars, or anyone I knew acted surprised. Every one of them told me they had expected it to be soon after the premier. They all spoke of how happy I had been that day and how I belonged on the screen.

The two weeks flew by. Each night Autumn and I spent hours packing. We would laugh and play while putting the stuff away. We went through our closet, playing dress up with old clothes and reminiscing about the night we had spent in there. We went through old boxes of papers and keepsakes, finding things that we needed to take, but throwing away things that weren't necessary.

We listened to music and made love on mounds of stuff meant to be packed. We took what would normally have been a long and terrible process and made it into something fun and silly. Every day with Autumn felt like a good day. Every task, no matter how menial, was made better because of her. Our love had been growing strong and steady since that first night at the theater.

Moving day came upon us fast. Within two hours we had the U-Haul completely packed and tied up. Autumn, Lil' Den, and I would take turns driving the U-Haul and the Jeep across country. The U-Haul would pull my car, but the Jeep would have to be driven. Gratefully Lil' Den had agreed to help out with driving, or we would have been in a touch situation.

The drive was long because we had to stop often for gas. The Jeep averaged around 11 miles a gallon and the U-Haul was even worse. There was one point, just past the California border, where we gassed up at the bottom of a valley filled with giant wind turbines. By the time we reached the top of that long gradual hill, the gas was already gone. It had taken less than two hours to drain the tanks because of the steep grade.

Finally, though, after almost 30 hours of driving, we arrived home. Autumn and I had found a cute little apartment while searching on the internet only days before. It was in West Hollywood, which is a great area. It wasn't very big, it was expensive, but it was perfect for us to call home.

The apartment itself was pretty small, only about 800 square feet, but sat on the side of the building with a view. It had a tiny foyer that you walked into where we had hung our favorite movie posters. The rest of the apartment, save for the bathroom and closet, was one long open space. This made it seem bigger and made it feel more like a home.

Lil' Den hung around and helped us decorate our new home. We painted walls, hung art, and added shelving where needed. We installed a projector for movie watching, displayed my DVD's, and even set up a full surround sound system. The last piece, my personal favorite, was a large canvas print I'd had made of Autumn and I. It was three foot tall and two foot wide. I proudly hung it above the fireplace for all to see.

One of the best things about our building was the view. Our roof, which had a pool, Jacuzzi, and grilling area, gave a 360 degree view of the city I loved. We could see downtown Los Angeles, Hollywood, Century City, and even the ocean. The first time I went up there I remember thinking back to my days sitting on the cliff at Mount Bonnell. That had been my sanctuary. Now, on the roof of my new home, was my new sanctuary. I took a quick look up to the sky and said, "Thank you," to whoever it was that had made sure I found this.

To thank Lil' Den for all of his hard work in helping us move, we took him all around the city. We took him to see the Hollywood sign and showed him the hiking path that goes right up behind it. We showed him the walk of fame, Mann's Chinese Theater, The Kodak theater where the Oscars are held, and other fun places at the Hollywood and Highland area. The next day we took him to the beach. The three of us playing on the sand, having a blast. I talked him into running full force into the ocean. He dove in before realizing how cold the Pacific Ocean is, then came streaking back out screaming. Autumn and I just laughed. That week flew by and soon he was back on a plane to Austin.

Autumn and I were left to start our careers. She immediately immersed herself in production work. She started out working as an unpaid intern on reality shows. Before long she was already getting paid as a Production Assistant and working her way up.

I jumped into acting classes. I took casting workshops and met with agents. It took me considerably longer to get things going than it took Autumn. I was very proud of her and the strides she was making, but I also felt a twinge of jealousy that she was able to break in so quickly while I took longer and struggled more.

She saw it and told me one day, "Don't feel that way. We are in this together. We are a team, a unit, a whole. I'm doing well because I have you as my support. Soon you will be doing well and I will have been your support. Don't get down on yourself, baby."

She was right. Doing what you love takes time. I wasn't going to be deterred from working toward my goal.

My career took a long time to get going. It was really slow at first. I met with a manager who told me she thought that I should take a workshop with a well-known commercial casting director. I took his workshop, working really hard to prove myself.

He pulled me aside after class one day and told me, "Chase, you have a great look and you're taking the direction well. I think I'd like to introduce you to a good commercial agent friend of mine."

I was, of course, extremely surprised that he had said that. I was elated that he had offered such a nice gesture.

"Thank you! I would, of course, love any connection you

may have," I stammered back at him. I was distraught and needed any leg up I could get.

I met the commercial agent for coffee a week later. We sat and chatted for a good hour before the conversation turned to the reason I was there. Confused and wondering if I was going to get to audition for her I finally asked, "Craig said you might be interested in bringing me on as a client, is that true?"

She laughed, "Honey, I trust Craig's opinion. He said you were great, so I already planned on signing you. I just wanted to chat with you and grab a cup of coffee before we did."

I was speechless. She smiled and nodded, then produced a folder with the necessary paperwork.

A week later, I got my first commercial audition. Then they started flooding in. I went from having one a week to two, to so many I could barely keep up. I started getting call-backs, that is when they bring just a few back to choose their favorite, on most of the auditions I was getting. Each audition, each call back, I felt closer to booking something. Closer to being able to do what I had been dreaming about since I was four.

"I hope you have the 27th open," my agent said over the phone to me one day.

"Yes I do. Why?" I said, a little unsure of what was going on.

"Because you booked!" she yelled.

She knew how hard I had been working. She knew the struggles I was going through and knew what it would mean. Autumn saw the look on my face and ran over to me, worried if I was okay. I turned to her, tears streaking down my cheeks, and reached for her. We held each other in silence, both letting the stress of our struggles wash away in those tears.

After shooting that commercial, I gained more self-confidence. Feeling pretty good about myself, I had my manager set me up a meeting with a fairly well known theatrical agent. Theatrical agents are the ones that book film and television. At first it seemed awkward as they didn't look all that impressed by me.

I wasn't going to walk out of the door with them feeling like that. Even if they didn't sign me, I wanted them to like me. I turned on my country boy charm, showed them that I wasn't the usual overly into himself "Hollywood guy" and then I showed them footage from METRO. That had done the trick. They saw me as a real actor; someone who was serious about getting his career going. We signed paperwork and I waited for my first audition.

I waited a lot. It was almost two months before my first. I admit to feeling a little disappointed. I felt like the agents weren't pushing hard for me. I became worried that they were overlooking me or forgetting about me. The first audition made all of that disappear. It felt good to go in, to slate for the casting director, to deliver my lines, to feel like an actor again.

After that, the auditions just started rolling in. It was awesome. 11 months after moving back, I finally booked my first part. It was a decent sized part in an independent film. I played a drug addict that wanted to find his father. Through many trials and tribulations he finally does, only to die once they are united. In the film I had to show a lot of emotion. I worked tirelessly to get into character, to feel what he felt. I must have done a pretty good job because the film garnered a lot of attention and got me noticed.

After that, I began working more and more steadily. Autumn was hired full time as a line producer on a network television show. I even, without her help, booked a job on that show and got to work with her. It felt like being back shooting METRO. I was in front of the camera, her behind, both of us doing what we loved. The whole time glancing at each other saying "Hey, I love you" with our eyes. Though it was no secret that we were together, we kept it professional on set. Well, everywhere on set except my dressing room.

That is how it went. For two years we both continued to grow and build our careers. Though money was coming in from both sides we never lived extravagantly. We stayed in our little apartment, choosing to buy investment properties in other states rather than to buy a house in Hollywood.

Sure, I bought a couple of nice cars and Autumn had the most up-to-date video cameras as they came out, but that was as fancy as we got. We never shopped for expensive clothes or jewelry. We were the happiest just being with each other, so material things were never a need.

With both of our careers now fairly solid, our finances in a good place, and my heart more sure than ever before that she was the one; I set a date to marry her.

"Let's get married on the ten year anniversary of when we met. Ten years from the day that you saved me from the doom of the mossy rocks."

That was only six months away, so I wasn't sure if she would be okay with it, but I had my fingers crossed.

"That sounds perfect, Chase. I'm ready to be Missus William!" she exclaimed.

We had been engaged for years. Though it worked fine for us, I knew it was better if we made it official.

"Just don't mess up between now and then," she added with a smirk.

Never temp fate.

22

I had loved Jennifer, there is no denying that, but the love I had for Autumn far surpassed it. Not only did we have a love that was felt equally from both parts, but also the same amount of respect for one another. We both put in effort. We both put in work. We paid bills together. We wrote scripts together. We took turns taking each other out. What we had was more real. I could feel it deep in my bones. I felt in my heart that there was no way I could hurt her. I couldn't have anticipated what was to happen next.

It was early on a Sunday morning that I had the urge to go up to the roof to write.

Autumn was working at the studio, so I was alone. I tossed on my board shorts, anticipating to get a little sun, and headed up. The roof was empty, which left me alone to work on the script I had been thinking about. I curled up on one of the comfy deck chairs and began to write.

I had been enjoying the sun for about an hour when my phone rang. With two agents, a manager, a fiancé, and countless friends, that wasn't unusual. It was unusual, however, to see Jennifer's name flash across the screen when I pulled the phone out of my pocket. I wasn't as affected by it as I used to be, but I do admit to having a moment of anger. Why was she calling now? What the hell could she want?

I ignored it. Autumn and I respected each other. One thing that would definitely break our trust would be for me to answer this call and have a conversation with my ex-fiancé. She called again. And again. And again. I could tell she wasn't going to stop.

I hit ignore again, then called Autumn and told her,

"Baby, I know you're at work and I hate to bug you, but I have a problem. About ten minutes ago, Jennifer called. She has been calling over and over again non-stop since. I haven't answered, but I kind of want to, just to tell her to stop calling. What's your opinion?"

Autumn wasn't my boss. Nor was I her boss. However, one thing we learned in our relationship was full disclosure and openness builds the strongest bond. I wasn't asking her for permission. I didn't need it. Nor would she want me to. I was making sure that she was okay with my decision.

"Of course, my love. Please, don't let her drag you into any weird conversations and please respect me," she said.

Damn, I love that woman. I hung up with her and waited for the phone to ring again. It only took about 15 seconds.

"Jennifer, what the hell do you want? Why are you bugging me? We haven't spoken in over ten years, for good reason, in case you forgot!" I had held nothing back. I was angry that she called and more annoyed that she kept calling.

"I know. I know I shouldn't be calling. I know I should leave you alone. I know you have a good life now. But, I... I... I don't know who else to call!" came her response.

It didn't sound like her; the voice was different. I knew that it was her, but she sounded weaker. Less sure of herself. Less in control. It made me feel bad for the way I had responded to her.

"I'm sorry for being harsh," I said, slowly but with meaning, "that wasn't fair. Though I don't think we need to be having a conversation, I won't be mean again. Are you okay?"

There was a long pause. It sounded as though she were crying softly with the phone away from her face.

"I'm dying," she said matter-of-fact.

I wasn't sure of what she had said. I mean, I heard it. I think I heard it, but it didn't sound right.

"What do you mean?" I said, feeling foolish.

"I'm dying, Chase," she choked back more tears, "I'm dying and I need your help."

What could I do? I was her ex-fiancé. I had a new love in my life, one I didn't want to hurt. Yet, she was claiming to be dying. Did she want a kidney? How in the world could I help?

Choosing my words carefully I said, "I'm not sure what you mean. If you're dying, I'm truly sorry for that. I don't even really know what to say. I'm not sure how I could help you. "

What do you say to someone that says they are dying? Her voice sounded so frail. She was obviously in pain. There was a lot of anger and hurt in my heart, but I would never wish for someone to be in pain or die.

"I really am dying. And I do need your help. I have breast cancer, Chase. We didn't catch it in time. We tried treating it over the past few months, but it has become terminal. It's eating away everything on the inside. They say I have less than a couple of weeks to live. They say there is nothing else they can do," her words trailed off at the end.

Hearing those words broke my heart. I had never had anyone tell me they were dying. And so soon. A couple of weeks? How was that possible? She was so young. My mind was whirling. I felt sick to my stomach. I packed up my things and headed back down to my apartment. I couldn't sit out in the sun while trying to grasp this conversation. This woman's body was failing her, but how could I help?

"Jennifer, I'm so sorry. I'm just, well, you know. I'm sorry. What can I do? Whatever you need I'll try to help with," I said in shock.

"I need you here with me," came her answer.

Okay, that was something I couldn't do. Wasn't her husband there to help her? Wasn't her family there? Why me? There was no way my heart could handle being in that situation. Plus, what about Autumn? How would she feel? How would she deal with me being there with my ex. What damage would it do to our relationship?

"I don't think I can do that. Is there anything else I can do? I don't mean to sound insensitive, but what you are asking is impossible. I'm sure what you're going through is beyond my comprehension and I won't pretend to understand how you feel or what you're going through. God, I don't know what to say, Jennifer. Isn't your husband there? Your family? Why me?!" I asked her.

"These past few months have been, well as you can imagine, really bad. I got really sick and we didn't know why. We had some tests done and found out that it was cancer. In the beginning, my husband was helpful and understanding. The worse I got the more distant he became. Last week, when we got the news that I was terminal, he left. He packed his things and left. He told us he couldn't deal with it..." she broke off. She was crying pretty steadily now. I didn't rush her. I didn't know what to say even if I did want to rush her.

After a long pause she started again, "He left me alone during this. He left me, Chase. My parents are here, at the hospital, with me. They are doing the best they can, but they don't like being in the room with me. It pains them. To be honest, it pains me too. I hate them seeing me like this. It could be different with you here. You have seen me in awkward moments before. You know me. I know you. Though we didn't end well, we did have love between us. If you were here, it would be easier for me to, ummm, take the next step."

She meant die. If I were there, it would make dying easier for her. Fuck. What do you say to someone who asks this of you? Even if I thought it would be ok, what about Autumn? How would she feel? I really was at a loss for words. I couldn't answer her yet, but I didn't want to stay on the phone either.

"I know you are hurting. I wish I could somehow make it better for you. I don't know if I can do what you ask, it really is a lot. I do know that time is very important and I know that you need an answer as soon as possible. I just can't give it to you yet. Let me take some time, do some thinking, and I'll call you back ASAP. Okay?" I had said all I could think to say.

"That is very fair. Thank you for considering it. I understand it is a lot to ask and I will understand if you say no. I just don't know what else to do. I'm scared, Chase, I'm so scared." Again, I could hear the hurt in her voice. She was trying to sound so strong. Trying to put up a front of someone who was okay. I knew better. I knew the real Jennifer.

We hung up the phone. I sat there, on my couch surrounded by my nice things that I had painstaking put to-gether, and cried. I loved Autumn. I loved her with all of my heart and knew she was who I wanted to be with. I had no doubt about that, but Jennifer had been a major part of my life. She had treated me terribly, but she was still a major part. Now she was hurting. Now she was feeling pain. Dy-ing. She was asking for my help.

I'm a country boy. I live and die by the Golden Rule. The Golden Rule says that I should do unto others as I would have them do unto me. When thinking about that rule, it made me think about if the tables were turned. How would I feel if I had to lower myself to call my ex for such a terrible reason? Would I expect that other person to come to my aid? Of course I wouldn't expect it, but I damn sure would hope for it.

Taking just that into account, the answer was easy. I had to go. A friend, granted a bad friend, but a friend nonetheless needed my help. The good man inside of me told me there was no other option but to go. I couldn't leave her to die, slow and alone.

Then, I thought about the bad. I thought about the pain that she had directly caused me. I thought about the deci-sions that she had made that had nearly ended my life. She was the cause of my biggest heartache. She was the cause of the worst year of my life. Going by the Golden Rule, wasn't she doing to me as she would have me do unto her? Going to her aid now, in her time of need, would be to say that every-thing she did to me was okay, which it was not.

But she was dying, God damn it! Her body had failed her. Now, in her young age, she was going to leave this Earth. Could I look at myself in the mirror each morning if I chose not to help? Could I look people in the eyes when they told me I was a good man? Could I teach my children the principals that I was brought up on if I was unwilling to live by them? A man, a real man, is there to help others in times of need. A well-lived life is a life lived for others.

Autumn. The incredible Autumn. She didn't deserve the anxiety that any of this was going to bring. She didn't de-serve the insecurities that me going to see Jennifer would surface. She knew I had loved Jennifer, but that I loved her more. She knew I only wanted to be with her, but putting myself in her shoes, I know that I would not feel great if she were to ask the same thing of me.

I had so much to think about. I had so little time to think, figure out, and decide. I had to weigh the feelings of a dying ex-girlfriend with the feelings of my own partner and myself. I walked out to the patio, pulled up a chair, popped open an energy drink, and closed my eyes. I took in the energy of the sun, letting it warm my soul. I opened my eyes and stared at the city that I loved. Life is beautiful. It really is. The miracle of birth. The beauty of nature and everything around us. I loved seeing life. I loved experiencing life. And, God willing, I would have many more years to do so.

Thinking about that gave me my answer. The truth is, I knew it all along. I just had to admit it to myself. The next step, the harder one, would be to tell it to Autumn.

She arrived home from set around 8 p.m. She was tired. I had cooked a filet mignon dinner with mashed potatoes and sweet corn. On the table, waiting for her, were candles, flowers, and a salad to start her meal. She gratefully accepted my offering and sat down to eat. We enjoyed the salads, then the main course, speaking mostly of how her day at work was and how good the food was.

Soon, the elephant in the room was awoken when she asked, "Okay, so tell me what she wanted. Did she beg for your hand in marriage?"

She had obviously been thinking about it. This next part was very hard. I took a deep breath, then started, "She didn't want my hand in marriage, but she did want something from me. She was recently diagnosed with breast cancer. It's terminal. She is dying, Autumn. They give her less than two weeks to live. She called because her husband left her. He just left her hanging there, in the hospital, to die. She wants me to come be with her while she passes. She's scared and alone."

I could see tears in her eyes. She was even more sensitive than I was. She said, "That is so sad to hear. Though I don't like her as a person, I would never wish this on her. What did you say to her?"

I knew what she was asking, but I took my time to answer, "I told her I didn't know if I could do it. It really is a lot to ask. She caused me a lot of heartache, not to mention what it could do to us."

She looked at me, "Chase, I don't know if I could handle it. I know that must seem so selfish, but you were a broken man when I met you. There was so much pain behind your eyes. It took me years to undo what she had done. Now, well, now she wants you to go back to her. I know it's her time of need. I know I'm terrible for feeling this way, but I love you so much. Seeing you hurting again would kill me." She was becoming more upset.

Autumn was the most beautiful woman I had ever dated. Not just because she was aesthetically pleasing to the eye, but because she had the biggest heart. I sat back looking at her. Her long shiny hair pulled back in a ponytail, the cute glasses she wore when she didn't feel like having her contacts in, those perfectly cute little lips, and those eyes that told me how she was feeling. I could see hurt in them. I could see worry. I could see that twinge of insecurity I had worried about.

"The truth is, I feel that I should go. I love you, my angel. I love you with all of my heart, but I'm the kind of man who prides himself on the fact that others can count on him in their time of need. I want to build my life with you. I want to grow old with you. I want to have children with you. I don't think that I could look my son in the eyes and teach him how to be a good man if I let a woman die alone who was asking for my help. I just don't think I could do that. I'm so sorry. I know this isn't going to be easy for you. I know, but I have to."

I got up from my chair, walked over to her, and hugged her. I held her tight. She really was the best woman on the planet. I was a better man because of her. I hoped with all of my heart that this would not be the end of us. If it was, I would understand. I was telling her that I was going to go spend time with my ex. Sure, she was dying. That didn't mean that feelings, emotions, insecurities wouldn't surface.

Those were the things Autumn was worried about.

She grabbed me back and held me just as strongly. After a long hug, she spoke.

"I can't promise you that I will still be here when you get back. You have to understand that what you're asking of me is more than most people could handle. I'm respecting your decision to be a good man, but you must also respect my decision to protect my heart. I'm damaged too. I have pain that I deal with. Please, understand that."

I couldn't argue with her. I knew about her past. I knew about the pain that she held in her heart. I had been as much of a rock for her as she had been for me. I knew that I was taking a chance in ruining that bond that we had built. It broke my heart. It made me feel so bad that I was the one causing someone else to feel negatively. I just didn't know what else to do. I could only hope she would allow me the opportunity to make things right once it was all over.

What a terrible, morbid thought. Once it was all over. That meant once another person's life had ended. Once a person I used to care about no longer had breath in her body. It was the saddest thing I had ever thought about.

We went to bed that night as different people. Though we held each other to start, we ended up rolling away and sleeping back to back. There was coldness in our bed. It wasn't her fault. She wasn't to blame. She was hurt. I was the cause.

23

I had always hated hospitals. I know that the adminis-
tration, doctors, nurses, and rest of the staff work hard to
make it a good place to come to. I know that many lives are
saved every day, but there is just a cold energy within them.
The walls are so white. Bright white. Bleached white.

Things had been awkward at first. As expected, there was
quite a bit of animosity between us when I first arrived. Her
family, however, had been incredibly kind. They couldn't
believe that I had decided to come help. They needed it as
much as she did. They came to the hospital every day, sometimes for hours on end. I texted them every hour, giving updates. They didn't want to be in the room when she finally
passed, but they did want to be close enough to come in and
say goodbye afterward. Until that time, they made sure to
come in and give her lots of love while she could accept it.

After the initial animosity stage, things were pretty good.
She was in high spirits in the beginning. She was happy that
I was there. We talked about the years that had gone by and
what each of us had gone through. Some of it felt like sitting
down to dinner with an old high school friend and chatting
about life and times gone by. Almost like we weren't sitting
there, knowing she would die.

Occasionally, we would get too close to certain subjects.
Those times would be followed by long bouts of awkward
silences. I never left though. There was a bathroom in her
room and the kitchen staff willingly brought me food every day. I stayed there, by her side, being as supportive as
I could.

We played board games, watched TV, ate, and slept. That

was our routine every day. Most of it was pretty boring and she slept more and more. Each day I noticed a little more of the spark leaving her body. A little more yellow color changing her skin. I knew what all of this meant from taking the medical classes.

There was no reason to scream for help or ring the nurses. She was terminal. There was nothing they could do but help to ease her pain as she passed. The cancer had spread to all of her major organs.

About a week and a half after getting there she began to lose the fight. She was sliding more quickly out of this world. I let her family know they needed to spend as much time as possible with her.

I texted Autumn updates as well, but I got no responses. I knew she was hurting and knew she was dealing with it in her own way. I kept sending them anyway. She had never told me not to come. She had never told me I was making a mistake. She knew it was the right thing. She knew I had to go. She just didn't know if she could handle it if I did. That is a strong woman, one who can let her man help an ex. I don't think I would have been able to do it if I were in her shoes.

I was fully aware that I might go home to a half empty house. There was a distinct possibility that she would be gone. There was nothing I could do about that. It was like I was losing both women I had loved at the same time. One would die, one would disappear.

Sometimes I don't understand God's plan. I don't know who/what I fully believe in. I don't know if God is the one I was taught in Bible school, the one that the Mormons believe in, or any of the others. I do know that there are energies floating through the universe. I believe in karma. I believe in the Golden Rule. I didn't understand why a woman so young and full of life was allowed to feel the way she did. Sure, she had hurt me, but it wasn't enough to deserve this. Not by a long shot.

My body ached from sleeping in an uncomfortable chair next to her bed. My stomach hurt from nearly two weeks of hospital food. My mind hurt from the conversations I had with Jennifer and the thoughts of Autumn leaving. It was my heart that hurt the most from watching a woman slowly die right in front of me.

It was a Saturday morning when I awoke with the realization that today was the day. I could tell by the look of her body she was almost ready to go. I knew that day was going to be a tough one.

24

The chair that I am sitting in is made of steel and cheap vinyl. Though I do appreciate that it's high enough for me to be at the same height as her bed. The vinyl is teal in color and sticks to my skin when I choose to only wear shorts. It is almost the only color in the room other than white, save for the shelf of cards, balloons, and flowers. So many flowers. I look at those flowers. They are probably the most appropriate. Soon, they too will lose their life and leave this world. Maybe they can follow her to Heaven, bringing color and joy to her next resting place.

"I am here. Your pain is too great. Let go, Jennifer. Let go and be free of this broken body."

She had been fighting for so long. Her body just couldn't handle what her mind wanted to believe. Though it hurt, I said the words that needed to be said. She couldn't keep holding on, dealing with the pain, while her body deteriorated.

Why hang on? Was she waiting for me to say something? Was she possibly waiting to feel something good before she could move on? What could I say to her? What could I do to help this poor, beautiful creature.

"I have and will always love you."

I say it without thinking. Though I mean it, I hadn't planned to say it. These words cause her eyes to look directly at me. It is the first time she has looked at me, really looked at me, in over a day.

She looks straight in my eyes, takes a long breath, blinks away a single tear, and finally lets go. I see her eyes change. I see the pain hidden within them release. I don't know if it was the words I said, or just the right moment, but she was able to let go. She is free of this body that has failed her. She is free of the world that has forgotten her. I let go of her hand, as my eyes could no longer hold back all of the tears held within them. A large, single drop left the corner of my eye. I felt it trickle down the side of my nose, up the curl of my lip, then fall gently on her face. Many more began to follow its path.

"Goodbye, Jennifer."

I lay my head on her chest. A stream of silent tears continue to flow while a deep sorrow grows inside of me for someone that I cared for so greatly. She had been taken from this world at the age of 37. She was only one year older than I. Breast Cancer. It had gotten her when she was so young, so vivacious, so full of life.

I lay there resting my head on her lifeless body. Minutes passed feeling like hours. Hell, it may have been hours. I was in no rush. I feel as though I have just run a marathon. I'm exhausted. Physically, mentally, but mostly emotionally. I am numb. As if I have fallen into a frozen Missouri pond in the dead of winter.

How did I get here? What led me to this moment? Was there enough good to compensate for all of this bad?

I began to ponder these things as I lay there. I close my eyes only for a second.

25

A sound of knocking wakes me. I wipe the corner of my mouth, looking around to find the source of the noise. I'm still quite groggy from the nap so it takes me a few seconds to realize that I had fallen asleep with my head on her body. She was gone. I could feel the cold creeping up through the sheets. Pain erupts from inside of me as I'm reminded that she has passed. A beautiful soul of a woman gone from this world. Though she made mistakes, she was still a person. A young person who had promise. Who may have changed and become better. Now the world will never know.

I turn around, trying to fully wake up, to see where the knocking sound had come from. It was Autumn. She was standing at the door and said, "I let you sleep for about 15 minutes, but I think the family will want to come in now."

I'm confused. How could she be here? How long had she been here?

"You're here," I say.

"Yes, I am. I always will be. I got your text this morning saying that you were sure today would be the day she left. It took some time, some deep soul searching, and a little bit of pride swallowing, but I decided I should be here for you. I came in, about a half an hour ago, and have been watching you. You are a good man, Chase. You are the man that I want by my side if something like this were to ever happen to me. It wasn't easy hearing you say those words to her, but, like you said, I'm your 'First, Last, Only... Always and Forever' and I'm here," she says while turning her hand sideways, showing the inscription on the ring to me.

I stand up, walk to her, and wrap myself around her.

My body, heart, and mind slump into her welcoming arms as I'm finally able to let go of the stress and pain I have been harboring. My heart releases all of the hurt it has held in watching another human pass. I cry so hard on her that I nearly fall down. She doesn't allow me. She holds fast. We stand in that embrace, the world fading around us, for a long moment. I'm in love with this woman. I always will be.

"These past two weeks have drained me. I'm saddened in my heart by the passing of a friend, but I'm happy in my heart by you being here," I said between painful sobs. I stepped back, lifted her chin up with my right hand, and looked her right in the eyes.

"You will never know what this means to me. I plan to spend the rest of my life showing you how much I love you and what I think you're worth," I say to her, with a heart full of joy and hope, then I softly kiss her lips.

"You already have, baby. You just don't know it."

She smiles at me, kisses me on the cheek, and we leave.

I don't know what the future holds. I don't know what curve balls the universe or God will throw at me with my relationship, my career, or my life. I have love in my heart and a willingness to accept whatever may come next.

Bring it on.

About The Author

James Craigmiles was born in Portsmouth, Virginia on a naval base. He moved to Missouri with his family at an early age and finally settled in Belle. It was in that small Missouri town that he learned what being a Midwest Man was all about. It was also in Belle where he found his calling as an artist. Through acting and writing, Craigmiles has found an outlet to tell his stories to the world. From age four to age 24 James excelled on stage, doing any part he could get his hands on (and learning the hard way that he was not meant for musical theater... as his voice could crack glass!). At 24 James moved his passion from stage over to film and television where he has been working ever since.

With roles in film, television, and commercials he is steadily building his resume and looks forward to the day when he will be the leading man. At the same time he has realized that acting jobs aren't there every day. So he put his pen to paper and has found a love of writing. This work is his first full length novel and he is busy working on his next ones. He also wrote his first film, *Right Side / Blind Side,* which stars himself and has a special appearance by his friend Leslie Jordan.

11514904R00158

Made in the USA
San Bernardino, CA
20 May 2014